FLORENCE

www.marco-polo.com

Sightseeing Highlights

Be it the world famous painting collection in the Uffizi Gallery, the unique building ensemble of the cathedral with the campanile or the church of San Lorenzo with Michelangelo's impressive New Sacristy – here are the sights that you definitely should not miss.

❶ ✶✶ Battistero San Giovanni
The baptistery became famous mainly because of the bronze doors, master-pieces of sculpture.
page 152

❷ ✶✶ Chianti
The classical landscape south of Florence is mainly known for its wine.
page 160

❸ ✶✶ Duomo Santa Maria del Fiore
The magnificent church is one of the most important structures in Europe.
page 165

❹ ✶✶ Galleria degli Uffizi
The Uffizi Gallery's collection of paintings is world class.
page 187

❺ ✶✶ Museo Nazionale del Bargello
This museum shows outstanding works of sculpture.
page 219

Do You Feel Like ...

... beautiful views of the city, modern art, special culinary pleasures or scents? Discover Florence along your personal interests.

BEAUTIFUL VIEWS

- **La Rinascente department store**
  Anyone who takes a well-deserved break in shopping in the café on the roof is rewarded with a magnificent close-up view of the cathedral dome.
  page 131

- **Palazzo Vecchio** ▶
  The symbol for the citizens' farsightedness, while itself being visible from all sides also offers a fantastic view of the old city. **page 246**

- **Bellosguardo**
  The name says it already: one of the most beautiful views of the city is available from Piazza del Bellosguardo above the San Frediano quarter on the south side of the Arno.
  page 264

MODERN

- **Nuovo Teatro dell'Opera**
  The new theatre is an impressive example of contemporary architecture and excellent acoustics. **page 127**

- ◀ **Museo Marino Marini**
  The museum – a 14th/15th cent. church in a 1980s concrete covering – that was dedicated to the modern sculptor bridges the gap between past and contemporary art. **page 217**

- **Museo Alinari**
  In the museum of the three photographer brothers Alinari rotating exhibits show the work of modern photographic artists.
  page 288

BACKGROUND

PRICE CATEGORIES
Restaurants (main dish without a drink)
€€€€ = over €22
€€€ = €15 – €22
€€ = €10 – €15
€ = up to €10
Hotels (double room)
€€€€ = over €200
€€€ = €150 – €200
€€ = €90 – €150
€ = up to €90

Note
Billable service telephone numbers are marked with an asterisk: *0180…

Dinner in the relaxed atmosphere of Piazza Santo Spirito

San Miniato al Monte

**Wonderful evening atmosphere in
the »Beauty on the Arno«**

BACKGROUND

What's worth knowing about the wonderful Renaissance city on the Arno in the heart of Tuscany, its population and economy, its history and the history of its art.

Cradle of the Renaissance

Florentia, Firenze, Florence – three flowers for the city with a lily in its coat of arms, where the rebirth of antiquity in art and science was first celebrated in Europe after the dark Middle Ages.

Few people took the time to look across the Arno to the flowery fields along its banks, which gave the city its name already in Roman times. The river was used for commerce and not for recreation; the poet Dante Alighieri and Giotto, the cathedral master builder, had already noticed this in the 14th century when the population of Florence was already over 100,000. As is fitting for a city with John the Baptist as its patron saint life in Florence was marked by hard work until a few citizens became so rich through textile production, trade and finance that they could devote all of their time to the finer things in life. The Florentines were the first to dare to break out of that dark time, so full of privation, called the Middle Ages to revive the bright, intellectual world of antiquity that so delighted in the sensuous. This Renaissance, the rebirth of Antiquity in the 15th century that was however steeped in Christian humanity, is the actual object of fascination in the artistic and rich city on the Arno, for nowhere else was in so short a time and in such variety the rediscovery of the world and of man carried out in such a revolutionary manner as in the bourgeois republican city of Florence.

Romantic Ponte Vecchio

While nobility ruled in other places and dictated local taste in art, along the Arno citizens' committees discussed art commissions. They made it possible for sculptors as diverse as Donatello or Michelangelo, creators of bronze works like Ghiberti or Verrocchio, daring master builders like Brunelleschi, Michelozzo or Alberti and the painter Masaccio, who is celebrated for having rediscovered perspective in art, as well as his successors Ghirlandaio and Botticelli to the brilliant Leonardo from the village of Vinci to give their works an enhanced expression, which they learned from nature and which was unknown until then. This artistic fundamentals were refined by the generation of Florentine Mannerists after 1520 and radiated to the rest of Europe, not to mention the epochal achievements of the literary Niccolò Machiavelli and the natural scientist Galileo Galilei. The fowering of Florentine bourgeois humanism in the 15th and 16th century was carried by a solid tradition of craftsmanship and cosmopolitan business sense, paired with knowledge of art and generosity

A stylish bar

among the elites. Magistrate, guilds and a wealthy aristocracy, including the famous ruling family of the Medici, competed aginst each other to beautify the city with art, not without ulterior motives of enhancing their own fame. Time was essential for soon Rome and Venice would force the city on the Arno from its premier position.

FASCINATING CULTURAL HERITAGE

Fortunately, the magnificent cultural heritage of the Renaissance could be preserved and it attracts people from all over the world until today. Despite all of the waiting in queues they are enthralled by the overwhelming parade of paintings in the Uffizi Gallery; they admire David and the Pietà by Michelangelo; they are amazed at the size of the cathedral dome and the wonderful paradise doors. You also can experience the clear spatial design of San Lorenzo and Santo Spirito, enjoy the tranquility of a monastery courtyard and the frescoed cells of San Marco, stroll across the lively squares or through the restful green of the Boboli Gardens. And when your legs and eyes protest after so much standing and admiring, treat yourself to a caffè on the Piazza, a glass of Chianti in a bar, a snack in a rustic vaulted cellar or a prosecco with tasty antipasti in a noble Renaissance palazzo. That will give you the necessary energy for a visit to Piazzale Michelangelo or the church San Miniato al Monte, located higher up. From there let your gaze wander along the silver-blue band of the Arno with its bridges to the tall towers of the churches as well as the beautiful palaces. In the distance, framed by cypresses and pines, numerous villas and Fiesole can be seen on the slopes of the Apennines. In short: Florence is a feast for the senses, but without being effusive, as is fitting for a proud and reasonable city of business.

Facts

Population · Politics · Economy

While Florence does not play a major role in the Italian economy it is still one of the country's major cities of art. This
makes it an enormous attraction for tourists, who are the
city's main source of income.

POPULATION

The rise of the city from Colonia Florentia, a Roman veterans'
colony, to the prosperous Florence of the Renaissance, took time.
In the Middle Ages the population expanded to about 100,000 by
the mid-14th century. The horrific **plague of 1348** took about half
of the residents, and the population sank to 40,000. Only in the
mid-19th century did the number rise again to 150,000 and then
continue to grow. In the 1980s it began to sink again due to emigra-
tion and a decline in the birth rate. In the past decades around
60,000 immigrants stopped this trend and today 366,000 people live
in Florence.

Changes in population

99% of the people of Florence are Roman Catholic. The city is the seat
of an archbishop, who traditionally is elevated to the rank of cardinal
by the pope. There are also churches of other Christian denomina-
tions and a synagogue.

Religion

ADMINISTRATION

In the Middle Ages Florence was divided into four quartieri
(quarters), which were named after the four city gates San Piero,
Duomo or Vescovo, San Pancrazio and Santa Maria. Later the
number was increased to six and they were called sestieri (San
Piero, Duomo, San Pancrazio, San Piero a Scheraggio, Borgo, Oltrarno). Today Florence is divided into **quartieri**, most of which
have the name of a church within the quarter, like Santa Maria
Novella, San Giovanni, Santa Croce, San Domenico, Santo Spirito.
There are also suburbs around the major traffic routes and outly-
ing districts on the hills: San Miniato, Belvedere and Bellosguardo
in the south, Careggi, Montughi, Fiesole and Settignano in the
north.

City districts

Galleria degli Uffizi, one of the world's major art galleries and an
absolute must for visitors to Florence

MARCO◉POLO INSIGHT

▶ In Italian:

Firenze

Location:
Tuscany

Area:
102 sq km/1098sq ft
Highest point: **70m/230ft above sea level**
Lowest point: **49m/161sq ft above sea level**

Population **366,000**
compared to: Rome 2.6 mil.
Milan 1.2 mil.

Population density:
3589 people/sq km
(9259 people/sq mi)

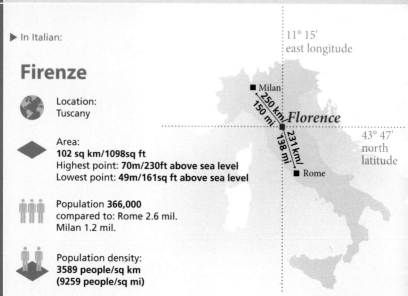

11° 15'
east longitude

■ Milan

250 km/
150 mi

Florence

231 km/
138 mi

43° 47'
north
latitude

■ Rome

▶ Administration

Capital city of the region of Tuscany
Main city of the province of Florence
Today's division into 5 districts:
A: Centro Storico
B: Campo di Marte
C: Gaviana-Galluzzo
D: Isolotto-Legnaia
E: Rifredi

Traditional city quarters
1: Santa Maria Novella
2: San Giovanni
3: Santo Spirito
4: Santa Croce

©BAEDEKER

▶ Coat of arms

Florence's coat of arms depicts a lily. It is widely known in art and heraldry as the Florentine lily. Differences to classic depictions of lilies include the two filaments (thus Ital. »Giglio bottonato = budded lily«).

▶ Partner cities

- Kassel and Dresden
- Reims
- Sydney
- Kyōto
- Budapest
- Philadelphia
- Edinburgh

▶ Economy

Service industry, clothing industry (Gucci headquarters), chemical and pharmaceutical industry, precision mechanics, tourism

over 8 mil.
overnight stays annually

▶ Climate

Average temperatures

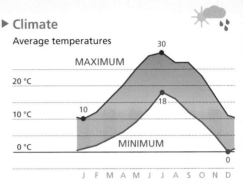

MAXIMUM
30
20 °C
18
10 °C
10
0 °C
MINIMUM
0

J F M A M J J A S O N D

Precipitation

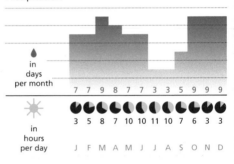

in days per month: 7 7 9 8 7 3 3 5 9 9 9

in hours per day: 3 5 8 7 10 10 11 10 7 6 3 3

J F M A M J J A S O N D

▶ Museums in Florence

There are more than 70 museums in Florence, and in the surrounding area there are even 170 (Paris: 140). The four most famous with their best known works of art:

Uffizi Gallery — **Galleria dell'Accademia** — **Museo Nazionale del Bargello** — **Palazzo Pitti**

SANDRO BOTTICELLI: PRIMAVERA (BIRTH OF VENUS)
FILIPPINO LIPPI: MADONNA AND CHILD
CIMABUE & GIOTTO
FRA ANGELICO
MASACCIO REMBRANDT
LEONARDO DA VINCI
PIERO DELLA FRANCESCA
MICHELANGELO
RAPHAEL TITIAN

MICHELANGELO: DAVID, THE SLAVES
PERUGINO
FILIPPINO LIPPI
FRA BARTOLOMEO DELLA PORTA
GIOVANNI MASACCIO
ALESSANDRO ALLORI
SANTI DI TITO
LORENZO BARTOLINI
LUIGI PAMPALONI
TADDEO GADDI

DONATELLO: MARZOCCO
LUCA DELLA ROBBIA
MICHELANGELO: BRUTUS, APOLLINO, DRUNK CUPID
DONATELLO
VERROCCHIO
GIAMBOLOGNA
BACCIO BANDINELLI
FRANCESCO MOSCHINO
BENEDETTO DA MAIANO

TITIAN: PORTRAIT OF TOMMASO MOTSI
RAPHAEL: MADONNA DELL' IMPANNATA
CARAVAGGIO: SLEEPING AMOR
PIETRO DA CORTONA
CIRO FERRI
ANDREA DEL SARTO
FRA BARTOLOMEO
RUBENS TINTORETTO
ANTONIO CANOVA

Administration

The Comune di Firenze is administered from the Palazzo Vecchio – the city government chose to use this name instead of Palazzo della Signoria or Palazzo Ducale. The most important political organ is the city council (consiglio comunale), which is elected every five years in local elections. The mayor (sindaco) is elected then, as are the assessori, who are responsible for individual departments like traffic, health and schools; together they form the city government (giunta comunale). In 1990 Florence was divided into **five new administrative districts**: Centro Storico, Campo di Marte, Gaviana-Galluzzo, Isolotto-Legnaia and Rifredi.

ECONOMY

International position

Since the Middle Ages the people of Florence have consistently brought wealth to their city as hard-working craftsmen, skilled merchants and good administrators. At times, the banks of Florence controlled the European money market and thus influenced European politics. The ruling family of Florence, the **Medici**, owed its rise to success in trade and banking. Since Florence did not succeed in gaining the same political power as other Italian states – the Republic of Venice, the Duchy of Milan, the Papal States and the Kingdom of Naples-Sicily – it lost its economic position and today is neither a leading trade nor banking centre.

Traditional economic sectors

Florence became wealthy in the late Middle Ages through the textile industry (weavers, dyers, tailors, silk trade), which is still an important economic sector today in the form of the **clothing industry**. Highly developed crafts (ceramics, porcelain, needlework, leatherwork, basketry) have preserved their special traditions. Chemical and pharmaceutical factories, precision engineering, the antiques trade, printing and publishing provide the most jobs. In addition, agricultural products of Tuscany are processed in Florence.

Service sector

The service sector is very important to Florence today; it employs more than two thirds of the workforce. There are numerous banks in the city; its fashion fairs (for example Pitti Immagine) are world famous, and its antique, medicine and crafts trade fairs attract local and foreign visitors. Since the regional, provincial and communal governments are all located in Florence, which is the capital of the region of Tuscany and the province of Florence, the government is an important employer in the city.

However, tourism with all its advantages and disadvantages remains the most important sector of the economy. About 8 million overnights and tourists and countless day-trippers visit the Renaissance city every year. Of these the USA, France and Germany lead the sta-

How would Florence live without tourism?

tistics. Even though many only come to Florence for a day, the city is in danger of drowning in the flood of visitors. During the high season in the summer and the main church holidays Florence is booked up, and visitors can count on **long waits at the museums** and other attractions. This has made Florence one of the most expensive cities in Italy, not only for tourists but also for residents. The Italian financial crisis of recent years has caused real estate prices to sink in Florence as well and sales in discount stores and on neighbourhood markets have increased. Competition by online reservation sites and the increasing availability of B&B accommodation have broadened the range of hotel prices, an advantage for tourists who do not want to pay the high prices of luxury hotels.

Welcome to Everyday Life!

Experiencing Florence away from the tourist crowds for once, meeting »normal« people or actual residents -- here are some tips.

PAINTING AND RESTORATION

Hardly any city moves people to explore the techniques of traditional crafts like Florence. The famous Florentine school of restoration Istituto per l' Arte e il Restauro Spinelli offers summer courses over several weeks in July and September. Participants are introduced to the techniques of painting, fresco, wall painting, gilding and restoration of works of art, sculptures and ceramics. Afternoon courses in Italian can also be booked.

Via Maggio 13
Tel. 055 282951
www.spinelli.it

LEARNING THE LANGUAGE ...

... is another way to get in touch with local people. People are generally very pleased to see you make the effort, and the language schools usually have plenty of tips on how to dive deeper into the culture. Here are some possible schools:

www.sculoaleonardo.com,
www.michelangelo-edu.it,
www.centromachiavelli.org/
Learnitalian

EVERYDAY MARKET

Visit Mercato Sant'Ambrogio, the morning market with fruit, vegetable, pulses, meat, fish, fresh bread and herbs on Piazza Ghiberti/Via de' Macci. Shopping where the local people shop will give you a chance to experience everyday life in Florence.
Mon-Sat 7am-2pm

LIVING WITH THE LOCALS

... with couchsurfing, where you can spend a night on the couch in a private home for free. The website www.couchsurfing.org has more than 4000 hosts registered for Florence and the surrounding area. Airbnb has rooms in private homes. There are also whole flats listed, which can be rented by the week or longer.
www.mwzflorence.com.
www.couchsurfing.org
www.airbnb.com

LEATHER WORK

The production of leather bags, wallets, belts and jackets is one of the oldest traditional Florentine crafts. The large leather market San Lorenzo testifies to this, but even more so the products of the traditional leather school next to the church of Santa Croce. The Scuola del Cuoio offers half-day and full-day courses in which you can create your own belt or handbag.
Piazza Santa Croce 16
Tel. 055 24 45 33/4
www.scuoladelcuoio.com

From Veteran's Colony to Illustrious City of Art

In the course of time the Roman veterans' colony on the Arno developed into one of the busiest and wealthiest banking, trading and textile cities in the Middle Ages. During the 15th and 16th centuries the ground-breaking innovations in all areas of the arts as well as the fame and glory of the Medici family radiated throughout Europe and Florence has benefitted from this until today.

THE BEGINNINGS OF THE CITY

59 BC	Founding of a Roman veterans' colony
4th century	The church of San Lorenzo becomes the first bishop's seat.
from 568	Lombard dukes rule Tuscany.

The hilly landscape around Florence has been settled and civilized for a long time. Florence itself, however, was not founded until around 59 BC. It then became a colony for Roman veterans under Caesar after Fiesole was destroyed. It was located in the still swampy but fertile Arno valley and given the name **»ager florentinus«**. The »blossoming place« was located at the junction of three important traffic routes: the Via Cassia from Rome to Fiesole, the Via Pisana from Pisa to Spina and the Volterrana from Volterra to Fiesole.

59 BC: founding of the city

Archaeological finds from Roman times, most of them from the 3rd century AD, give an approximate picture of Florentia: in a walled, square-shaped area the forum was at the centre – where the Piazza della Repubblica is today – with a temple and thermal baths as well as a theatre near today's Palazzo Vecchio. The street grid, which marked the insulae or residential blocks, can still be seen in the centre. The main source of income was the trade in wool, river transport and military service. Florentia was the seat of the governor of Tuscany and Umbria under emperors Aurelian and Diocletian.

From the 2nd century Christianity was brought to Florentia by traders from the eastern Mediterranean area, above all Syrians. **St Minias** (San Miniato) was martyred around 250 on a hill outside the city; the church of San Miniato al Monte was later built over his

2nd–4th cent. AD

Palazzo Pitti: the Italian kings lived in the magnificent Appartamenti Reali

grave. In the 4th century the city became an episcopal see, and the church of San Lorenzo was dedicated in 393 by St Ambrose as a cathedral. In 412 St Zenobius, a later patron saint of the city, is attested as bishop.

5th–6th cent.: Great migrations

Florentia declined after the collapse of the Western Roman Empire. In its indefensible location in the valley it was more vulnerable to enemy attacks than other towns on the hills. Florentia was plundered and destroyed above all by **Goths and Byzantines**; in the 6th century the city covered only about one third of the area of the Roman colony and had a population of no more than 1000.

More peaceful times began in 568 with the **rule of the Lombards**, who founded the Duchy of Tuscia. In Florence ten new churches were built, but the city then lost its leading position to Lucca and Pisa, the new residences of the Lombard dukes.

MEDIEVAL RULE BY NOBLES

from 774	Florence is part of the Frankish march of Tuscia.
1055	Autonomous city rights awarded
1250	Patrician rule replaces noble rule for good.

From 774: Frankish rule

Charlemagne defeated the Lombard Desiderius in 774 and made Tuscia a Frankish march. Florence was given a new defensive wall up to the Arno. The population grew to 15,000 thanks to gradual economic growth. Under **Emperor Lothar I** in 854 the counties of Florence and Fiesole were united, which brought the city more economic power.

Around 1000

Around 1000 **Margrave Hugo** moved his residence from Lucca to Florence. The colours of his coat of arms became the city colours. In 1055, in the time of Emperor Henry III, Florence became an **autonomous commune** subject only to the Holy Roman Emperor, and was able to gain its own territory by 1125 by forcibly taking control of surrounding castelli and the neighbouring city of Prato and destroying its competitor Fiesole. After patrician families had more say in the city government in 1177, its rise to become the most important trade and banking city in central Italy began. Conflicts between influential families after 1215 led to internal destabilization and the division of the residents into two camps. These factions fought for

MARCO POLO INSIGHT

? *Coat of arms*

The lily in the Firenze coat of arms probably refers to the campi fiorentini, the lily-covered meadows along the Arno, a motif that was combined with the red and white colours of the dukes of Tuscia (Tuscany) to form a red lily on a white background?

control of the city under the guise of pursuing higher interests as Ghibellines (loyal to the emperor) and Guelphs (loyal to the pope).

Finally, after a popular uprising in 1250, the first citizens' government without Ghibellines was formed, and a **capitano del popolo** (city captain) managed the city's affairs along with various councils at his disposal. The nobility even had to reduce the towers of their fortified palaces to a certain height. Economically strong, in 1252 the city began to mint a gold ducat, the **florenus** (florin) – thus the abbreviation fl. for guilder, which soon spread throughout Europe. Moreover, the guilds, which had already existed for some time, were reorganized after 1266. The guilds started as unions of wealthy merchant families, who eventually became involved in city politics.

1250: first constitution

CITY GOVERNMENT IN THE HANDS OF THE CITIZENS

1293	Nine-member Signoria begins to rule the city state.
1348	Great plague reduces population by half.
1378	Social dissatisfaction leads to the Ciompi uprising.
1406	The acquisition of Pisa and Livorno makes Florence an international trading city.

In 1282 resurgent battles between the Ghibellines and Guelphs led to a change in the **city constitution**. For the first time it gave decisive political influence in the city government to the heads (priori) of the seven most important guilds, which had become wealthy through banking and trading. A few years later serfdom was abolished in order to gain more cheap labour for the production of textiles. From 1293 the Ordinamenti della Giustizia, communal principles of law, were the basis for a government of merchants and citizens that was based on the guilds. The governing body was the Signoria, consisting of eight priori and the gonfaloniere della giustizia, the banner bearer of justice. The Signoria, which existed until the beginning of the Medici dukedom in 1532, was chosen by a combination of lot and election, with rotation of its members. For this reason the town hall square is still called the Piazza della Signoria.

1282–93: consolidation of republican government

The office of capitano del popolo, also called podestà, has been preserved in the name of a palace that was later called the Bargello, meaning bailiff. The city grew to 100,000 residents and expressed its self-confidence in new buildings. A new **city wall**, five times larger than the old one, was built; the massive communal palace, the Palazzo dei Priori, later Palazzo Vecchio, was built and the construction of the cathedral began.

In the 14th century the city experienced a series of political defeats, catastrophes and economic losses: battles against Pisa and Lucca were lost; the **Arno flood in 1333** destroyed many bridges and buildings; famines and several plagues (1340–48) decimated the population; several large banks went bankrupt.

Economic difficulties, weakening of civil power and dissatisfaction with the lack of a political voice led to the **uprising of the Ciompi** (1378) as the wool carders were called because of their dirty working conditions. They succeeded in forming a government of the lower classes and lower guilds for a short time in 1378. However, the higher guilds of the wealthy merchants were able to defend their position and in the **new constitution** of 1380 the political supremacy of the higher guilds was determined once and for all. A few rich families like the Albizzi, Peruzzi, Capponi, Soderini, Rucellai and Strozzi then determined the fate of the city.

During the war with the equally powerful Milan between 1389 and 1402 **individual families controlled the city government**. The conquest of Florence was only prevented by the sudden death of Duke Gian Galeazzo Visconti of Milan. After this, in the early Renaissance period, civic humanism was able to flourish to its full extent in Florence. By subjugating Pisa in 1406 and acquiring the ports of Livorno and Portopisano, Florence was able to develop its position of power in Tuscany and gain access to international markets.

CITY REPUBLIC UNDER THE MEDICI

from 1434	Beginning of the political rule of the Medici
1436	The cathedral is dedicated by Pope Eugene IV.
1478	Lorenzo the Magnificent and his brother are attacked.
1494	The Medici are driven out and a theocracy is set up under the Dominican Savonarola for four years.
1512	The Medici return as rulers of the city.

Rise of the Medici

Times of political change were an opportunity for rising families like the Medici, who were probably pharmacists or physicians. At the end of the 14th century the Medici were increasingly successful in the banking business, so that Giovanni d' Averardo de' Medici, known as **Giovanni di Bicci**, moved the headquarters of his uncle's bank to Florence in 1397, opened other branches and as the pinnacle of his career was named banker to the popes, who returned to Rome in 1417 from exile in Avignon.

1434–64: Cosimo the Elder

His son Cosimo de' Medici, later called »il Vecchio« (the Elder), inherited his father's property in 1429 and was able to make it secure, which made others jealous. In the battle of San Romano in 1432 the

Florentine troops were victorious over a Sienese-Milanese army, but after defeat in the war against Lucca the oligarchy dominated by Albizzi had Cosimo the Elder taken prisoner in 1433 and banished from the city for ten years. However, after Rinaldo degli Albizzi failed to be re-elected as gonfaloniere, the oligarchs recalled Cosimo, who was supported by the pope, in 1434. On the surface he respected republican institutions, but in fact he governed as the sole ruler. He had his opponents banished and gave government positions to his supporters. **Milan's war against the city**, which was incited by Albizzi, ended with a Florentine victory in 1440 at the battle of Anghiari. Then Venice became the next political and economic rival, while peaceful relations with Milan were established when the mercenary Francesco Sforza took over control there after the Peace of Lodi in 1454. Cosimo the Elder was very generous to Florence his native city. He supported the arts and sciences, financed church buildings and had an imposing family palace built. He founded the Academy of Plato as a school under the leadership of the philosopher Marsilio Ficino and the famous Medici library (today: Biblioteca Medicea Laurenziana), so that by the time of his death he was rightfully honoured as »pater patriae«.

> **MARCO ⊕ POLO INSIGHT**
>
> ### ? *Mysterious spheres*
>
> The spheres »palle« in the Medici coat of arms might symbolize money, but more likely pills, since the name means »physician«. The patron saints of the Medici were the two physicians Cosmas and Damian.

1464–68: Piero de' Medici

Several patrician families united to form the Poggio party against the weak Piero de' Medici, called »il Gottoso« (»the gouty«), the son of Cosimo, out of revenge for being deprived of power under his father. Piero was able to defeat the confederates in 1466 with the help of Milan and his son Lorenzo. Two years later another uprising of the Poggio, which Venice supported, ended in the indecisive battle of Imola.

1469–92: Lorenzo de' Medici, the Magnificent

Florence experienced its greatest economic and cultural prosperity under Lorenzo Il Magnifico (the Magnificent), who respected the republican forms of government despite his position as city ruler. But Lorenzo was less successful as an entrepreneur. Lack of coordination and mismanagement weakened the Medici bank. With the approval of the pope, two members of the de' Pazzi banking family attempted to assassinate Giuliano and Lorenzo de' Medici in the cathedral in 1478. Lorenzo escaped with minor injuries. After the conspirators were arrested and hanged, Lorenzo's position took on an almost royal character. The fame of his family and Florence's position on the European political stage were equally important to him. His successful mediation as a diplomat in several conflicts between competing Italian states gained him international recognition.

1492–98:
Piero
de' Medici
After Lorenzo's death his son Piero II de' Medici ruled the city in a highly autocratic manner. His unauthorized negotiations with Charles VIII of France in 1494, who had invaded Italy, led to his downfall and the banishment of the Medici.

The situation was made even more difficult by the appearance of the Dominican monk Fra Girolamo Savonarola, who preached an ascetic life of repentance to a growing audience from the middle and lower classes and demanded religious and political reforms. In the next four years Savonarola founded an increasingly authoritarian **theocracy**, which was rejected in the end by religious as well as secular circles. When Savonarola opposed the pope, he was captured and executed publicly in 1498 at the behest of Pope Alexander VI.

1502–12:
republic
under
Soderini
The republican city government that followed under Pietro Soderini was so successful that an amendment to the constitution (1502) made Soderini ruler (gonfaloniere) for life, but he was not able to prevent the return of the Medici. Their connections throughout Europe and

Savanarola's execution in 1498 on the Piazza della Signoria

their support in the local opposition to the oligarchy enabled Giovanni de' Medici, the son of Lorenzo the Magnificent, to regain rule over the city in 1512 with the help of Pope Julius II. In 1513 Giovanni became Pope Leo X.

The republican form of government was abolished. The young **Lorenzo II de' Medici**, the ward of his uncle Giulio de' Medici, became the ruler. The early death of Lorenzo in 1519 and the ensuing takeover by Giulio prevented a rebellion against the ruling family. After being elected in 1523 as Pope Clement VII, Giulio retained control over Florence; Cardinal Passerini acted as his viceroy. After the opposition rebelled in 1527 Passerini was forced to leave the city.

1512: return of the Medici

The newly formed republican government allied itself to France. When King François I dropped his Italian allies in the conflict with Emperor Charles V, Florence was isolated. In 1529 the city was occupied by imperial troops and in the following year lost its status as a republic.

1527–30: short-lived republic

RESIDENCE OF GRAND DUKES

1532	Alessandro de' Medici becomes Duke of Florence.
1569	Cosimo I becomes Grand Duke of Tuscany.
1737	With the death of Gian Gastone the Medici dynasty dies out.

From this date Florence was the **fortress and residence of the Medici dukes** and subject to an autocratic regime that was not able to bring about new economic and cultural prosperity. Emperor Charles V named Alessandro de' Medici, the last of the Medici before they were ennobled, as regent and in 1532 made him Duke of Florence. In 1536 he married Margherita of Austria-Parma, a daughter of Emperor Charles V. Alessandro's tyrannical rule made him extremely unpopular, and he was murdered by his adviser Lorenzino de' Medici in 1537.

1531–37: Duke Alessandro de' Medici

Then Cosimo de' Medici, the descendant of a different branch of the family and son of the mercenary Giovanni delle Bande Nere, was named regent. He ruled his duchy autocratically from the Palazzo della Sigria and suppressed a rebellion of republican emigrés. Following the example of his predecessors, the arts were to be a visible expression of his power. Thus the interior of the government palace was redecorated and construction of the Uffizi began. His wife Eleonora of Toledo transformed **Palazzo Pitti** into a magnificent palace, the residence of the future Medici dukes. In 1554–55 Cosimo conquered

1537–87: Cosimo I de' Medici

Art and Commerce

The Medici – the name stands for Renaissance art and art patronage, but also for immeasurable wealth and large-scale financing. Unlike other upper-class Florentine families, they did not gain wealth and influence in the 14th century. Their rise took place later, within the century known as the quattrocento, a glorious age for Florence.

Giovanni di Bicci de Medici (d. 1429) laid the foundation for the family's wealth by giving generous loans to the popes during the schism of 1378. When Rome grew as the papal residence, the Medici were already well established as the pope's bankers, and the young Cosimo, later called the Elder, was able to continue his lucrative business deals. The Rome branch of the banking house made about 50-60% of the Medici profits at that time. The Medici managed this without much personal capital, since the high deposits made by the Curia were used to make loans that brought in a return of up to 20%. The bank had branches in many cities: in Venice for trade with the Orient, in Bruges for trade with northern Europe, in Geneva for central Europe, in London for the English court and the wool trade, and in Milan and Naples. The Medici also had a commercial monopoly on alum, traded in wool and silk, and sold luxury goods.

Banking Business

Their account books from 1397 to 1420 document profit increases of 5000 gold florins annually – multiply this figure by 100 for today's value in gold in euros. When Cosimo the Elder took over the business, profits exceeded 8000 gold florins annually until 1434, and lat-

er even increased to 13,000 gold florins annually. Cosimo was generous in making gifts but cautious in lending and kept a close eye on the creditworthiness of his clients, who were generally associated with the Curia or were members of ruling houses and could also increase the political influence of the Medici. Cosimo also hired excellent bankers for his branch offices and reinvested a large part of the profits. In contrast his grandson **Lorenzo il Magnifico** was not interested in business and loved to live beyond his means; by the time he died in 1492 the banking house was almost broke. However, the Medici position was also strengthened by international connections, and despite being exiled after 1513 they continued to rule the city with the help of the popes.

Art Patronage

Wealthy Florentine citizens put a large amount of their wealth into charitable foundations. Thus Giovanni Tornabuoni, head of the Medici bank in Rome, had Domenico Ghirlandaio decorate the main choir chapel of **Santa Maria Novella** with wonderful frescoes »as an act of respect and love for God and to praise his house and family«. Other motivations for patronage can be seen in the writings of the international merchant Gio-

In Botticelli's *Adoration of the Magi* several members of the Medici clan had themselves portrayed here

vanni Rucellai (1403–81), who financed the façade of the church: »I believe that I have earned more honour by spending money than by making it.« The dimensions of this kind of publicity can be seen in the records of Lorenzo the Magnificent, who figured from the family account books of 1434 to 1471 that his family had paid out about 664,000 gold florins to the poor, to foundations and taxes. Of these 8000 gold florins went to the decoration of the Franciscan church of Santa Croce, 40,000 gold florins to the reconstruction of the monastery of San Marco, 60,000 gold florins to the reconstruction of the parish church of San Lorenzo by Filippo Brunelleschi and 60,000 gold florins to the building of Palazzo Medici. That meant an annual expense of 18,000 gold florins, which were not covered by the 13,000 gold florins of profit that were made every year, but possibly through real estate. But why these immense expenditures? On the one hand, alms were given to ease the conscience of the donor, since loaning money was considered to be shady business and was condemned by the church. Pious patronage allowed the church to make use of the money, and thus it indirectly condoned the business practices by accepting the donations. By choosing the buildings and the artists that they supported, the patricians showed their level of education, virtuous motives and the cultured use of their wealth. Their generosity also served political purposes, for the many large private contracts created jobs, were visible proof of the economic power of the families and brought them votes for communal offices. The conviction that not the person but the art he had made possible would outlast time and increase the family fame was also important. The **Sassetti Chapel** in the church of Santa Trinita shows how subtly piety on the one hand and wealth and political power on the other can be demonstrated artistically. Francesco Sassetti had become rich as the branch head of the Medici bank in Lyon; from 1469 he was an advisor to the young Lorenzo de' Medici. In the chapel next to the choir in **Santa Trinita** he documented his social rise and his close contact to the Medici family. The confirmation of the Franciscan order by Pope Honorius III in 1223 is depicted in the political centre of contemporary Florence. The Sassetti and Medici families are spectators in the foreground. Near the papal throne on the right stands the bald Francesco Sassetti with his son Federico, next to him the dark-haired Lorenzo de' Medici as well as the greying Antonio Pucci, a relative of the Sassetti and Medici supporter. On the left opposite are Sassetti's three sons Teodore I, Cosimo and Galeazzo. The children of Lorenzo the Magnificent are depicted as they climb the stairs with their tutor: little Giuliano first, then Piero and finally Giovanni, followed by their teacher Matteo Franco and the poet Luigi Pulci. It is interesting that the setting is not the cathedral but the political centre of Florence, a clear indication that Sassetti was more interested in a demonstration of power than in a depiction of St Francis of Assisi.

Elevation to the Nobility

The **Procession of the Magi** in the private chapel of the Medici palace makes it evident that the Medici already enjoyed the prestige of princes in the mid-15th century; it was painted by Benozzo Gozzoli in 1459–60 and depicted the family as kings. The monumental mural refers to three grand events in Florence in which the Medici played a decisive role: the council for the unification of the eastern and western Christian churches in 1439, the great festival for Pope Pius II and Duke Galeazzo Sforza in 1459, and the processions of the Brotherhood of the Magi. Further proof of the Medici claim to kingship is the **Adoration of the Magi** (around 1475) in the Uffizi Gallery, in which Sandro Botticelli immortalized the Florentine upper class. Even though the kings – portraits of Cosimo the Elder with his sons Giovanni and Piero – are subordinated to the Holy Family, they still occupy the centre of the picture. The younger Medici, Cosimo's grandsons, stand at the side: the pensive **Lorenzo** in dark clothing and his vivacious brother **Giuliano**, who was murdered during the Pazzi conspiracy in 1478, in bright clothing. The actual theme of the picture is upstaged and serves only an excuse for ostentatious representation of the Medici and their supporters. The eldest king, who is kneeling before Mary and the Christ child, is Cosimo the Elder and his son Piero is the figure in the centre with a red cloak.

Siena and expanded his power. After the deaths of his daughter, two of his sons and his wife, in 1562 Cosimo handed the reins of government to his son Francesco, who married Johanna of Austria, the daughter of Emperor Ferdinand, in 1565. The **Palazzo Vecchio** was decorated and the Vasari corridor built for this event. But Cosimo's greatest triumph was his **elevation to the rank of grand duke** in 1569 by Pope Pius V; the ceremony took place the following year in St Peter's Basilica in Rome. However, the rule of Grand Duke **Francesco I** (1574-1587), who was interested in art and the natural sciences, was weak. After the death of his wife he married his mistress Bianca Cappello, first having her husband murdered. Medici interests were expanded internationally through the marriage of his daughter Maria with the French king, Henri IV.

Florence repeatedly suffered from plague, here in 1630

Francesco died in 1587 and was succeeded by his brother Ferdinando I When a flood (1589) and several famines struck the city the regent, who until then had been known as a scholar and patron of the arts, took control of the situation skilfully. He also granted religious freedom. Under his rule the **Fortezza de Belvedere** was built to secure Medici power, and the massive **ducal chapel** was built as an extension of San Lorenzo.

1587–1609: Grand Duke Ferdinando I de' Medici

In the 17th and 18th centuries there was a succession of mediocre and weak rulers in the house of Medici: Cosimo II (1609–21), Ferdinando II (1620–70), Cosimo III (1670–1723) and Gian Gastone (1723–37). Florence's economic condition continued to decline. The wool and silk industries died out. The nobility lived from their rural estates and the people became poorer. With the death of Gian Gastone in 1737 the male line of the Medici died out. Anna Maria Luisa (1667–1743, ►MARCO POLO Insight p.77), the last Medici and wife of Elector Johann Wilhelm of the Palatinate, turned the **Medici art**

17th and 18th centuries

treasures over to the city, which made them the basis of the outstanding Florentine museum collections. In an international agreement, the Grand Duchy of Tuscany passed to Duke Francis Stephen of Lorraine (from 1745 Holy Roman Emperor Franz I, married from 1736 to Archduchess Maria Theresa of Austria).

FROM HABSBURG-LORRAINE TO THE KINGDOM OF ITALY

1737	The Grand Duchy of Tuscany passes to the house of Habsburg-Lorraine.
1796–1814	French rule in Tuscany
1860	Florence joins the kingdom of Italy in a plebiscite.
1913	Socialist city government
1944	Cultural heritage destroyed in the war

1765–90: Peter Leopold

Under Francis Stephen of Lorraine, the Grand Duchy of Tuscany was only a pawn in the European power game; but under Grand Duke Peter Leopold reforms were introduced. The guilds and ecclesiastical privileges were abolished, as was the death sentence, torture and the inquisition; the redistribution of large estates to small landowners led to a more balanced social structure. A moderate taxation policy allowed agriculture and free trade to flourish. The mezzadria (semilease) system in agriculture, despite some disadvantages, guaranteed that the smaller landowners got a share of the harvest. When the grand duke was elected **Emperor Leopold II** in 1790 he left Florence and handed power to his brother Ferdinand, who only ruled a few years as **Grand Duke Ferdinando III**. He had to flee from the French revolutionary army in 1796–97. After his return he was forced to leave again in 1803, and was compensated with the titles of Elector of Salzburg and later Grand Duke of Würzburg.

1804–14: Napoleon's intermezzo

Tuscany was an integral part of the French empire from 1804 to 1814 under Napoleon I; after the Congress of Vienna, Ferdinando III returned to Florence as Grand Duke of Tuscany. From 1824 the government of **Grand Duke Leopold II** gradually transformed Florence into a modern city, which also became a centre of liberal schools of thought. After 1847 liberals participated in the government of the grand duchy. Following military conflicts during the 1848 revolution, the situation calmed down; the peaceful conditions were used to develop the railway network and free trade in the port of Livorno.

1860: joining the kingdom of Italy

After the short rule of Grand Duke Ferdinando IV (1859–60), in 1860 Florence and Tuscany joined the Kingdom of Sardinia-Piedmont by plebiscite in the wake of the Italian national movement, when King Vittorio Emanuele, Count Cavour and Giuseppe Garibaldi brought about the unification of Italy. As a consequence of the expansion of Vittorio Emanuele's kingdom, the **capital was moved from Turin to Florence**, where the king lived in Palazzo Pitti until Rome took over as capital in 1871. A building boom changed the appearance of the Florence for good. The city wall was razed and large ring roads built in its place. Piazzale Michelangelo was built as an observation point.

With the transfer of government to Rome, Florence fell behind the rest of Italy in political and economic development. The preservation of the city's great cultural heritage was not enough to maintain its prosperity, and by the end of the 19th century the economic situation had deteriorated greatly. Liberal, democratic and socialist movements took conflicting positions of how to react to social changes. In the mean time Florence had become an **innovative intellectual centre**, where numerous writers and landscape painters felt at home. In the local elections in 1913 the Socialists gained the majority of the votes. During the First World War social tensions increased under the deprivations of war. Industrialization created workers' groups and leftists fought Fascists in the streets in the postwar period.

1871–92: social tension

In 1922 the Fascists came to power. Numerous political opponents went underground and later became guerrillas. Many Florentines supported Mussolini, but few were politically active.

1922–39: Fascism

After Mussolini was deposed in 1943 and a new government negotiated a ceasefire with the Allies, German troops occupied Florence on 11 September 1943. The city was then bombed by the American air force. In the Resistenza, which was mainly supported by left wing parties, the opposition gathered to plan a radical political reorganization of Italy. In August of the following year the Germans destroyed all bridges across the Arno except for the Ponte Vecchio before the city was liberated by the Allies. During a referendum in 1946 the people of Florence voted against keeping the monarchy and in favour of a republic of Italy.

1943–44: Second World War

A FRESH START

since 1946	Frequent left-wing liberal city governments
1966	Devastating Arno floods
1993	Bombing in the city centre
2009	Florence elects one of Italy's youngest mayors

**The bombing by the mafia in 1993 damaged buildings
and works of art**

Rapid change
After the war social and economic change was rapid. An economic upswing brought prosperity to broad sections of the population. From 1946 to 1951 a coalition of Communist and Socialist parties governed the city. Up to 1964 the popular Christian Socialist mayor **Giorgio La Pira** left his mark by helping the socially marginalized groups. He was succeeded by centre-left and after 1975 mostly by Communist-Socialist city governments.

The city was devastated when the Arno burst its banks on 4 November 1966. The water was up to 6m/20ft deep in the streets, homes, museums and libraries. It resulted in countless deaths, loss of homes and enormous damage to the historic buildings and to many works of art.

After the Europe-wide **student protests in 1968** the university city of Florence regularly experienced political unrest, which questioned traditional values. The emancipation of women as a part of the **feminist movement** played an important role in this. This protest movement, however, lost its attraction through the association of some of its proponents with the drug scene or terrorist groups.

The 1980s were marked by a new **economic upswing**, not least due to the tourism boom. In 1981 the historic centre of Florence was added to the **UNESCO World Heritage list** and in 1986 it was the European cultural capital. In order to reduce growing noise and emissions, the use of private cars was severely restricted in the centre.

A bomb attack by the mafia on 27 May in the city centre killed six people and wounded about 30. The Uffizi was damaged and numerous works of art were destroyed or damaged.

1993: bombing

The city centre has meanwhile been made into a pedestrian zone. In November 2002 Florence was the scene of a large peace demonstration in the form of a human chain of one million people through the city's streets.
One of Italy's youngest mayors was elected in June 2009, Matteo Renzi (b. 1975), who is a rebellious reformer of the Partito Democratico on the national level. With that he has continued the tradition of left-wing city government in Florence.

Turn of the millennium

A look into the future of Florence promises great innovations in the area of infrastructure, namely the extremely ambitious project of a railway station for high-speed trains. It was designed by Norman Foster and Ove Arup and will be built in the neighbourhood of the former slaughterhouses in the northwest of the city. Despite high costs and civil protest the preparations are under way.
 The large project Nuovo Uffizi is also making progress. By 2015/2016 the restoration, expansion and renovation of the Uffizi Gallery should be complete. Meanwhile several new rooms have been opened to the public.

2015/2016

Art and Culture

Art

Florence is a first-class art and cultural city. From the 14th to the 16th centuries, especially during the Renaissance, the creative achievements of this city's artists made an enduring impression on European art and cultural history.

ANTIQUITY

Although the hilly landscape around Florence is **an ancient area of civilization**, the city itself was not founded until 59 BC, by Caesar, as a Roman veteran's colony with the name Florentia.

The art and culture of the **Etruscan period** and the Roman republic was concentrated in Faesulae, today's Fiesole, above the Arno valley. Only in the course of the **imperial Roman era** in the 1st and 2nd centuries AD did Florence begin to flourish. During this period marble-covered temples, colonnades and baths were built near the forum (Piazza della Repubblica); outside the city walls a theatre occupied the site of today's Palazzo Vecchio.

In the course of the 19th-century city development, many Roman remains were found by archaeologists, including mosaics, fragments of statues, parts of temples and homes, and coins, which can be seen today together with Etruscan art from central Italy in the archaeological museum of Florence.

The many ancient statues in the Uffizi Gallery, in Palazzo Pitti and the Boboli Gardens are not originally from Florence but were brought here from Rome and southern Italy by several members of the Medici clan.

Bloom during imperial Roman period

EARLY MIDDLE AGES

Early Christian churches from the late 4th and early 5th century have been verified as the precursors of Santa Felicità, San Lorenzo and Sant' Ambrogio. Excavations in Santa Felicità exposed gravestones in the catacombs with Greek inscriptions from the year 418. Much was destroyed in the 6th century during the Lombard campaigns of conquest. In the following period and up to the 11th century Florence produced no important cultural and artistic achievements.

Early Christian churches

San Miniato del Monte: excellent example of Romanesque, Florentine-Tuscan influenced architecture

ROMANESQUE PERIOD

Architecture

Around the middle of the 11th century Florence developed into a **centre of the ecclesiastical reform movement**, when the Burgundian cleric Gerard became bishop of Florence in 1045 and introduced the reform ideas of Cluny. This had an effect on church-building. As Pope Nicolas II he laid the foundation stone of the baptistery of San Giovanni in 1059. Presumably in the same year, at the behest of the papal legate, the later Pope Gregory VII, the monastery of San Miniato al Monte, a Cluniac Benedictine abbey, was expanded. Since both buildings have been preserved without changes, they represent excellent examples of Florentine Romanesque architecture of the late 11th and the 12th century. The close connection to Roman antiquity can be seen in the outer design and the interior of the buildings.

The church of **San Miniato al Monte** (▶ill. p. 38) possesses a brilliant white and green incrusted façade. Incrustation is the covering of a brick structure with thin marble slabs of various colours, a technique known from ancient Roman building that was revived in the 11th century in Florence. Geometrical patterns, triangles, squares and rectangles inserted in the large Romanesque arches decorate the three-storey church façade. The interior has no transept, but a raised choir and an exposed roof structure, it gives the impression of an early Christian columned basilica. Lateral arches and the alternation of columns and piers give the nave an unusual rhythm. The magnificently decorated choir screen with marble pulpit (12th century) and the inlaid floor (1207) are remarkable late Romanesque works.

The 12th-century **Baptistery of San Giovanni** was thought to be an ancient building during the Renaissance because of its regular proportions and marble cladding, and thus was considered to be exemplary. It harks back to early Christian baptisteries in having an octagonal form, but surpasses them in its monumental dimensions. Each of its three storeys has different decoration through marble incrustation in rectangles and arches. In its balance and regular forms the Baptistery, which was modelled on ancient Roman structures, can be compared to Renaissance art, which is why it has been described as Proto-Renaissance, anticipating individual attributes of style even though it was built three hundred years before the Renaissance actually began. Inside the walls are again articulated in geometric marble areas of different colours, but the overall spatial impression is dark and medieval. Little light comes in through the windows, and massive granite columns and pilasters shape the interior, which has an octagonal, double-skinned vaulted dome. It is decorated with important 13th-century mosaics that depict the Creation, the story of Joseph, the life of Christ and the story of John the Baptist and other scenes. The mosaics are by Venetian artists who worked in Florence after 1230 and introduced Byzantine mosaic art, as it had already been imitated in Venice and Ravenna.

The church of **Santi Apostoli**, first documented in 1075, was built about the same time as the Baptistery. Its interior gives the impression of an early Christian basilica with an open roof structure and narrow clerestory windows. Constructive and decorative parts like columns with entasis, composite capitals – two are ancient originals – and stepped arches are influenced by classical architecture and give the Florentine Romanesque style a Roman classical look.

GOTHIC

The Gothic style arrived in Florence only in the late 13th century. After many internal political squabbles the fortified Palazzo del Podestà, later called the **Bargello** after the Italian word for bailiff, was built between 1250 and 1261 as the seat of the captain of police. He was a neutral official who was bound by strict laws and did not come from Florence; his role was to maintain law and order in the city. The imposing fortress-like structure made of dressed and natural stone with a high tower originally had wooden balconies. Inside there is an impressive courtyard with broad arcades as well as several stone-vaulted assembly rooms and a frescoed chapel. In 1292, after the organization of the guilds finally coalesced into a ruling college of nine men, called the Signoria, a new administrative seat was needed. The Palazzo dei Priori – called the **Palazzo Vecchio** since the 16th century – was built after 1299; its core was completed by 1314. The outward appearance of this city hall is still that of a medieval fortress. The massive façade is only decorated with bossed stone and Gothic twin windows set in the upper storeys. It is crowned with a crenellated walkway. The row of coats of arms here shows the eventful medieval history of Florentine government. To the left of the Palazzo Vecchio and set back a little is a smaller palazzo, the former commercial court, built around 1359, whose Gothic

Architecture

Fortified Bargello

Santa Maria Novella has an epochal Renaissance façade

façade is also decorated with coats of arms of the seven large and 14 smaller guilds.

The residential architecture of the 13th century was still dominated by the family towers, which were razed when the commune consolidated its position, as the tower of the Palazzo Vecchio, the symbol of communal power and the pride of the citizens, was supposed to rise above the other buildings. Of the Gothic palazzo architecture only **Palazzo Davanzati** with its loggia and the crenellated, 14th-century **Palazzo Spini-Ferroni** have been preserved.

Around 1300 **Santa Maria Novella**, the first Gothic Dominican church, was built in the shape of a spacious pillared basilica with a groin vault. The **Cathedral of Santa Maria del Fiore**, a monumental Gothic construction, was begun in 1296 and dedicated in 1436 after many delays due to repeated design alterations; the façade was not completed until the 19th century in neo-Gothic style. In none of the Gothic churches in Florence is the filigree skeleton construction

typical of Gothic architecture clearly evident. The usual flying buttresses, tracery and sculpted façades are largely absent. The interiors
also display Florentine characteristics. The cathedral interior is a
pillared basilica in the form of a Latin cross. The nave, divided into
only four bays, has a sober, hall-like appearance. The compactness
and breadth is emphasized by the cross-ribbed vault, which rests on
the massive arcades without a triforium. There is hardly anything
similar to the slender, soaring forms of Gothic architecture in northern and western Europe.

In the field of painting Cimabue (1240/45–1302) is one of the first   Painting
masters to move away from the rigid system of forms found in Byzantine icon painting, which had dominated art for centuries, towards
a style with greater depth and differentiation of colours. **Cimabue's**
Madonna Enthroned (c 1275, Uffizi Gallery, ▶ill. p. 194) and painted
crucifix in Santa Croce (c 1287) bear witness to this.
Giotto di Bondone (c 1266–1337) was the first to break completely
with the incorporeal and non-spatial portrayals of Byzantine medieval painting. With his frescoes in Santa Croce and altar panels (*Madonna of Santa Trinita*, Uffizi Gallery), which were created in the first
30 years of the 14th century, he is considered to be the founder of
modern European painting, since he created a view of the world and
of man that was based on observing reality.
In the course of the 14th century a series of painters in part followed
Giotto's style, and in part the International Gothic style. The major
Florentine works include the frescoes of the Last Judgement, Paradise
and Hell (around 1357) by **Nardo di Cione** in Santa Maria Novella,
a stylistically conservative work steeped in medieval spirituality. The
important cycle of frescoes (1365-1367) by **Andrea Bonaiuto da
Firenze** (d. 1377) in the Spanish Chapel of Santa Maria Novella is
more cheerful, with a wonderful series of pictures (1365–67) that depict man's way to salvation. In the Franciscan church of Santa Croce,
where Giotto left exemplary works, his pupil and immediate successor **Taddeo Gaddi** painted a cycle of frescoes in the Cappella Baroncelli with scenes from the lives of Jesus and the Virgin (c 1335). The
cycle of frescoes by **Agnolo Gaddi** on the Legend of the Cross in the
main choir chapel of Santa Croce was painted between 1380 and
1390. Both painters by and large incorporated Giotto's monumental
style of figures and his indication of spatial depth in his pictures without arriving at new solutions in terms of composition.

In the area of Gothic sculpture the works of **Arnolfo di Cambio**, the   Sculpture
first bronze door of the Battistero San Giovanni by Pisano and the
marble tabernacle by Orcagna in Orsanmichele are among the most
outstanding achievements. Arnolfo di Cambio (c 1245–1302) was the
cathedral architect in Florence from 1296. The few sculptures that

have been ascribed to him (including St Reparata, Madonna and Child, Pope Boniface VIII, cathedral museum) are monumental figures with a block-like outline and somewhat antique-style tendencies in pose, facial expression and gesture.

Around 1330 **Andrea Pisano** (around 1295–1348), another pioneering sculptor and goldsmith, appeared on the scene. His most important and his only certain work is the oldest bronze door of the baptistery (1330–1336) with 28 quatrefoil reliefs. The scenes from the life of John the Baptist have a spatially clear construction and a balanced composition of calmly moving figures with dynamic gestures, some modelled in the round and dressed in richly draped robes. The style reflects Giotto's legacy and Roman sarcophagus reliefs.

Andrea Orcagna (1343/1344 first mentioned in Florence; died 1368) was active not only as a sculptor but also as a painter and architect. Few of his works have been preserved. The marble tabernacle with scenes from the life of the Virgin (1352–59) in Orsanmichele is among Orcagna's best works.

EARLY RENAISSANCE (▶MARCO POLO Insight p. 50)

Architecture   The most urgent building project at the beginning of the 15th century in Florence was the completion of the **cathedral**, especially the construction of a dome over the crossing. **Filippo Brunelleschi** (1377–1446) achieved this between 1420 and 1436 by means of an unsupported, double-skinned, parabolic construction which was seminal for Baroque dome construction. Brunelleschi is the true creator of Renaissance architecture, which was based on a thorough study of ancient architecture and aided by linear perspective projection, vital to architectural drawing, which he rediscovered between 1410 and 1420. In this way precisely calculated, well-proportioned secular and sacred structures were built based on ancient classical and early Christian building methods (▶MARCO POLO Insight p. 170).

The **Spedale degli Innocenti** (Foundling Hospital), begun in 1419, is the first modern secular building with the epoch-making columned portico of an ancient temple instead of medieval supporting pillars. The vaults of this loggia consist of a series of sail-domes that replace the medieval groined and cross-ribbed vaulting. In church architecture Brunelleschi an produced innovative plan for a central space with the Old Sacristy of San Lorenzo (around 1420), a domed structure developed out of a cube and sphere. Brunelleschi also brought new ideas to the construction of a church nave. **San Lorenzo** (begun around 1420) and **Santo Spirito** (begun 1436) are examples of a basilica that was developed out of the building concepts of late antiquity and early Christian times with the ground plan of a Latin cross and a clearly structured, extremely harmonious interior.

Along with Brunelleschi, **Michelozzo** (1396–1472) was the major architect and sculptor in Florence. He succeeded Brunelleschi as cathedral architect (1446–1452). With the **Palazzo Medici-Riccardi** (1444–60) Michelozzo created the prototype of a Florentine city palace with a fortress-like façade in undressed ashlar, double-arched windows as a further development of a Gothic biforium, a cornice all around the building and an arcaded courtyard. The Medici also gave him the commission for the conventual buildings of the Dominican monastery of **San Marco** (between 1437 and 1452). The single cells are grouped around a courtyard without a dormitory; they have barrel vaults and a common open-structured roof. The design is an expression of the individualism that entered monasteries, too, in the 15th century. With the church of **Santissima Annunziata** – today in Baroque style – the first hall church without aisles but with a series of wall chapels was constructed between 1444 and 1453 under the guidance of Michelozzo. This pattern was later used in many Baroque churches.

Palazzo Medici-Riccardi, prototype of a city palace

In the field of painting the traditional forms of the international Gothic style were still being used at the beginning of the quattrocento (15th century). For all his expertise in realistic detail **Gentile da Fabriano** (c 1370–1427) was a late Gothic painter who represented courtly society in an ostentatious and festive manner, as his *Adoration of the Magi* of 1422 in the Uffizi shows. The creator of Italian Renaissance painting is considered to be **Masaccio** (1401–28), who with the aid of the new linear perspective that Brunelleschi discovered, gained a depth and realism in figures, space and landscapes that had never before been achieved. The altar painting *Virgin and Child with St Anne* (1424–25, Uffizi), the cycle of frescoes on the life of the apostle Peter in the Brancacci chapel of **Santa Maria del Carmine** and the Trinity fresco (1426–27) in Santa Maria Novella, a masterpiece of spatial perspective, are examples of this. Paolo Uccello (c 1397–1475) followed Masaccio's example around 1435 and with his equestrian portrait of the Florentine mercenary leader Giovanni Acuto (John Hawkwood, cathedral) of 1436 achieved a great and im-

Painting

posing three-dimensional depiction. In the fresco on the Flood (around 1448; Chiostro Verde, **Santa Maria Novella**) and in the *Battle of San Romano* (around 1456, Uffizi Gallery) he proved himself to be a passionate perspectivist, who came up with unusual, sometimes anti-natural, abstract compositions.

Andrea del Castagno (1421–1457) specialized in rendering the three-dimensionality of the human figure and showed the strong influence of early Renaissance sculpture on his work. Between 1445 and 1450 in the cycle of frescoes in Sant' Apollonia (Cenacolo di Sant' Apollonia) he created scenes of the Passion and a Last Supper with life-size, voluminous figures that communicate with one another through all sorts of looks and lively gestures.

The Dominican monk **Fra Angelico** (around 1387 to 1455) painted his altar pictures and frescoes (San Marco and Uffizi Gallery) with sparse spatial composition and unarticulated body language, but with delicate figures in colourful, flowing garments on an ornamented gold background. With the aid of circular or semicircular groups of figures he achieved a convincing composition that united the area and space of the picture.

The painter monk **Fra Filippo Lippi** (1406–69) oriented himself more to the three-dimensional figures of Masaccio. he created several paintings of the Virgin (Uffizi Gallery, Palazzo Pitti) in an attractive style with beautiful lines and restrained gestures. **Sandro Botticelli** (1445–1510) was another painter in the service of the Medici. In the *Adoration of the Magi* (1475; ▶ill. p. 31; Uffizi Gallery) three generations of Medici appear as the Magi and their companions, surrounded by literary and humanist figures, and the painter himself. But Botticelli's allegorical pictures *Spring* and *Birth of Venus* (both Uffizi Gallery) are more famous; they show the painter's preoccupation with humanist ideas around 1480 as a daring synthesis of neo-Platonist and Christian thought. Despite several nude subjects, Botticelli's painting is still Gothic in its emphasis on S-shaped body lines, flowing robes and exalted looks instead of realistic Renaissance figures based on anatomical studies.

In **Domenico Ghirlandaio** (1449–94) the Florentine upper class found a painter who loved to tell a story. His frescoes in the main choir chapel of Santa Maria Novella with scenes from the life of the Virgin and John the Baptist (1486–1490) are an homage to upper-class Florence. Many famous contemporaries, local sights, homes of the well-to-do, landscape panoramas, festive meals and dances are the subjects, all of which reflect the sensuous life of the second half of the quattrocento, the period of Lorenzo the Magnificent.

Sculpture   When putting a date on the rebirth of European sculpture that spread from Florence, there is only one candidate: 1401, the year of the public competition for the second door of the Baptistery. The competing

This fresco by Ghirlandaio depicts the life of John the Baptist

reliefs with the Sacrifice of Isaac (1402) by the leading masters Ghiberti and Brunelleschi have been preserved and are in the Bargello. Brunelleschi's expressive realism and Ghiberti's decorative illusionism are examples of the main traits of early Renaissance sculpture. Between 1403 and 1424 **Lorenzo Ghiberti** (1378–1455) created a pioneering work with his bronze door. As soon as the second door was completed, Ghiberti was commissioned to make the third, east door of the **Baptistery**, later called the **Paradise Door**. Ghiberti worked for over 20 years (1425–1452) on this door, too. Its completion was delayed for mainly technical reasons, since many attempts had to be made at casting the bronze and gilding it. This craft had been neglected after ancient times and had to be re-learned. Ghiberti's ten gilded bronze panels with scenes from the Old Testament, in which high and low relief are combined, achieved an effect of pictorial illusion that had never before been attained. Ghiberti was primarily a goldsmith and bronze sculptor. For the church **Orsanmichele** he created monumental bronze figures of John the Baptist (1414), St Matthew (1419–22) and St Stephen (1429). A further outstanding project for the sculptors of Florence was the sculptural decoration of the **Cathedral of Santa Maria del Fiore**.

Paradise Door

Nanni di Banco (c 1370/75–1421) worked around 1403 on the Porta della Mandorla, the most richly decorated door of the cathedral, for which he created a gable relief of the Assumption of the Virgin. In 1408 he sculpted the marble figure of Luke the Evangelist for the cathedral façade, a ground-breaking seated figure with an eloquent facial expression, demonstrating complete mastery of posture. A series of the statues for the outside niches of **Orsanmichele** followed. On all of them, for the first time, the adoption of the ancient contrapposto figure is apparent, and the treatment of the heads is reminiscent of Roman portrait busts.

Nanni's work stimulated **Donatello** (1382/86–1466) to outstanding achievements that made him the **true founder of modern sculpture**. His Marble David (1408–09, Bargello), and sculpture and relief of St George (around 1415–17, Bargello) testify to his dramatic handling of the human figure, which is dominated by opposites and rests on the use of the contrapposto of straight and bent leg, as well as on the resulting shift of the body's axis combined with the inner emotion that is reflected in the facial expression of the figure. The monumental niche figures for the cathedral show similar characteristics: *the Prophet with a Scroll*, *Habakkuk* and *Jeremiah*(1425–35; all in the cathedral museum), in which Donatello combines classical poses with Gothic draped figures and gives the statues passion as well as prophetic power. The softly sculpted youthful bronze figure of David (around 1435, Bargello) contrasts with this and is the first freestanding nude figure since ancient times. With his choir loft (1433–1439, Museo dell' Opera di Duomo) Donatello created a lively ensemble of joyful dancing cherubs. In the field of sculpture in wood, Donatello showed his great talent with the crucifix (1412–1420) of **Santa Croce**, which emphasizes the human nature of the Son of God with its expressive naturalism. His late *Maria Magdalena* (cathedral museum), a wooden figure that was made after 1453, shows poignant tragedy in its haggard old figure in comparison to the immaculate beauty of the *Bronze David* of 1435 and demonstrates Donatello's artistic versatility.

Luca della Robbia (1400–82) made a fine marble relief with his choir loft (1431–38; Museo dell' Opera di Duomo), a counterpart to Donatello's depiction of children making music and dancing, as well as an important bronze work in the northern sacristy door of the cathedral; but he focussed mainly on ceramics. He was the founder of an important family workshop in the 15th and 16th centuries, where Andrea (1435–1525) and his sons Giovanni and Giuliano della Robbia also worked. They produced fired reliefs, which were glazed with enamel or lead glaze at first in blue and white and later in various colours, and can be seen in many churches (**cathedral**) and public buildings (**Spedale degli Innocenti**) in Florence.

Desiderio da Settignano (c 1428–1464) was influenced by Donatello but his work was less passionate and expressive. The tomb for the humanist Carlo Marsuppini (around 1453) in **Santa Croce**, the sacramental tabernacle (1461) in **San Lorenzo** and his portrait busts (including Young Lady, Bargello) show his characteristic love of ornamental detail and sensitive, almost drawn treatment of the surface of the marble.

The architect and sculptor **Bernardo Rossellino** (1409–1464) was his contemporary. Rossellino's wall tomb for the state chancellor Leonardo Bruni (around 1450) in Santa Croce was the model for a series of other tombs of the Florentine patriciate. His brother Antonio Rossellino (1427–1479) designed the tomb of the Cardinal of Portugal (1461–1466) in San Miniato al Monte as well as outstanding lifelike portrait busts.

Donatello: *Penitent Magdalene*

Benedetto da Maiano (1442–1497) made important contributions to Florentine sculpture with such works as the extremely realistic portrait bust of Pietro Mellini (1474; Bargello) and the marble pulpit in **Santa Croce** with reliefs of the *Legend of St Francis* and figures of the virtues from the same period, as well as the incomplete late works *Madonna with Child* and *St Sebastian* (Misericordia Chapel); these already hinted at the coming style of the High Renaissance.

The outstanding sculptor and bronze caster of the second half of the 15th century was **Andrea del Verrocchio** (1436–1488), who also showed talent as a painter (including *Baptism of Christ*, Uffizi Gallery). His tomb for Piero and Giovanni de' Medici (completed 1472) consists entirely of ornamental decoration in various shades of marble and bronze. The *Bronze David* (1472–1475, Bargello) is the delicately modelled, naturalistic figure of a shepherd boy in a confident pose. The powerful and realistic figure of the *Putto with Dolphin* (Palazzo Vecchio) concentrates even more on multiple perspectives, which foreshadows the artistically »revolving« fountain sculptures of the Baroque period. The marble bust of a *Lady with a Bouquet* (Bargello) shows an excellent surface treatment of the marble, so that not only the head and hands but also the different layers of fabric are rendered with great effect. His masterpieces in the area of bronze sculpture include the Christ and Thomas group (1466–83) in **Orsanmichele**, niche figures which gave important impulses to Baroque sculpture.

HIGH RENAISSANCE

Within a few decades, by about 1500, the style modelled on ancient Greece and Rome had taken over in Italy; this phase lasted until the death of Raphael (1520) and is called the High Renaissance.

Definition

»Rebirth« of Antiquity

In the early 15th century major Italian architects began to get interested in the way antiquity used forms. They began to use Greek and Roman structures as models for their own work. Filippo Brunelleschi is considered to be the creator of Renaissance architecture. He drew up the plans for the dome of the cathedral of Florence and drew his knowledge from the study of Greco-Roman buildings. In painting the rediscovery of the central perspective was important as is made possible the portrayal of three dimensions on canvas.

ITALY

▶ **The most important people and works**

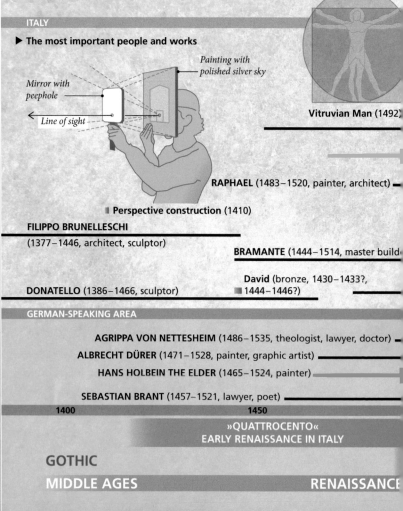

Painting with polished silver sky

Mirror with peephole

← Line of sight

Vitruvian Man (1492)

RAPHAEL (1483–1520, painter, architect)

■ **Perspective construction** (1410)

FILIPPO BRUNELLESCHI
(1377–1446, architect, sculptor)

BRAMANTE (1444–1514, master build

David (bronze, 1430–1433?),
■ 1444–1446?)

DONATELLO (1386–1466, sculptor)

GERMAN-SPEAKING AREA

AGRIPPA VON NETTESHEIM (1486–1535, theologist, lawyer, doctor)

ALBRECHT DÜRER (1471–1528, painter, graphic artist)

HANS HOLBEIN THE ELDER (1465–1524, painter)

SEBASTIAN BRANT (1457–1521, lawyer, poet)

1400	1450

»QUATTROCENTO«
EARLY RENAISSANCE IN ITALY

GOTHIC

MIDDLE AGES   **RENAISSANCE**

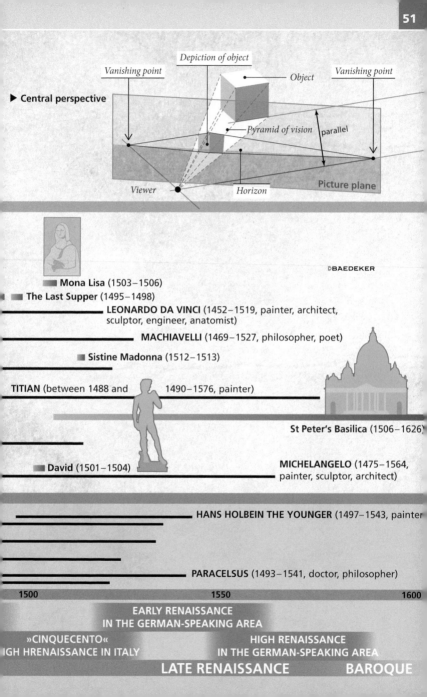

▶ **Central perspective**

Vanishing point

Depiction of object

Object

Vanishing point

Pyramid of vision | parallel

Viewer

Horizon

Picture plane

ⒷBAEDEKER

🔲 **Mona Lisa** (1503–1506)

🔲🔲 **The Last Supper** (1495–1498)

LEONARDO DA VINCI (1452–1519, painter, architect, sculptor, engineer, anatomist)

MACHIAVELLI (1469–1527, philosopher, poet)

🔲 **Sistine Madonna** (1512–1513)

TITIAN (between 1488 and 1490–1576, painter)

St Peter's Basilica (1506–1626)

🔲 **David** (1501–1504)

MICHELANGELO (1475–1564, painter, sculptor, architect)

HANS HOLBEIN THE YOUNGER (1497–1543, painter

PARACELSUS (1493–1541, doctor, philosopher)

| 1500 | 1550 | 1600 |

EARLY RENAISSANCE
IN THE GERMAN-SPEAKING AREA

»CINQUECENTO«
IGH HRENAISSANCE IN ITALY

HIGH RENAISSANCE
IN THE GERMAN-SPEAKING AREA

LATE RENAISSANCE   **BAROQUE**

Architecture

The buildings of **Giuliano da Sangallo** (1445–1516) are pioneering works of the High Renaissance in Florence. He developed Brunelleschi's concepts further and thus helped Florentine architecture to attain maturity. The Villa Medicea (1480–1485) in Poggio da Caiano was built under his direction. In Florence he was responsible for the sacristy of Santo Spirito, an octagonal building with a double-skinned dome (1488–1492) and a barrel-vaulted portico with antique-style decorations such as richly decorated capitals. From 1480 to 1500 Sangallo directed the remodelling of Santa Maria Maddalena dei Pazzi. He added side chapels to the nave, which emphasized the impression of a hall church without aisles.

His contemporary, the architect **Cronaca** (1457–1508), used the same principle in designing San Salvatore al Monte (1487–1504), but in the interior was innovative in the two-storey division of the walls with a palace-like façade. With Palazzo Gondi (1490–1494), Giuliano da Sangallo developed designs for a city palace that pointed the way to the High Renaissance architecture of Rome. The building of Palazzo Strozzi had begun only a year earlier. Sangallo the Elder, Benedetto da Maiano and Cronaca successively directed the work between 1489 and 1500.

Unlike Palazzo Gondi, where the rustication of the ashlars is reduced with each of the three storeys, the stylistically more conservative Palazzo Strozzi has a continuous rustication of the façade with regular rows of arched windows and carefully worked cornices that divide the three storeys. Both palazzi have beautiful courtyards.

Painting

The painting style of **Filippino Lippi** (1457–1504) stands at the cusp of the High Renaissance. After additions to the frescoes in the Brancacci chapel (Santa Maria del Carmine) between 1481 and 1483 he returned to the early Renaissance concept one last time in the altarpiece the *Vision of St Bernard* (1486, Badia). He integrated a portrait of the donor, landscape, architecture and still life by means of warm colours and a balanced composition into a unified work. The *Adoration of the Magi* (1496, Uffizi Gallery), on the other hand, presents a restless picture of numerous poses and much motion of the figures, which can also be seen in the frescoes of the Cappella Strozzi in **Santa Maria Novella** with scenes from the life of the Apostle Philip and St John the Evangelist; Lippi completed them in 1502. Turbulent lines dominate; the architecture seems monumental and over-decorated; the figures have animated gestures, all of which introduces the style of Mannerism.

Leonardo da Vinci (1452–1519), painter, sculptor, architect, technician and natural scientist, learned to paint in Florence under Andrea del Verrocchio; his great talents were shown in two early works, the *Baptism of Christ* and the *Annunciation* (1472–75, both Uffizi Gallery), which were painted with the help of Verrocchio. The *Adoration* *of the Magi* (Uffizi Gallery) is his own work, but was never completed, as Leonardo entered the service of the Duke of Milan in 1482. The Christmas story, in Leonardo's restless, expressive version of a world in upheaval, shows a new dimension to the salvation of the world. Leonardo's contribution to High Renaissance painting lies mainly in the field of rendering light and darkness, with soft transitions between areas of light and shade which give his pictures great atmospheric quality.

Raphael, actually Raffaello Santi (1483–1520), came from Urbino, was a pupil of Perugino and produced his great works in Rome. He lived in Florence for only four years between 1504 and 1508. During this time he painted a double portrait of Agnolo and Maddalena Doni, (1505–06, Palazzo Pitti), a work of sharp skills of observation, the *Madonna of the Goldfinch* (around 1506, Uffizi Gallery) and the *Madonna del Granduca* (1505–06, Palazzo Pitti), both »sweet« depictions with a slightly melancholy air that left a one-sided impression of Raphael's work for centuries. The portraits that Raphael painted in Rome of Pope Leo X (1517–18, Uffizi Gallery), a beautiful Roman woman Donna Velata (around 1514, Palazzo Pitti), and of Cardinal Inghirami (around 1516, Palazzo Pitti) bear witness to Raphael's mastery of portraiture. Raphael represents the pinnacle and also the conclusion of High Renaissance painting, with a thoroughly optimistic view of life despite the critical times – it was the era of the Reformation. Harmony and beauty, pride and dignity determined his concept of man.

Andrea del Sarto, actually Andrea d' Agnolo (1486–1530), was influenced by Raphael, Leonardo and Michelangelo, but he worked almost exclusively in Florence. Several of his frescoes are in the church of **Santissima Annunziata** including the *Birth of the Virgin* (1514), a strictly geometric composition but full of motion with its walking figures. Del Sarto's change of style can be seen clearly in the cycle of grisaille paintings with scenes from the life of John the Baptist in the **Chiostro dello Scalzo**, on which he worked uninterruptedly from 1510 to 1526. The powerful and heroic John the Baptist in the Palazzo Pitti is impressive; and the *Assumption of the Virgin* (around 1527), a work with a dense atmosphere through effective use of light and shade, with deep religious feeling.

It was **Michelangelo Buonarroti** (1475–1564; ▶MARCO POLO Insight p.56) who helped the High Renaissance style break through into sculpture with his early work in Florence , before he went to Rome

Sculpture

from 1496 to 1501. He studied ancient models and was taught by Ghirlandaio and Bertoldo; his early works (all of them are in the Casa Buonarroti), the *Madonna of the Steps* (1491), the *Battle of the Centaurs* (1492) and a wooden crucifix (1494), show, with daring shortening and full of contrast, his strong perception of and at the same time revolutionary renewal of ancient art. *Bacchus* (begun 1497, Bargello) is at first glance only an adaptation of classical antiquity. The shoulder over the right leg, however, is turned not back but forward, which makes the figure seem to sway, something as unknown in antiquity as the expressive naturalism of the slightly vulgar, paunchy figure with a sagging mouth.

Michelangelo was less interested in the balanced, perfectly harmonious ancient concept of the figure than in the interplay of different parts of the body resulting from tension and contrast.

This is expressed in the world famous colossal statue of **David** (1501–1504, Galleria dell' Accademia; ▶MARCO POLO Insight p.186; ▶ill. p. 184), a classical contrapposto figure with strong contrasts between rest and movement, relaxation and tension. Michelangelo's David was planned for the outer façade of the cathedral, but then set up in front of the Palazzo Vecchio. It is the conclusion of a series of Old Testament heroes that was begun in 1400 in Florence. Along with their religious meaning they served as models of knightly courage and by extension of civic responsibility.

MANNERISM

Definition | The expression Mannerism has been adopted for Italian art in the late Renaissance, between 1520 and 1600. It refers to an anti-classical style that gave dynamism to all forms of expression and permitted distortions of reality, even depictions of the abnormal and the unreal, in place of the previous idealization of natural models.

Architecture | The most important example of Mannerist architecture in Florence is the **Biblioteca Laurenziana**. The building was begun in 1524 to plans by **Michelangelo** but was completed only after his death in 1571. The vestibule, rather than the reading room, represents one of the most idiosyncratic spaces created by Michelangelo and his era. The high and narrow, monumentally structured vestibule, a triumphal setting for entering and ascending to the library, is unique in the history of architecture. Visitors are at first unsure whether they are on a main floor or mezzanine, in an inner room or an antechamber. The space is divided by columns into individual sections. The staircase also has an unusual appearance, since it must span a large difference in height in a short space. The central flight of steps flows broad and rounded out of the entrance, and a feeling of insecurity arises when climbing the side flights, which are without a balustrade. This evocation of insecurity by reversing architectural forces is a characteristic of Mannerism.

Giorgio Vasari (1511–1574), painter, architect and writer, oriented himself to Michelangelo's architectural style. With the building of the **Uffizi Gallery** (1560–80), an administrative building for the Grand Duchy of Tuscany, he created an extremely foreshortened, court-like architectural view. The lines of sight are not focussed on a central section of the building, but lead out into the distance through the open loggia. In the so-called Studiolo (study) of Grand Duke Francesco I in the Palazzo Vecchio Vasari produced his Mannerist showpiece (from 1570), a philosophically inspired creation with interpenetrating architectural, painted and sculptural forms which erase all borders between real and artificial space.

The most versatile Mannerist architect in Florence was probably **Bernardo Buontalenti** (1536–1608), who was equally in demand as an interior decorator, builder of fortresses, landscape architect, theatre engineer and costume designer. The Tribuna (around 1581), an artistically adorned, stately octagonal hall in the Uffizi Gallery, the grottoes in the Boboli Gardens (around 1585, design by Vasari), and the interior of the Palazzo Vecchio (1588) were all constructed for the duke's pleasure. Palazzo Nonfinito (1593), the fortress Forte di Belvedere (1590–1595) and the façade of Santa Trínita (1593) are other important buildings by Buontalenti.

One of the first Mannerist painters in Florence was Giovanni Battista Rosso (1494–1540), called **Rosso Fiorentino**. A fresco of the Assumption of the Virgin (1517, Santissima Annunziata) and the panel painting *Madonna with Four Saints* (1518, Uffizi Gallery) are his earliest works. They show skills that he presumably acquired from Andrea del Sarto. The altarpieces *Madonna with Four Saints* (1522, Palazzo Pitti) and the *Betrothal of the Virgin* (1523, **San Lorenzo**) stand out for their asymmetrical composition, iridescent colours and the sophisticated construction of the robed figures. The strong contrast of colour and direction in the composition of *Moses Defending the Daughters of Jethro* (1523, Uffizi Gallery) with doll-like human bodies is also unusual. **Jacopo da Pontormo**, actually Jacopo Carrucci (1494–1557), in his early fresco of the Visitation (1514–1516, Santissima Annunziata) still looks back to the monumental style of his teacher Andrea del Sarto. In Pontormo's Annunciation fresco and *Deposition from the Cross* (1526–1528, both in Santa Felicità), the figures seem almost weightless because of the sophisticated draping of the robes in cool, transparent colours. Pontormo's posthumous depictions of the Medici, Cosimo the Elder and Lorenzo the Magnificent, are very delicate and sensitive.

Painting

Genius from Tuscany

The universal genius Michelangelo worked as sculptor, painter, builder, poet and scientist. His restless spirit is also evident in his numerous moves between Florence and Rome. He did ground-breaking work in both cities in various fields: in Florence as the sculptor of the world-famous statue of David in the Accademia and the figures in the New Sacristy of San Lorenzo, in Rome as painter of the Sistine Chapel in the Vatican and as the architect of the building of St Peter's basilica.

▶ **Milestones**
Time in

▮ Bologna
▮ Florence
▮ Rome

Michelangelo was born on 6 March 1475 in Caprese.

▶ **Michelangelo as sculptor**

Ⓐ Battle of the Centaurs
Time period: 1492–93
Location: Casa Buonarroti, Florence
Supervised by: Lorenzo de' Medici, the Magnificent

Ⓑ Pietà
Time period: 1498–99
Location: St Peter, Rome
Commissioned by: Cardinal Jean Bilhères de Lagraulas, Abbot of St-Denis and French ambassador to the Holy See

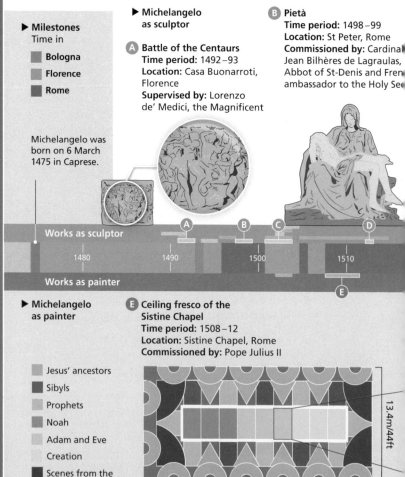

Works as sculptor

1480   1490   1500   1510

Works as painter

Ⓐ   Ⓑ   Ⓒ   Ⓓ

Ⓔ

▶ **Michelangelo as painter**

Ⓔ Ceiling fresco of the Sistine Chapel
Time period: 1508–12
Location: Sistine Chapel, Rome
Commissioned by: Pope Julius II

▮ Jesus' ancestors
▮ Sibyls
▮ Prophets
▮ Noah
▮ Adam and Eve
▮ Creation
▮ Scenes from the Old Testament

13.4m/44ft

40.9m/134ft

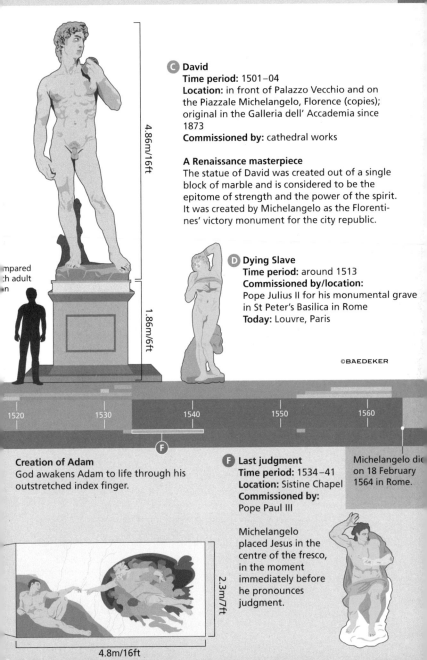

C David

Time period: 1501–04
Location: in front of Palazzo Vecchio and on the Piazzale Michelangelo, Florence (copies); original in the Galleria dell' Accademia since 1873
Commissioned by: cathedral works

A Renaissance masterpiece

The statue of David was created out of a single block of marble and is considered to be the epitome of strength and the power of the spirit. It was created by Michelangelo as the Florentines' victory monument for the city republic.

4.86m/16ft

1.86m/6ft

compared
th adult
n

D Dying Slave

Time period: around 1513
Commissioned by/location: Pope Julius II for his monumental grave in St Peter's Basilica in Rome
Today: Louvre, Paris

©BAEDEKER

1520 1530 1540 1550 1560

Creation of Adam

God awakens Adam to life through his outstretched index finger.

F Last judgment

Time period: 1534–41
Location: Sistine Chapel
Commissioned by: Pope Paul III

Michelangelo die
on 18 February
1564 in Rome.

Michelangelo placed Jesus in the centre of the fresco, in the moment immediately before he pronounces judgment.

2.3m/7ft

4.8m/16ft

Grotto by Buontalenti

Characteristic examples of Mannerist sculpture are the figures for the tomb of Pope Julius II, the so-called Slaves (around 1519, Accademia) and the Medici tombs (1520–1534) in the New Sacristy of San Lorenzo by **Michelangelo** Buonarroti. They have an unprecedented complexity of motion and intensification of expression in order to reveal emotions and passions. Since none of them are complete they can only give an impression of Michelangelo's work process. And yet the incomplete sculptures seem almost timelessly modern as basic depictions of an existential battle between freedom and bondage, between spirit and matter. Michelangelo repeatedly analysed the Christian teaching on salvation in the central theme of the pietà. The *Pietà* in the Museo dell' Opera di Duomo and the *Pietà di Palestrina* (Galleria dell' Accademia) are incomplete works with a poignant, tragic character.

Benvenuto Cellini (1500–1571) was one of the leading Mannerist goldsmiths and bronze sculptors. His masterpieces include a bust of Cosimo I (1545, Bargello) with exaggerated details on the armour and a life-size statue of Perseus (1545–1554, Loggia dei Lanzi, Piazza della Signoria). Characteristic of his style is the momentary movement of the human figure, which is always balanced and is delicately modelled.

Sculpture in Florence culminated at the end of the 16th century in the works of **Giambologna** (1529–1608), who was Flemish and came from Boulogne sur Mer. His most important contribution to sculpture, not least in view of Baroque sculpture, is the »figura serpentinata«, a figure whose body can be viewed from many sides and whose spiralling movement forces the viewer to walk around the figure. The marble group *Florence Defeats Pisa* (1570, Bargello) and *Rape of the Sabine Women* (1583, Loggia dei Lanzi, Piazza della Signoria) are excellent examples of this. In the field of bronze sculpture Giambologna created a masterly statue in the Winged Mercury (around 1580, Bargello), which seems to defy the laws of gravity. The equestrian monument for Grand Duke Cosimo I de Medici (around 1594) on the Piazza della Signoria is considered to be the first public equestrian monument of the era of Absolutism. A public monument to the ruler in an imperial pose, mounted on a horse above the heads of the people, is the most extreme form of glorification of ducal power and highlights the political conditions in Florence. By the late 16th century the republican-minded citizens had turned into subjects who paid homage to their duke.

BAROQUE

Florence was on the sidelines in the Baroque period. Economic slowdown and a rigid political system had caused a decline in artistic work in Florence since the beginning of the 17th century. It then devoted itself to caring for and preserving the cultural assets of the past centuries.

Not a Baroque centre

The biggest building project in Florence in the 17th and 18th centuries was the **ducal chapel** in **San Lorenzo**, a giant domed octagon begun in 1608 as a stately mausoleum for the Medici grand dukes. After many changes to the plans and other delays it was completed in 1737, but the interior was not completed until the 20th century with the inlaid altar of 1939. The expansion of the **Palazzo Pitti** as the ducal residence involved the extension of the façade (1620–40) by Giulio and Alfonso Parigi and of the wings (between 1764 and 1783), which resulted in a forecourt similar to those in French Baroque palaces. **Palazzo Corsini** (1648–56), built by Gherardo Silvano, is a good example of a Baroque city palace with a monumental staircase. In the area of church architecture, the choir of **Santa Maria dei Pazzi**, an important work in which Pier Francesco Silvani (architecture) and Ciro Ferri (painting) cooperated, was remodelled in 1685.

Architecture

Around 1600 painting in Florence was still dominated by the last echoes of Mannerism. **Alessandro Allori** (1535–1607) first gained a reputation as a portrait painter, but under the influence of Michelangelo he created a fresco of the Last Judgement in 1560 in **Santissima Annunziata**. Around 1570 he tended towards ecstatic Counter-Reformation motifs and finally painted subjects from mythology and ancient history with a series of nudes. The *Sacrifice of Isaac* (1589/1601, Uffizi Gallery) is an episodic portrayal with a strong tendency to landscape painting. His *Virgin and Child* (around 1590, Palazzo Pitti) shows a well-developed realism that returns to the painting of the quattrocento. **Pietro da Cortona** (1596–1669) painted several

Painting

Giambologna's
Winged
Mercury

rooms of the **Pitti Palace** for the Medici dukes. The sensual pathos of his trompe l'oeil wall and ceiling paintings can be seen in the rooms of Venus, Mars, Jupiter and Apollo as well as in the Sala della Stufa (Stove Room), which he painted between 1637 and 1641.

Pietra dura　An important craft in Baroque Florence was the mosaic work called *pietra dura*, inlay work in stone (often gemstones) that can be seen especially in the Medici crypt in San Lorenzo. In 1588 Grand Duke Francesco I de' Medici established the workshops, which were soon famous all over Europe and still exist today (Opificio delle Pietre Dure).

19TH AND 20TH CENTURIES

Architecture　The classical and historicist styles mainly left their mark in residences. For the **Piazza della Repubblica**, a civic showpiece and place for promenading, the medieval quarter with the Mercato Vecchio and the Ghetto were torn down in 1890 and replaced by a triumphal arch, the so-called Arconte (1895), surrounded by a series of administrative palaces whose antique style was reminiscent of the Roman forum that once stood here. In church architecture the marble façade of **Santa Croce** (1853–60) was completed by Niccolò Matas, presumably on the basis of ideas by Cronaca (15th century).

The façade of the **Cathedral of Santa Maria del Fiore** was constructed from 1875 to 1887 in the neo-Gothic style to plans by the Florentine Emilio de Fabris. Of the 20th-century buildings, **Stazione di Santa Maria Novella**, the main railway station, by Baroni, Berardi, Gamberini, Guarnieri, Lusanna and Micheluzzi in 1933, and the **bank building** of 1958 by G. Micheluzzi are worth mentioning. A more recent example of ambitious contemporary architecture is the aesthetically and technically ultra-modern music theatre Nuovo Teatro dell' Opera, which opened in 2012.

Painting　Around the mid-19th century a group of Tuscan artists called **Macchiaioli** (*macchia* means »spot«) made a name for themselves. They deliberately distanced themselves from academic art and moved toward open air painting, as did the French schools of Barbizon and Impressionism with their more relaxed use of the brush, natural colours and realistic themes (►MARCO POLO Insight p.62). The works of these artists, including G. Boldini, G. Fattori, S. Lega, can be seen in the **Galleria d' Arte Moderna** in the Palazzo Pitti. In the early 20th century Futurism had its followers in Florence. During the Mussolini dictatorship abstract art was not popular, and in part even forbidden. Florence did not link up with modern art movements again until after the Second World War.

The most famous classical sculptor in the 19th century in Florence was **Pio Fedi** (1816–1892), whose *Rape of Polyxena* (1866) has a place of honour among the statues in the Loggia dei Lanzi. Around the turn of the last century there were several sculptors who imitated Rodin's style in Florence. Heroism and pathos dominated sculpture during the Fascist period. After the Second World War the borders between painting and sculpture became less defined. Installations, environments and happenings are common in contemporary art, and in this way acquire a new dimension for sculpture as well.

Sculpture

Cultural Life

Since the Renaissance Florence has maintained its position as a centre of culture and art. More importantly, the city has kept much of the appearance it had in its golden age. The churches and palaces, piazzas and bridges, frescoes and paintings that were created in the decades of cultural prosperity were pre-served.

Thus the city not only attracts tourists with general interests but especially artists, art historians, humanists and art restorers. Universities and scientific research institutes, theatres and orchestras, opera and libraries bear witness to the vitality of Florentine intellectual life.

Centre of the arts

Next to the state university, which was founded as such in 1924 – but first established in 1349 – there are the following schools: Università di Parigi, Università Europea (located in Fiesole), Università Internazionale dell'Arte, Università Libera per Attori. Nine public libraries are available to the general public and to scholars.

Universities, libraries

Along with its buildings, churches, palaces and museums, Florence offers unique opportunities to study art and history. Thus numerous academies and institutes **nurture science and culture**, as the Accademia della Crusca per la Lingua Italianaum promotes the Italian language. Moreover, there are other schools with an international character such as the British Institute of Florence.

Academies and scientific societies

Twelve theatres, with the **Teatro Comunale** or the new **Opera Theatre** as the foremost, cater to every taste in classical and modern plays and operas. There are concerts to satisfy the most demanding

Theatre, music

Modern Art as Well

Florence is dominated by the brilliant creations of great artistic person-alities of the past. In a setting like this, can there even be room and air to breath for modern artists? Basically the interest in art is there; one might even say that it's in Florence's DNA.

Everything revolves around art here. In hardly another city do as many art restorers and art histori-ans live as in Florence. But the main topic is the great art of the past. Doesn't this suppress or in-hibit artists living in the present? Or it challenges them – as the many trips to Florence by artists of the past centuries show. Many even stayed in Florence and died there. Painters like Arnold Böcklin and Hans-Joachim Staude are bur-ied in the Cimitero Evangelico de-gli Allori (Via Senese 184).

To make it possible for young art-ists to travel to Florence the Ger-man government maintains an art-ists' house, Villa Romana, with studio apartments for scholarship holders. The Villa regularly hosts exhibitions of current art works (Via Senese 68, www.villaromana. org).

In recent times Florence has re-peatedly sent out artistic impulses. For example the Macchiaioli move-ment of the mid 19th century around artists like Giovanni Fattori and Telemaco Signorini introduced social subjects into art with their anti-academic, anti-romantic and anti-classicistic input; they trans-formed the linear brush stroke into »spots« (»macchie«) and in this way set off modern painting in Ita-ly.

In the 20th century it was the Flor-entine design scene of the 1960s and 1970s with groups like Archiz-oom and Superstudio, that started the Italian design boom. The Flor-entine school of applied arts Isti-tuto d' Arte as well as the faculty for architecture are famous throughout Italy.

There is no outstanding collectors' scene or an exciting museum of contemporary art like almost all other Italian cities have in the meantime. But the Museo dell' Arte del Novecento in the me-dieval former hospital Le Leopol-dine on Piazza Santa Maria Novella is being planned, in which collec-tions of 20th century art like the Raccolta Alberto della Ragione, which are scattered over various locations, will be combined. A few galleries are doing good work and providing a stage for Florentine contemporary artists, like the Gal-leria Biagiotti (Via delle Belle Donne 39 r, www.artbiagiotti. com), Otto luogo dell' arte (www. ottoluogodellarte.it) and the Cen-tro d' Arte Spaziotempo (Via Val di Marina 15).

There is a whole row of addresses for contemporary art in the area around Florence, with the museum of contemporary art Luigi Pecci in Prato, and in the middle of the me-dieval centre of San Gimignano in an old cinema the Galleria Contin-ua surprises with excellent contem-porary art. Not to forget the bril-liant sculpture park of the

Museo Marino Marini, one of the few museums of modern art in the city

dedicated collector of contemporary art Giuliano Gori near Pistoia: Fattoria di Celle (www.goricoll.it). Pistoia is moreover connected to Florence through a great 20th century Italian artist, the native of Pistoia and sculptor Marino Marini (1901–1980), whose enormous oeuvre fills two museums (and many other collections in Italy), the Museo Marino Marini in Florence and the one in Pistoia. The dedicated director of the Florentine Marini museum also organizes very interesting exhibitions of works by young contemporary artists.

Today's art has also found a showplace in Palazzo Strozzi, in the Centro di Cultura Contemporanea Strozzina (www.strozzina.org). Large exhibits of contemporary art are also held in Forte Belvedere. Fabbrica Europa has conducted interesting and very successful events on new forms of art in dance, theatre, visual art, media art and much more for 20 years. These are held in various different venues like the old railway station Stazione Leopolda and the former prison Le Murate (www.fabbricaeuropa.net). Florence is indeed giving modern art a chance.

Modern art can also be seen in the Pitti Palace

audience, especially the performances of the **Maggio Musicale Fiorentino**, (Musical May in Florence, from May to late June), which was first established in 1933.

Museums About **50 museums and art collections** are open to the public in Florence. The Uffizi Gallery is famous around the world. The Galleria dell' Accademia, the Museo Nazionale del Bargello, the Palazzo Pitti with their art treasures as well as numerous smaller museums also hold priceless works of art.

Nevertheless, in view of this overwhelming tradition of art, modern or contemporary art have a hard time finding room and attention in Florence. But interesting temporary exhibitions, the International Biennale of contemporary art in the Fortezza da Basso (www.florencebiennale.org) as well as the museum of the famous Tuscan sculptor Marino Marini, which opened in 1988, form bright spots.

Works of art A large part of Florence's art is not kept in museums but is or was originally displayed outdoors. In order to protect sculptures and architectural ornamentation from pollution, in the past many pieces were restored and then put in museums; copies were placed in their original locations. Some of them were made of artificial materials. It is clear that this method will have to be used in the future for many other art treasures. In Florence the question has been raised, however, whether to use original materials instead of artificial ones for this. Great efforts are being made to preserve art treasures. Restoration is in progress everywhere, not only on the paintings in the Uffizi Gallery, but also on churches and their works of art and other buildings. These **restorations** are supported by municipal, state and EU funds, but also by sponsors.

Famous People

FRA ANGELICO (AROUND 1395–1455)

The son of a wealthy farmer from the Mugello valley and actually   Painter
called Guido di Pietro by name or Giovanni da Fiesole, he entered a
Dominican monastery in Fiesole at the age of twenty and spent many
years there decorating his home monastery with frescoes. His reputation as a painter – a mostly self-taught natural talent – spread rap-
idly and when in 1436 the Dominican monastery of **San Marco** in
Florence was remodelled, Fra Giovanni got the commission to decorate the cells with themes from the Passion of Christ.

His painting, despite its strong tendency towards a flat Gothic style,
is astonishingly sculptural and close to reality. His realism was so effective that some of his brothers in the order fainted when they saw
his depiction of the Crucifixion, because there was so much blood.
This compassion was undoubtedly deliberate and gave new emotional impulses to the art of painting. Moreover, the painter monk was an
important innovator in composition who used mainly the semicircle
and circle as the constituting elements of a picture. Iridescent colours, exalted facial expressions and the heartfelt piety of Fra Angelico's figures, especially on his altarpieces, are characteristic of his
painting style. Posterity has exalted his life and artistic achievements
by giving him the name »il beato Angelico« (»the blessed angelic
one«). He died while in Rome in 1455 and was buried in Santa Maria
sopra Minerva. In 1984 he was officially beatified by Pope John Paul
II and made the patron saint of artists.

GIOVANNI BOCCACCIO (1313–1375)

Boccaccio was probably born in Paris as the illegitimate son of a   Poet
wealthy merchant from Certaldo; he grew up in Florence and first
took on his father's profession. Business trips took him to Naples in
his early twenties, where he made contact with courtly society, decided to study classical languages and then stayed there for some
years as an author of Latin and Italian literature. Around 1340 he was
in Florence again, where he met the humanist and scholar **Petrarch**,
with whom he then worked to revive Latin and Greek language and
literature. At that time Boccaccio's works included his psychological
romance *Fiammetta* (1343), which goes back to a love affair of his
own at the Neapolitan court. Boccaccio survived the Great Plague of
1348, which took over half of the population of Florence, and under
the influence of this disaster wrote the cycle of novellas **Il Decamer-
one** (1348–1353), which is now considered to be the first work of
Italian prose and which had a decisive influence on world literature

Florence did not treat its great poet Dante very well

(Shakespeare, Rabelais, Lessing). In 100 stories, which are told by ten people over ten days, questions of the zest for life and joy of existence as well as the morality of love are presented in full, realistic imagery. The subject covers everything from the high art of love to sexual love, against the background of a plague epidemic that suspends all restrictions of law, religion and morality. In addition many other works in Italian and Latin, Boccaccio, as an admirer of Dante, also wrote a historically controversial *Vita di Dante* (around 1360). In 1373 the city of Florence gave him the public professorship for the interpretation of Dante's *Divine Comedy*.

SANDRO BOTTICELLI (1445–1510)

Painter   The painter Alessandro di Mariano Filipepi was born in Florence and got the nickname Botticelli (little barrel) as a boy. He was trained as a goldsmith and then became a student of Filippo Lippi. Early on he gained the favour of the Medici family, who supported him through many commissions; he was even a close friend of Lorenzo the Magnificent, who was the same age. Botticelli was greatly receptive to humanistic ideas, which he also incorporated into his paintings. He gained impulses from the Platonic Academy in Florence, but in later years tended toward mysticism and became a **follower of Savonarola.**

His main works – including the famous *Primavera* and *Birth of Venus* – were painted between 1470 and 1495; in the collections of the Uffizi the development of his style is represented well. His paintings unite the glittering lifestyle of the era of Lorenzo the Magnificent with humanist education, great sensitivity, a sharp understanding combined with a delicate, elegant use of the brush and rhythmic composition of colour. Although he painted some nudes, Botticelli's style is basically neo-Gothic, since he deliberately abstained from the dimensional realism of the Renaissance and instead gave his pictures an ethereal, mysterious charm. After the death or exile of all his Medici patrons in 1494 Botticelli had a personal and creative crisis, which was in part expressed in religious pictures, but without examining the new painting of a Leonardo, Michelangelo or Raphael. It is not surprising that toward the end of his life he made more than 90 pen and ink drawings on Dante's *Divine Comedy* and analysed the idea of salvation mystically.

FILIPPO BRUNELLESCHI (1377–1446)

Filippo Brunelleschi, a native of Florence, is the true founder of Re-   Architect,
naissance architecture. His innovations required an intensive study of   sculptor
ancient architecture. Brunelleschi even went to Rome with his friend
Donatello, the sculptor, in order to study ancient ruins on site. The
results of his measurements and computations were geometric and
stereometric forms that served as the basis for his buildings. Between
1410 and 1420 he derived his ground-breaking discovery of **central
perspective projection** from Euclidean optics; this is a scientifically
accurate depiction of a three-dimensional space on a flat surface,
which opened up unimagined possibilities, especially in painting.
Brunelleschi's great feats of engineering include the massive unsupported, double-skinned structure of the **cathedral dome** in Florence,
which was built between 1420 and 1436 (▶MARCO POLO Insight
p.171). In secular building he charted a new course in the Ospedale
degli Innocenti, the orphanage, by using sail-domes. In church architecture he achieved revolutionary naves in San Lorenzo and Santo
Spirito, which made Gothic architecture appear completely obsolete.
In a daring synthesis of early Christian basilica and ancient architecture (columns, pilasters, capitals, entablature) Brunelleschi created a
space that was flooded with light and had balanced proportions; the
space was constantly in interplay with the individual forms. In **San
Lorenzo**, for example, the semicircle of the nave arcades is repeated
on a smaller scale in the clerestory windows, in the arches of the chapel openings and in the arches of the domes in the aisles. In **Santo
Spirito** the crossing square (intersection of the nave and transept) is
the standard of measure for the whole building. For buildings with a
central plan Brunelleschi followed the example of Byzantine domed
structures. The **Old Sacristy** of San Lorenzo, a square-domed space,
and the **Pazzi Chapel**, the chapter house of the Franciscans of Santa
Croce, where he combined a domed rectangular plan with a square
plan, offer interesting variations of modern central-plan structures. As
a sculptor Brunelleschi took part in 1402 in the competition for the
second bronze door of the Battisterio San Giovanni with a relief of *The
Sacrifice of Isaac*, but Ghiberti's design won; both reliefs are in the
Bargello museum today. Competing with his friend Donatello he created a crucifix with a beautiful, idealized portrayal of Christ modelled
on ancient classical nude figures (**Santa Maria Novella**). The great
architect found his final resting place in the cathedral of Florence.

DANTE ALIGHIERI (1265–1321)

Dante, the son of a respected patrician in Florence, was born in 1265   Poet
and grew up at a time when the cities of northern Italy were the bat-

tleground in a war between rival noble families; the supporters of the emperor were called the Ghibellines, the supporters of the pope the Guelphs. Often these families were less interested in the authority of the pope or emperor than in their own power in their home cities. Dante's family was part of the Ghibelline party, which called itself the **White Guelphs** in Florence, and had to go into exile several times when the city was once again ruled by the papist Black Guelphs. Dante was born during a period of Black Guelph dominance, and part of his family lived in exile. In Bologna he studied

law and then went into politics at the age of 20. In 1295 he was a member of the Council of the Capitano del Popolo, in 1296 of the Council of the One Hundred and in 1297 of the Podestà, until in 1300 he was elected to the Signoria as one of the priori. In that year bloody battles broke out again between noble groups in the city. The pope sent Charles of Valois to Florence to restore order. The White Guelphs were accused of conspiracy and their leaders were banished from the city. As one of their supporters Dante was put on trial: in 1302 he was sentenced to exile for life; five years later the sentence was changed in his absence to the **death penalty**. Embittered and dependent on charity, Dante lived in various northern Italian cities, in Verona, in Treviso and Ravenna, where he worked as the ambassador of Guido Novello della Polenta and died in 1321. He was buried in Ravenna. In Santa Croce in Florence there is a memorial to him.

During his years of exile Dante wrote his most important politico-philosophical and literary works. These include the Latin treatises *Monarchia* and *De Vulgari Eloquentia* as well as the *Commedia*, which was written in the Tuscan dialect, the precursor to the Italian national language and which later got the addition »Divina« to its name. It is an allegorical didactic poem consisting of 100 songs in verse form. It is a comprehensive collection of the most important medieval intellectual discussions on theology and philosophy, church and state as well as the political and social situation of Italy in Dante's time. In the *Divine Comedy* and in a series of poems the female character Beatrice appears again and again. She was a friend from Dante's boyhood, who in the course of time became for him the personification of redeeming love. With this portrayal of ideal love Dante remained closely connected to medieval thought.

DONATELLO (AROUND 1386–1466)

Donatello – his name was actually Donato di Niccolò di Betto Bar- *Sculptor*
di – was **the most important sculptor of the 15th century**, unsurpassed in his time for his power of expression, variety of subjects
and the amount of his output. He was a pupil in Ghiberti's workshop and with Nanni di Banco; as a master he sculpted figures for
the façade, the outer walls and the campanile of the cathedral of
Florence, his hometown, as well as for the church of Orsanmichele.
His encounter with Roman antiquity took him far beyond the concepts and techniques of medieval art. He created the first nude
(*Bronze David*, around 1430, in the Bargello) and the first completely free-standing group monument (*Judith and Holofernes*,
1440, in front of the Palazzo Vecchio) that were made in modern
times. The tabernacle with the *Annunciation* in the church of **Santa
Croce** (around 1434) and the **choir loft** with dancing children for
the cathedral (1433–40, in the cathedral museum) are further major works. His realistic sculpting mastered both beautiful and ugly
subjects and expanded the dimensional shape of figures in an exemplary manner for following artists. The Medici honoured the
sculptor by having him buried in the crypt of Cosimo the Elder in
San Lorenzo.

GALILEO GALILEI (1564–1642)

Born in Pisa, Galilei grew up in Florence and studied literature and *Scientist*
mathematics there (▶MARCO POLO Insight p. 72). At the age of
25 years he went to the University of Pisa to lecture in mathematics,
but the best scientific studies were being done in Padua at that time,
where he taught for more than 18 years. In 1610 he returned to Florence – as the court mathematician under the protection and in the pay
of the Medici, which made it possible for him to devote himslef completely to his research in mathematics, physics and astronomy. He
improved scietific apparati, like a telescope, which allowed him to gain
new knowledge on the character and movement of heavenly bodies.
In one of his main works he supported the teachings of Copernicus,
according to which the sun is in the middle of the solar system, not
Earth. He dedicated the *Dialogo* to the Medici prince Ferdinando II,
but it also got him a conviction by the Inquisition. At that time under
the threatening pressure of the Reformation and the arising Enlight-
enment the church could not deviate from its received world view. He
died on his estate Arcetri near Florence in 1642, old and venerated,
and **was buried in the church Santa Croce**. Galileo Galilei's studies
on gravity, the laws of motion, scientific empiricism to one of the
greatest physicists of all time. 350 years later, in 1992, the Roman
Catholic church officially rehabilitated him as well

And Yet It Moves!

Dass Galileo Galilei diesen Satz sagte, nachdem er offiziell der kopernikanischen
The fact that Galileo Galilei made this statement after he officially renounced
Copernicus' theory is more of a legend. But it is true that the Roman Catholic
Church only rehabilitated Galileo in 1992 – 360 years after condemning his
teachings as heretical.

▶ **Geocentric conception of the world (schematic; according to Ptolemy/ Aristotle)**
The geocentric conception of the world placed Earth and consequently also people in the centre of the universe. It was part of the fundamental convictions of the Roman Catholic Church.

SATURN
JUPITER
MARS
SUN
VENUS
MERCURY
MOON
EARTH

ERIS PLUTO
• • · • - - Dwarf planets - - - - - - - -

▶ **Planets and their respective distance from the sun in mil. km (schematic representation)**

NEPTUNE 4496
URANUS 2896

▶ **Stations in the life of Galileo Galilei**
Galileo was professor of mathematics in Padua

PADUA
PISA FLORENCEE
ROME

Galileo's birthplace and first place of learning

The family came from Florence; after his trial Galileo spent most of his arrest period in Arcetri nearby

Galileo was brought to trial in Rome

▲ **Sector**

▶ **Life, discoveries and inventions of Galileo Galilei**

1564 Birth of Galileo Galilei

1592–1610 Professor of **mathematics** at the university in Padua

1593 Galileo invents a water **pump** that is driven by horses. In 1594 he receives a patent for it from the Venetian senate.

1597 Galileo invented the sector, an instrument used to calculate proportions. Its areas of use included surveying and navigation.

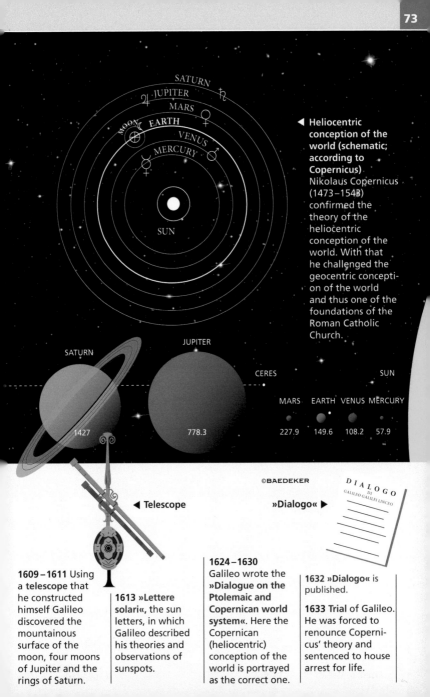

SATURN
JUPITER
MARS
MOON EARTH
VENUS
MERCURY

SUN

◀ **Heliocentric conception of the world (schematic; according to Copernicus)** Nikolaus Copernicus (1473–1543) confirmed the theory of the heliocentric conception of the world. With that he challenged the geocentric conception of the world and thus one of the foundations of the Roman Catholic Church.

SATURN
JUPITER
CERES
SUN
MARS EARTH VENUS MERCURY

1427   778.3   227.9 149.6 108.2 57.9

©BAEDEKER

◀ **Telescope**

»Dialogo« ▶

DIALOGO
DI
GALILEO GALILEI LINCEO

1609–1611 Using a **telescope** that he constructed himself Galileo discovered the mountainous surface of the moon, four moons of Jupiter and the rings of Saturn.

1613 »Lettere solari«, the sun letters, in which Galileo described his theories and observations of sunspots.

1624–1630 Galileo wrote the **»Dialogue on the Ptolemaic and Copernican world system«**. Here the Copernican (heliocentric) conception of the world is portrayed as the correct one.

1632 »Dialogo« is published.

1633 Trial of Galileo. He was forced to renounce Copernicus' theory and sentenced to house arrest for life.

GIOTTO DI BONDONE (AROUND 1266–1337)

Painter, architect

Giotto is generally considered to be the **founder of modern European painting**, since he created important, ground-breaking works around 1300 that departed from the non-spatial and incorporeal compositions of Byzantine-influenced medieval painting. He observed nature and reality closely and thus achieved a realistic picture of the world and of people in his frescoes and altarpieces, even though they still had religious themes. He stressed the corporeal in his figures, who also radiate human emotions and appear to act on their own. His realistic, monumental style together with clear principles of composition (triangular composition) and bright colours created a new school of painting and inspired generations of painters. Giotto was also an architect and sculptor. In 1334 in Florence he was given the office of **cathedral architect**, where in his few remaining years he mainly spurred on the building of the campanile. He had a large workshop and apart from Florence was also active in Assisi, Padua, Rome, Rimini, Naples and Milan.

The works attributed to him with certainty are the six frescoes on the life of St Francis (around 1320) in the Bardi chapel and three scenes from the lives of St John the Evangelist and John the Baptist (around 1325) in the Peruzzi chapel of **Santa Croce** in Florence, as well as the *Enthroned Madonna* (around 1310) in the Uffizi Gallery and the crucifix in the sacristy of **Santa Maria Novella**, an early work of 1290.

NICCOLÒ MACHIAVELLI (1469–1527)

Historian, author

As a historian Niccolò Machiavelli was the **great annalist of his native city** and left to posterity an eight-volume history of Florence. As secretary of the chancellery of republican Florence from 1498 until he lost the position in 1512, Machiavelli was a staunch supporter of

the republican system as the one in which people could best develop freely, despite the internal political conflicts of his time. His model for this was the Roman republic, which placed the common good of all citizens above the good of the individual, as Machiavelli explained in his *Thoughts on Politics and Statesmanship* (*Discorsi*). In various works he analysed his own era and especially in his writing ***The Prince*** (*Il Principe*) he came to insightful, but largely negative conclusions on laws and behaviour in politics. Machiavelli's writings were known only to a small circle of intellectuals during his lifetime. It was their effect in later times that made him famous as a defender of raison d'état, even though Machiavelli only demystified the medieval state, which hid behind a guise of religion, exposed its actual mechanisms of power and maintained that reason, will and instinct rule the world. Only they could stand up to human instability and quirks of fate. It is not generally known that Machiavelli also wrote novellas, poems and very original comedies.

MASACCIO (1401–28)

Masaccio (Tommaso di Giovanni di Simone Guidi) is considered to be the **creator of Italian Renaissance painting**. On the basis of Giotto's style of the early 14th century he was able to achieve an unprecedented depth and reality in figures, space and landscapes by making exact and rigorous use of the teaching on perspective that Brunelleschi had rediscovered between 1410 and 1420. The emotional power of his painting brought about the most perfect expression of the Renaissance concept of man. Masaccio was a pupil of Masolino and worked in Florence from 1422, where together with his teacher he painted the series of frescoes from the life of the Apostle Peter in the Brancacci Chapel in **Santa Maria del Carmine** between 1424–25 and 1427–28, including works he painted by himself: *The Expulsion*, the first realistic nude in Renaissance painting, the *Distribution of Alms*, *St Peter Healing with his Shadow*, *St Peter Baptizing and Preaching in the Cathedral* as well as the famous depiction of the *Tribute Money* with the people's eloquent expressions and gestures. His fresco of the Trinity (around 1426–27) in **Santa Maria Novella** with the kneeling donors is the masterpiece of perspective spatial depiction in early Renaissance painting.

Painter

ANNA MARIA LUISA DE' MEDICI

▶MARCO POLO Insight p.77

LORENZO DE' MEDICI, THE MAGNIFICENT (1449–92)

He was the **embodiment of the Renaissance spirit** in his style of rule, life, world view, education and patronage of the arts – Lorenzo de' Medici, called »Il Magnifico« (»the Magnificent«) by the people. Lorenzo gained a special position for Florence in Italian culture and politics by using the means of the Medici bank and his support

Regent

among the Florentine population. His brother Giuliano fell victim to the Pazzi conspiracy in 1478 in the cathedral of Santa Maria del Fiore. Lorenzo, though wounded, was able to flee to safety in the sacristy. He promoted the Platonic Academy and was active in literature. In the Medici Gardens by San Marco he collected ancient sculptures, drew sculptors together and had young talents like Michelangelo trained. Andrea del Verrocchio, Ghirlandaio and Sandro Botticelli worked for him. When Lorenzo died at the age of 43 from a mysterious illness Niccolò Machiavelli wrote: »Never before has someone died in Italy with a reputation for such great intelligence, nor to so great a dismay of his fatherland. All of his fellow citizens mourned his death, no one refrained from showing his grief at this event.« Lorenzo was first interred in the Old Sacristy of San Lorenzo, later together with his brother in the New Sacristy built by Michelangelo.

MICHELANGELO BUONARROTI (1475–1564)

Painter, sculptor, architect, poet, natural scientist

With the universal genius Michelangelo Buonarroti (►MARCO POLO Insight p.56), painter, sculptor, architect, poet and natural scientist, the transition from High Renaissance to Mannerism, with its pioneering use of colour and form, is complete. At the age of 13 Michelangelo began studying in the workshops of the Florentine painter Domenico Ghirlandaio. Along with his love of painting he developed more and more a passion for sculpting. In 1489 the young Michelangelo was admitted into the sculptor's academy in the Medici Gardens. In 1494 he left Florence (before the Medici were expelled and the political upheaval – the Dominican monk Savonarola soon took power) and after a short stay in Venice he worked in Bologna. His next place of residence was Florence again (1495–96). Then Michelangelo travelled to Rome and stayed there from 1496 to 1501. From 1501 to 1505 Michelangelo stayed in Florence again. He created the **David** (Galleria dell'Accademia), the round relief *Madonna Pitti* (Bargello) and the painting *The Holy Family* (Uffizi Gallery). His restless spirit and commissions kept him moving from 1505 to 1534 between Florence, Rome and Bologna. In these years the **funerary chapel of the Medici** near San Lorenzo, the *Slaves* (Galleria dell' Accademia), *Apollo* (Bargello) and *Vittoria* (Palazzo Vecchio), as well as many drawings. With short interruptions Michelangelo stayed in Rome from 1534 until he died. In this time he completed projects

Noble Donor

Anna Maria Luisa (also Lodovica) de' Medici, who was from 1691 until 1716 the wife of Johann Wilhelm von Pfalz-Neuburg and the Palatine electress at the court in Düsseldorf, is to be thanked for the wealth of art that still belongs to the museums of Florence today.

Unlike in other noble dynasties, where the treasures collected over generations were scattered to the four winds when the dynasty died out Anna Maria, the last Medici, succeeded in leaving the immeasurable family wealth in paintings, sculptures, reliquaries, precious gold and silver jewellery, carpets, porcelain, fine furniture, scientific collections and much more to the city of Florence in her will. The bequest was bound by the condition that everything should remain in the capital of the duchy, in Florence. In this way Anna Maria showed herself to be the wise heiress of the humanist foundation of the Renaissance and its modern consequences.

Her father, Grand Duke Cosimo III, had married her to the German elector and provided her with a stately dowry. She loved Flemish and Dutch painting, infected her husband with her love of art and together they travelled incognito to Amsterdam and Rotterdam and bought art, including Rubens and Rembrandt. For Italian art, which was in great demand at the European courts at that time, she of course had her own special contacts. So the collection that she gathered in Düsseldorf soon contained more than one thousand works, not to mention fine porcelain and jewellery that fill the silver museum and the porcelain museum in Palazzo Pitti today. But when Johann Wilhelm died in 1716 she had to return to Florence. The couple had no heir. A small part of the collection, 50 paintings, remained in Düsseldorf. The largest part went to Munich to the heirs of the elector of Düsseldorf, the Bavarian branch of the house of Pfalz-Sulzbach, and formed the basis of the collection in the Alte Pinakothek museum. What Anna Maria paid for out of her own pocket went along with her to Florence, including many Dutch works that can be admired in the blue rooms of the Uffizi today. The Medici dynasty in Florence was also dying as the last duke, her brother Gian Gastone, had no children. But the last Medici heiress was able to save the family's immense artistic property for the city through her will, which was called the »Family Pact«.

for the Biblioteca Laurenziana. His late work, including the marble *Pietà* in the cathedral museum in Florence, emphasizes Christian salvation again. Michelangelo's body was brought from Rome to Florence and interred in the church of Santa Croce.

RAPHAEL (1483–1520)

Painter   Raphael (his name was actually Raffaello Santi/Sanzio) is the artist who **»expressed High Renaissance painting in its most pure, perfect and comprehensive form«**

(J. Jahn). Raphael was born in Urbino; he joined the workshop of Perugino in Perugia at the age of 17. In 1504 he moved to Florence, where he devoted himself to the study of the old and »modern« painters. From 1508 on he lived in Rome; after the death of Bramante he was placed in charge of the construction of St Peter's Basilica. During these twelve years in Rome he reached his artistic peak in the frescoes of the *Stanze di Raffaello* in the Vatican. Raphael was the only artist honoured by being buried in the Pantheon in Rome. Raphael's many notable paintings in Florence include, in the Uffizi Gallery, *Pope Leo X with Two Cardinals*, *Pope Julius II*, *Madonna with the Goldfinch* and *Portrait of Perugino*, and in Palazzo Pitti *La Donna Velata*, *La Donna Gravida* and *Madonna del Granduca*.

LEONARDO DA VINCI (1452–1519)

Painter,   The Italian Renaissance produced many personalities but only the
sculptor,   **genius** of Leonardo da Vinci united the abilities of a painter, sculp-
architect, tor, architect, natural scientist and engineer. Michelangelo alone can
natural   be compared. As an artist he brought the Renaissance to its highest
scientist, attainments and his technical discoveries and inventions show the
engineer   breadth of his mind. Leonardo da Vinci was a pupil of Verrocchio
and in 1472, at the age of just 20, was admitted to the painters' guild in Florence. From 1482 to 1498 he worked at the court of Duke Lodovico Sforza in Milan. He lived in Florence again from 1500 to 1506, then in Milan, finally from 1513 to 1516 in Rome. In 1517 he accepted the invitation of King François I to go to France.

Almost all of the works from his last 20 years of life are lost, or preserved only as copies made by his students. The **_Mona Lisa_**, probably his most famous work, is in the Louvre in Paris. Leonardo also worked as a fortress builder, dedicated himself to intensive scientific studies, dissected corpses, wrote a treatise on human anatomy and illustrated it with drawings. He also conducted experiments on flight, observed the flight of birds, examined the laws of air and water currents, and conducted botanical and geological studies. His many drawings, studies on the movement of the human body, experiments in the natural sciences, designs for buildings and technical projects prove the universality of this Renaissance genius.

ENJOY
FLORENCE

Where can you find out more about Florence? Which are the best
hotels? Where are the good restaurants? Read it here, ideally
before the trip.

For Every Taste

Under the roofs of Florence there are no less than 12 mil. overnight stay every year, in hundreds of hotels, from numerous luxury accommodations with 5 stars to simple guesthouses with one star, but also countless holiday flats and B & B rooms.

The luxury hotels, but also many of the middle class hotels or residences are located in historic palazzi, in the Renaissance palaces (►MARCO POLO Insight p. 84). Many hotels were renovated in recent years. The competition with B&B has served to improve the standards of mid-range and simple hotels.

Residences, that is furnished flats or rooms with a kitchenette that can be rented by the day. Anyone who is plan to stay longer or who wants to experience everyday life in Florence should stay in a holiday flat, which can be booked with numerous agencies by the week.

Accommodation possibilities

The city government has been collecting a visitor's tax (tassa di soggiorno) on overnight stays in recent years, which is added to the price of the hotel room. For a night in a youth hostel or in a B&B room in a private home the tax is €1 and it goes up to €5 per night for stays in luxury hotels.

Visitor's tax

When choosing a hotel, keep the city centre in mind. The historic sights and a rest during the hot noon hours are close by. On the other hand, the noise factor must be taken into account, since Florence is busy until after midnight. Do not underestimate the lack of parking in the centre of town or the high costs of parking in garages or lots.

Close to the centre

A list of hotels called *Guida all' Hospitalità* is available at tourist offices (►Information) and on the Internet: www.firenzeturismo.it. In any case, make reservations early.

Hotel prices vary greatly according to season. Most hotels can be booked online, which makes for additional price flexibility (e. g. www.booking.com, www.hrs.de). In this way luxury hotels can be affordable at times even for normal budgets.

There are also many B & B rooms in Florence (Internet: www.bbitalia. it, www.bed-and-breakfast.it).

Prices and reservations

Hotel Four Seasons is located in an old palazzo

Living in History

Palazzi, palazzi, palazzi – the Renaissance left us not only all of the valuable works of art or magnificent churches, but also a unique lifestyle that was expressed in the residences of Florentine nobility and patrician families.

Renaissance palazzi are characterized by their elegant and balanced forms, their inner courtyards, loggia and gardens. The interior furnishings impress with artistic stone floors, painted ceilings and rafters, carpets, luxurious fabrics, bronze fittings and unadorned furniture, all of them testimonies to crafts that are still alive in Florence today. Hundreds of these palazzi still stand in the interwoven lanes and alleys of the city, many of them now house large and small museums, foundations, offices, administrative offices and collections of antiques. Many of them are also home to the descendants of the families that built them. It is possible to stay in a Renaissance palace even when only on a short trip to Florence since a number of the palazzi are being used as hotels.

One of the most recent examples of this trend is the luxury hotel **Four Seasons** (▶hotel list), which was opened in 2008 in the **Palazzo della Gherardesca**. It was built around 1480 as a Renaissance villa with a profound square inner courtyard and a park and passed to the ownership of the later Medici pope Leo XI in 1585; his sister, who had married the nobleman Ugo della Gherardesca, inherited it. Even more recent (2010) is the transformation of a wonderful Renaissance villa in Fiesole into the luxury hotel **Il Salviatino** (www.salviatino.com), which had belonged to families like the Bardi, the Orsini and the Rucellai in the 15th and 16th centuries.

Villa Mangiacane (▶Hotel list) outside of Florence in the hills is an enchanting hotel in a Renaissance villa. It originally belonged to the Machiavelli family; later it was acquired by the influential patrician family Mazzei.

Jacopo Mazzei, a descendant of this family, is now one of the managers of a luxury residence in **Palazzo Tornabuoni** consisting of 36 elegant apartments, which are now open after years of restoration. This gigantic palace from the middle of the 15th century even goes back to a design by Michelozzo, one of the star Renaissance architects, who was commissioned by the Tornabuoni family. Their feeling for art was no less than that of the Medici, for they financed the expensive fresco work of the large main choir chapel in Santa Maria Novella by the painter Domenico Ghirlandaio.

Villa Bellosguardo (▶hotel list) on a hill at the edge of Florence, is also a wonderful Renaissance hotel that was named after its medieval tower. A good friend of Dante, the poet Guido Cavalcanti, had it built as a hunting tower with a wide view. In the 16 cent., the villa was added; the

Florence lies at your feet in Hotel Torre di Bellosguarda

original frescos have been preserved until today. In 1913 the villa came into the possession of the German baroness Marion Hornstein; she used it as a meeting place and guest house for artists and politians. Her grandchild, Baron Amerigo Franchetti, has been running a small but fine hotel in the villa since 1988.

But you can live in a Renaissance palace even if you don't want to spend a lot of money, for example, in Hotel Palazzo Guadagni (►hotel list) or Hotel La Scaletta (►hotel list). Palazzo Tolomei is decorated throughout with frescos from the Renaissance; today it houses a residential hotel (www.palazzotolomei.it).

If the have **hotels accommodated travellers on the Grand Tour** since the 18th cent., like Pension Pendini (►hotel list) or Pension Loggiato dei Serviti (►hotel list) in a monastery (16th cent.), located on Piazza Santissima Annunziata no less, they could certainly tell many stories.

A different story is connected to Hotel Principe in a charming villa (1820). King Vittorio Emanuele II chose it personally as his hotel when Florence became the capital of the freshly united Italy from 1865 until 1871.

Recommended adresses

PRICE CATEGORIES
€€€€ over €200
€€€ €150 – €200
€€ €90 – €150
€ up to €90

❶ etc. ▶plan p. 112–113

HOTEL RESERVATIONS
Consorzio Firenze Albergo
tel. 055 2 70 72 78
www.firenzealbergo.it

LUXURY
❶ Brunelleschi €€€€
Piazza S. Elisabetta 3
tel. 0 55 2 73 74 87
www.hotelbrunelleschi.it 96
rooms
Well-appointed hotel near the cathedral, renovated in 2012, stands out for its excellent service as well as modern design and the best materials in an interesting building complex. With the medieval Torre Pagliazza, which was only discovered in 1989 when the hotel was being built and once served as a prison; roof terrace with a wonderful panoramic view.

❷ Four Seasons €€€€
(▶ill. p.82)
Borgo Pinti 99
tel. 055 2 62 61
www.fourseasons.com
This dream hotel was opened in 2008 in the largest private park in the city; it stands for pure luxury: elegant top-class restaurants, beautifully stylish furnishings in generous suites, the wellness, pool and fitness area. And all of this in a Renaissance villa estate, which was once the residence of the age-old Tuscan noble dynasty of the della Gherardesca.

❸ Helvetia & Bristol €€€€
Via dei Pescioni 2
tel. 0 55 2 66 51
www.hotelhelvetiabristolflorence. com, 67 rooms
Located opposite Palazzo Strozzi, this fabulous luxury hotel is now part of the Leading Hotels of the World. It was built in the late 19th century and soon became one of Florence's best; prominent guests include Pirandello, Stravinsky and de Chirico; the magnificent rooms are in Florentine and English style; beautiful winter garden.

❹ Regency €€€€
Piazza d' Azeglio 3
tel. 0 55 24 52 47
www.regency-hotel.com, 35
rooms
Small elegant villa decorated in English style, with a pretty garden for a romantic breakfast.

❺ Villa Mangiacane €€€€
San Casciano
Val di Pesa
Via Faltignano 4
tel. 0 55 8 29 01
www.villamangiacane.it, 26
rooms and suites
With Villa Mangiacane another luxury accommodation for Florence holiday-makers with high standards opened; for British clientele. This completely renovated Renaissance villa sits on a hill in the middle of olive groves and vineyards. The view from the fab-

Noble atmosphere in Hotel Villa Mangiacane

ulous loggia is unforgettable and shows that Florence is only 12km/7mi away.

❻ Principe €€€€
Lungarno Vespucci 34
tel. 0 55 28 48 48
www.hotelprincipe.com, 20 rooms
Stylish house with rooms with a garden or river view.

❼ Torre di Bellosguardo €€€€
Via Roti Michelozzi 2
tel. 055 2 39 81 45
www.torrebellosguardo.com, 16 rooms

Insider Tip

Anyone who wants a quiet and dignified place to stay should choose this beautiful Renaissance villa on a hill south of the centre with a wonderful view of the city. There is a pool in the park.

❽ Westin Excelsior €€€€
Piazza Ognissanti 3
tel. 0 55 2 71 01
www.starwoodhotels.com, 171 rooms
Luxury hotel in splendid 19th-century style right on the Arno; there is a wonderful panoramic view from the restaurant and bar on the roof.

❾ Gallery Hotel Art Insider Tip
€€€ – €€€€
Vicolo dell' Oro 5
tel. 055 2 72 63
www.lungarnocollection.com, 71 rooms
Two chic hotels are part of the Ferragamo style empire in Florence. The location is ideal, very close to the Ponte Vecchio on the southern banks of the Arno River. Contemporary elegance and beautiful materials in shades of brown, beige, white; discrete service; light, Asian-inspired cuisine in the restaurant; good cocktails, all of this makess the house a comfortable oasis. The high point in the truest sense of the expression are the three suites each with its own roof terrace.

❿ Loggiato dei Serviti
€€€ – €€€€
Piazza Santissima Annunziata 3
tel. 0 55 28 95 92, 38 rooms
www.loggiatodeiservitihotel.it
Elegant hotel with atmosphere that comes from its location on a beautiful square and the historic premises, a house built in 1527 for the Servite order.

⓫ Palazzo Guadagni
€€€ – €€€€
Piazza Santo Spirito 9
tel. 055 2 65 83 76
www.palazzoguadagni.com, 14 rooms
Stay in formal rooms furnished with Tuscan antiques in the third and fourth floors of a Renaissance palazzo right on the Piazza Santo Spirito. High point of the Grand Tour atmosphere and wonderful location is the loggia

terrace for looking, reading and relaxing.

⓬ Villa Carlotta €€€
Via M. di Lando 3
tel. 0 55 2 33 61 34
www.hotevillacarlotta.it, 32 rooms
Patrician villa near Palazzo Pitti with a beautiful garden; restaurant with Tuscan specialities.

⓭ Alessandra €€
Borgo SS. Apostolo 17
tel. 055 28 34 38
www.hotelalessandra.com, 25 rooms
This quiet hotel on the upper storeys of a medieval palazzo in a quiet side street is very pleasant; the rooms are all bright and nicely furnished, some without bathrooms; some rooms have a pretty view of the Arno.

⓮ Annalena €€ Insider Tip
Via Romana 34
tel. 0 55 22 96 00
www.hotelannalena.it, 20 rooms
This romantic hotel in a 15th-century Medici palace is just right for travellers who like a little greenery outside their windows: it is located right next to the Boboli Garden; the rooms – some with a view of the garden – are decorated in various styles.

⓯ Beacci Tornabuoni
€€ – €€€€
Via dei Tornabuoni 3
tel. 0 55 21 26 45
www.hoteltornabuonibeacci.com, 29 rooms
Centrally located, elegant hotel in a 15th-century palace on the re-

nowned shopping street; breakfast on the roof terrace.

⑯ Casci €€
Via Cavour 13
tel. 0 55 21 16 86
www.hotelcasci.com, 25 rooms
Simple hotel, once the residence of the composer Gioacchino Rossini. Central location with modern rooms; the dining room has a painted ceiling.

⑰ Classic €€
Viale Machiavelli 25
tel. 055 22 93 51
www.classichotel.it, 19 rooms
Pleasant hotel in a villa with a beautiful garden south of the Boboli Gardens with a parking lot; tastefully furnished rooms.

⑱ Crocini €€
Corso Italia 28
tel. 0 55 21 29 05
www.hotelcrocini.com,
20 rooms
Affordable hotel near the Teatro Comunale with a pretty garden; simply furnished, quiet rooms, some in a quite old-fashioned style; the breakfast room faces a courtyard with plants.

⑲ Il Guelfo Bianco €€ – €€€€
Via Cavour 29
tel. 0 55 28 83 30
www.ilguelfobianco.it, 40 rooms
Centrally located 18th cent. patrician house with pretty Florentine style guest rooms. Many pretty details, the owner's respectable art collection and the nice service make the house a popular address.

⑳ Liana €€
Via V. Alfieri 18
tel. 055 24 53 03/4
www.hotelliana.com, 24 rooms
Quiet hotel in an Art nouveau house, formerly the British embassy; small garden and elegant rooms..

㉑ Palazzo dal Borgo €€ – €€€
Via della Scala 6
tel. 055 21 62 37
www.palazzodalborgo.it,
34 rooms
Near the railway station this small but fine hotel is located in a palace (1480). Some of the rooms still have original Renaissance stucco decoration; shady, green inner courtyard for breakfast.

㉒ La Scaletta €€ – €€€
Via Guiciardini 13
tel. 0 55 28 30 13
www.hotellascaletta.it, 11 rooms
Hotel in a tasteful historic building; a beautiful view of the city from the idyllic roof terrace.

㉓ Johanna & Johlea € – €€€€
Via San Gallo 80
tel. 055 4 62 72 96
www.johanna.it
Behind this name are a whole selection of especially cheerful and stylishly decorated guest houses, B & B rooms and holiday flats spread out over the historic centre of Florence. The guest house Antica Dimora Johlea even has a charming roof terrace.

㉔ B & B Orti di Cimabue €
Via Cimabue 25
tel. 055 9 06 40 34
www.ortidicimabue.it, 4 Z.rooms

In a residential area within walking distance of the Arno and Santa Croce this house offers functional, clean and liveable rooms. Two of the rooms open to the garden, where the house guests can relax. Very nice breakfast.

㉕ B & B In Centro €–€€
Via del Ponte Sospeso 22
Handy 0039 34 74 31 40 58
www.bbincentro.com, 5 rooms
These five charming, modern guestrooms are located south of the Arno in south-western Florence. Guests get their breakfast in a nearby pasticceria with oven-fresh cornetti. The residential neighbourhood lies outside of the restricted traffic zone in the centre of the city, so the chances of finding an affordable parking place are good.

RESIDENCES
㉖ Le Stanze del Duomo €€
Via De' Martelli 8
tel. 055 290012
www.lestanzedelduomo.it,
11 rooms
A more central location isn't possible: This recently restored house with B&B rooms with breakfast in a nearby bar or studios with kitchenettes, all in an imaginative boutique style and with air conditioning and Wifi, is located between San Lorenzo and the cathedral.

㉗ La Medicea €
Via dell' Ariento 31
Mobile 0039 33 58 11 66 88
www.residencelamedicea.com,
11 flats
Central location near San Lorenzo, this restored palazzo with a roof terrace offers comfortable, well-equipped apartments of varying sizes. Only a few steps from the large open Mercato Centrale.

FURNISHED APARTMENTS
Acacia
Via dei Pepi 7, tel. 055 24 47 50
www.acaciafirenze.it

Florence and Abroad
Via San Zanobi 58
tel. 055 48 76 03
www.florenceandabroad.com

www.oh-florence.com
Online portal lists more than 150 holiday flats in Florence, in all sizes from plain to elegant.

YOUTH HOSTELS
㉘ Ostello Archi Rossi
Via Faenza 94
tel. 0 55 29 08 04
www.hostelarchirossi.com, 30 rooms
The well-equipped youth hostel is near the main railway station; affordable meals; large terrace.

㉙ Ciao Hostel
Via Guido Monaco 34
tel. 055 32 10 18
www.ciaohostelflorence.com, 15 rooms
The hostel has 15 rooms, including double rooms, family rooms, 8-bed rooms; it is new and has modern furnishings, orderly and clean. West of the main railway station, about a 10-minute walk.

㉚ Florence Youth Hostel
Via della Condotta 4
tel. 055 21 44 84

www.florence-youth-hostel.com,
14 rooms
Inexpensive and friendly youth
hostel with 3 and 4 bed rooms
near the Piazza della Signoria.

CAMPING
Information
http://en.camping.info/italy
Extensive list of camp sites.

Confederazione Italiana
Campeggiatori
Via Vittorio Emanuele 11
I-50041 Calenzano
tel. 0 55 88 23 91
www.federcampeggio.it

Camping Michelangelo
Viale Michelangelo 80
tel. 0 55 6 81 19 77
240 places

Children in Florence

Playing and Fun

Even a city of the arts like Florence, where most of the sights are museums and churches, there are still things to do to make a holiday fun with children – beginning with the countless ice cream shops and a climb into the dome of the cathedral Santa Maria del Fiore.

In the large public and municipal museums children up to the age of 18 get in free of charge With children it is especially worthwhile to reserve tickets to the Accademia and the Uffizi Gallery ahead of time (▶p.119) and thus avoid long waits in queues. Florentine museums are generally very child-friendly, and many of them offer creative activities (mostly in Italian). Many museums surprise with exciting exhibits, like the ▶Museo Stibbert with its lifesize cavalcade of horses and riders, the machines invented by Leonardo da Vinci (MARCO POLO Tip p. 53) and the mammoth skeletons, fossils and anatomical models in the science museums. But you can also go rafting on the Arno, splash in the pool in the Cascine, solve crimes on a city tour or learn how to make pizza and ice cream in a cooking course.

Attractions

In the not particularly green centre of Florence, apart from the ▶Giardino di Boboli, which charges admission, there are some other pretty green areas where children can romp. These include the free park of ▶Museo Stibbert, not far from Piazza della Santissima Annunziata the green space on Piazza M. D' Azeglio with all sorts of play equipment for small children and near San Marco monastery the Botanical Garden in Giardino dei Semplici (▶p. 274, admission charge) with its impressive cactus collection is also interesting for children. Finally there is Giardino delle Rose below the Piazzale Michelangelo. The park of Villa Vogel (Viale Canova, open daily from 8am) is located in the southwest district on the edge of the city centre; take Bus 1 from the railway station; it has playgrounds, a roller skating track and trampolines.

Parks

In the **Parco delle Cascine**, the largest park in Florence, on the banks of the Arno in the northwest there are large lawns that are great for playing football, picnicking in the shade of trees; bikes and rollerblades are available for rental. There are also playgrounds and mini-rides along the banks of the Arno. In the summer kiosks sell drinks, pizza and ice cream, and in the middle of it all is the pretty swimming pool Le Pavoniere (Viale della Catena 2) with a children's pool, and a bouncy castle for the tots. Café Magnificenza with a restaurant and cocktail bar provides grown-ups with sustenance.

Encounters of a special kind

Selected Tips

Agenzia Accord
Via Condotta 27 r
tel. 055 239 94 93
Mobile 0039 34 08 33 75 00
www.accordsolutions.it
This Historical WhoDunit Tour allows participants to solve a murder mystery set in the Renaissance; the decisive clues form an exciting tour of the city. Three-hour tour daily, children up to age 5 free admission, age 6 to 12 years 50 % disocunt. The agency also offers pizza-making courses as well as rafting tours in large inflatable boats on the Arno. Children from the age of 4 may take part, 4 – 7 years free admission.

Biblioteca delle Oblate
Via dell' Oriuolo 26
Cafeteria and library:
Mon 9am – 2pm, Tue – Sat 9am – 12 midnight
Children's reading room:
Mom – Sat 9am – 6.40pm
The large city library in the middle of Florence near the cathedral has cozy corners, where you can take a break to read your own books. Or watch cartoons or relax undisturbed in the inexpensive cafeteria in the expansive cloisters as long as you want.

Lago di Bilancino
This large artificial lake lies in nearby Barberino di Mugello north of Florence, near the big outlet centre. It was built as the city water reservoir and is now used for water sports of all kinds: canoeing, windsurfing, sailing and swimming. It is a great place to go on hot days in Florence.

Museo dei Ragazzi
Palazzo Vecchio
Piazza della Signoria
tel. 055 2 76 82 24
www.museifirenze.it
Daily 9am – 6pm
This initiative for children in museums is exemplary. Museum educators lead exciting tours through city museums with experiments, playtime, simulations, workshops on fresco painting and much more. Daile programmes are available in the Palazzo Vecchio. They are mainly in Italian but more and more are being held in English, and many can be done without knowing the language.

Parco Avventura Il Gigante
Pratolino bei Vaglia
Via Bolognese
April – Oct Tue – Sun
9.30am – 7.30pm, other times only on weekends, admission:
adults €18, children up to 12 years €14,
children 3 – 6 years €10
www.parcoavventurailgigante.it
The largest adventure park in all of Tuscany is located only 10 minutes by car from Florence in northern Pratolino near Vaglia. It offers 7 adventurous »hang-outs« from tree to tree on ropes, nets, ladders etc. for children from the age of 3.

Parco Avventura Vincigliata
Fiesole
Via Vincigliata 12

At least the boys should like the suits of armour

tel. 055 3 98 40 36
www.treeexperience.it
June – Oct daily 10am – 7pm
Admission: children up to 11 years
from €10, 11 to 18 years from
€15, adults €18
This shady and well appointed adventure park, locataed near Fiesole, charges no general admission, instead guests pay for each
course separately.

Villa Demidoff
Pratolino-Vaglia
Via Fiorentina 276
May – Oct Sat, Sun
10am – 10pm
This large and beautiful villa park,
open to the public, is located opposite the Il Gigante adventure
park. The Medici duke Francesco I
placed wonderful surprises in it,
like a huge stone fountain and a
giant who is supposed to represent the Apennine mountains . It
is a great place to have a picnic.

Tradition Preferred

How do the people of Florence celebrate? Urbane events take place in especially beautiful venues in this city. Just think of the Firenze Estate and Estate Fiesolana in Fiesole with its many events held outdoors, classical and pop music concerts as well as dance performances, which are held in the inner courtyards of old palazzi, in the Roman theatre in Fiesole, on the banks of the Arno, on grand squares and in churches.

A highlight of the cultural calender not only for the city, but for all of Italy is the Maggio Musicale Fiorentino, a festival of the best opera, concert and dance performances, which begins in May. It was started in 1933 by the Fascist government official and Florentine nobleman Luigi Ridolfi Vay da Verrazzano and the orchestra conductor Vittorio Gui. It celebrates the beginning of spring in May, which has always been celebrated in Tuscany with Calendimaggio festivals. world famous conductors, musicians and singers are invited to the festival every year.

Maggio Musicale Fiorentino

Due to financial problems the festival faced its end in 2013. But the residents and Florence and musicians wouldn't allow it: they performed without costumes and for half the usual pay. Donations are keeping the festival afloat until better times.

Florence also has a very traditional, folkloric soul, which comes to the fore a couple of times a year. This happens, for example, on the feastday of the city's patron saint on June 24, the Feast of St John, when the residents meet in the afternoon on the grandstands on Piazza Santa Croce to cheer on their own team in the somewhat violent historic version of football, Calcio in Costume (▶MARCO POLO Insight p. 100).

Traditional festivals

ACF Florence plays in the Italian premier league, Series A. The Fiorentana's heyday are long past. They won their last championship in 1969.

Premier league football

Homegames are played in Stadio Artemio Franchi (Viale Manfredo Fanti; near Campo Marte railway station). The stadium was built in 1930 at the initiative of Verrazzano, the founder of the Maggio Fiorentino. Tickets and further information at http://en.violachannel.tv.

Scoppio del Carro crackles and burns

Festival calendar

HOLIDAYS

1 January: New Year's Day (Capodanno)
6 January: Epiphany (Epifania)
March/April: Easter Monday (Lunedi di Pasqua)
25 April: Liberation Day 1945 from the German army (Anniversario della Liberazione)
1 May: Labour Day (Festa dei Lavoratori)

2 June: Republic Day (Fondazione della Repubblica)
15 August: Assumption of the Virgin (Ferragosta)
1 November: All Saints' Day (Ognissanti)
8 December: Immaculate Conception (Immacolata)
25/26 December: Christmas Day/ Boxing Day (Natale)

Events

JANUARY
Epiphany (Jan. 6)
La Cavalcata dei Magi
This parade was first documented in 1417. At that time the Medici would occasioanlly take part as the three kings. The spectacular costume parade starts at Palazzo Pitti and proceeds via Ponte Vecchio and Piazza Signoria to the cathedral with the Christmas nativity scene.

MARCH/APRIL
Scoppio del Carro
▶MARCO POLO Insight p. 100

La Notte Bianca
Open museums and art events in the night of the last Saturday in April
www.lanottebianca.firenze.it

APRIL – SEPTEMBER
O Flos Colende
The title of a series of concerts of sacred musics for afficianados, from mid-April to early September in the cathedral. There is generally no admission.
www.firenzeturismo.it

MAY
MOSTRA DELL' IRIS
May 2 – 20: An enchanting show of iris, the flower on Florence's coat of arms, in the pretty garden below the Piazzale Michelangelo.

MAY
Festa del Grillo
Sunday after Ascension Day: (▶MARCO POLO Special p.100).

MAY/JUNE/JULY
Maggio Musicale Fiorentino
Despite the current financial difficulties this festival has stood for years for top class opera and concerts with international artists. Performances are held in Teatro Comunale and Teatro (www.maggiofiorentino.it), the main summer venue of the Maggio Fiorentino in July – open air concerts, ballet – is the courtyard of the Palazzo Pitti.

SUMMER
Firenze Estate
Every year new venues are added for the great variety of music and entertainment events, which en-

Parades in historical costumes have a fixed place in the calendar of festivals

liven the Florentine summer: rock concerts on the open air stage in Park Cascine, live and DJ music on the Arno beach at San Niccolò, ethnic music in the former prison Le Murate (www.festival-au-desert.org), cultural events in the inner courtyard of the Bargello museum or in the gardens of the Stibbert Museum or Villa Strozzi and summer cinema on the Piazza Santissima Annunziata.
www.firenzestate.it

Estate Fiesolana
In Fiesole: concert, theatre, film and ballet, many of the events outdoors in the Roman theatre or in the cathedral.
Infos: www.estatefiesolana.it

JUNE
Calcio in Costume
June 24
▶MARCO POLO Insight p.100

AUGUST/SEPTEMBER
Festa Democratica
the annual festival of the Italian leftist parties used to be called Festa dell' Unità, but today it's called the Festa Democratica. From late August until mid-September the local people mark the end of summer with food and concerts.

SEPTEMBER
La Rificolona
On September 7 adults and children celebrate the Virgin Mary

Florentine Festivals

Florentines have managed to preserve their traditional festivals until the present; they continue to value them and celebrate them with great devotion.

It almost seems as if the virtues of the knights and the Renaissance have survived in these festivals, in competitions and feats of skill, in the art of the flag bearers that accompany all festivals. Often there is also a religious aspect.

The round of popular festivals begins on Easter Sunday with **Scoppio del Carro**, a kind of fireworks on the Piazza del Duomo to announce the resurrection of Christ. After Easter mass a rocket called »la colombina« (the dove) is shot from the high altar on a cable to the square, where it »blows up« the »carro« (cart), which is decorated with firecrackers and shaped like a hearse, and is pulled to the square from across the Arno by two white oxen. If the explosion is strong and results in a lot of smoke, it means that farmers and businesspeople will have a profitable year.

Many people meet on Ascension Day in Parco delle Cascine in order to eat merenda (supper) and listen to the chirping of the crickets, the sound of the Italian summer, which is why this holiday is called **Festa del Grillo**. People used to catch the crickets themselves but now they are sold in little wooden or straw cages to be given to the children. Now the crickets are mechanical and the festival has lost much of its charm as the traditional market stalls sell only junk.

Tough guys in Calcio in Costume

On the Feast of St John, 24 June, the festivities honouring the city's patron saint are louder and pack a punch. Everyone meets on Piazza Santa Croce in order to support the local teams in the **Calcio in Costume**. This traditional ball game in historic costumes was first played in 1530 when the people of Florence wanted to show occupying troops that they were not at all intimidated by them, and were cool enough to take time for a ball game. A colourful procession from all parts of the city goes from Santa Maria Novella to Piazza Santa Croce. The four teams wear costumes with their local colours. The game is a kind of football with liberal use of hands and elbows and somewhat abstruse rules.

with a procession with paper lanterns. The main celebration takes place at the Piazza Santissima Annunziata.

Nextechfestival
This festival in the first week in September at the Fortezza da Basso Florence offers one of Italy's most inetersting events in electronic music.
www.nextechfestival.com.

OCTOBER
Mostra Mercato Internazionale dell' Antiquariato:
The famous antique exhibition in the first half of October in the magnificent rooms of the Palazzo Corsini sull' Arno shows wonderful furniture with Florentine intarsia or Renaissance paintings (in every odd-numbered year).
www.biennaleantiquariato.it

DECEMBER
Festival Internazionale del Film Documentario
In the first week in December this traditional film festival on social documentaries shows many outstanding productions from all over the world; locations include the beautiful old Odeon cinema.
www.festivaldeipopoli.org

Country Cooking

The Tuscan sense of moderation and quality influences the kitchen as well; cooking is simple and has a hearty taste. There are hardly any differences between urban and rural cooking.

Restaurants in Florence serve the same rustic dishes that are served in the farms and trattorias in the hills of Chianti. The connection between city and country have always been very close in Tuscany; most of the upper class families in the cities at one time had estates in the country. They built beautiful **country villas** with cypress-lined lanes leading up to them that could be seen from far off; the land was divided among farmers in semi-leases. Their hard work on the somewhat infertile ground of the hilly, even wild landscape is the reason for the beauty of the Tuscan landscape with its orderly olive groves and vineyards.

Close connection between city and country

The farms where vegetables and fruit are grown also raise **small domestic animals** like rabbits and every kind of poultry, mostly chickens and above all ducks. When Katherina de' Medici 1533 went to the court of Henry II in France as his bride, she brought along Florentine Renaissance culture. This included fine table manners and her cooks, whose recipe for duck a l'orange would become a French classic.
The farms also raised **pigs** for sausages like finocchiona, a soft salami spiced with fennel seeds, or for air-dried ham. The dark meat of wild boar, which live in the brush of the local forests, is also used for roasts and sausage. The forests also bear rabbits, chestnuts and mushrooms.

Livestock: basis of cuisine

When there is hardly any arable land no basic feeling for luxury could develop. That is why it was so important to make the best of what they had. Moreover in a semi-lease the crops had to be shared with the landowner. That meant that the upper class ate the same beans as the farmer. So pulses are the basis for the many soups, as are cabbage and grains like spelt (farro) from Garfagnana. The there is the typical Tuscan bread without salt, which unlike the rest of Italy takes the role of pasta (►MARCO POLO Insight p. 100). Using everything meant not only old bread but also **innards**. So crostini, roasted bread slices covered with chicken liver paste, become the antipasto. It is only here in Florence that you will find snack bars that sells rolls with marinated trippa (tripa) or lampredotto (beef maw); it tastes surprisingly good.

Rustic cooking for everyone

The heavens are full of ham and Chianti wine in the Trattoria Il Latini

Good meat The fact that these dishes continue to be served shows how closely Tuscans hold their food traditions. And why should they change when they suit modern life so well, with vitamin-rich olive oil, lots of vegetables, good quality meat since only meat from local breeds of cattle far removed from factory farming.

Around Siena and south of Florence a special breed of pig is raised, the Cinta Senese, which live half wild in the forest and feed on beechnuts and acorns. In the Chiana Valley and in the Maremma large white **cattle** graze, which deliver the meat for juicy bistecca alla fiorentina, the famous Tuscan t-bone steak. In order to meet the demand, however, the steak comes from Argentina these days. The raw meat on the bone with the fillet and rump steak weighs up to 800 g (28 oz), enough to feed two people. Lamb is also served; the sheep herds can be seen grazing over the hills of southern Tuscany. They also produce the milk for pecorino sheep's cheese, sometimes mild and sometimes more, which goes well with the caramelized figs and wild honey.

Wine Meals finish off with a small glass of the sweet dessert wine called **vin santo**, into which hard almond biscuits called cantuccini are dipped. Apropos wine: one of the best known red wines in the world comes from Tuscany. **Chianti** is made from the dry, earthy Sangiovese grape, and can be either a rustic or a fine table wine. Popular table wines include Morellino di Scansano from the southern Maremma or Vino nobile di Montepulciano. The so-called Supertuscans are also world famous, including Sassicaia, Ornellaia, Solaia or the classic Brunello di Montalcino. Among the few white wines are the fresh Galestro or traditional Vernaccia di San Gimignano. Some of the larger vineyards have wine rooms with snack bars, wine tasting and sales rooms in Florence.

Restaurants There is a large variety of restaurants in Florence. Many bars and bistros also serve warm dishes and salads along with the usual panino. There are osterias and trattorias everywhere in the typical rustic style with the classic menu selections, with lunches usually being cheaper. Recently better restaurants have started serving lunches as well. Remember that kitchens close at 2.15pm, that there is a cover charge and that a waiter will escort you to a table. **Smoking is not allowed** in restaurants and bars, unless there is a separate closed-off smoking room with separate ventilation. Don't count on the good graces of the owner as fines go up to €2200.

Cafés Some traditional cafés like the Gilli, the Paszkowski, the Giubbe Rosse, all very elegant and with restaurants, line the **Piazza della Repubblica**. So the expansive square is turned into one big streetside café in the summer. Guests sit under awnings or umbrellas in areas

Dinner in the relaxed atmosphere of Piazza Santo Spirito

divided by flower planters. Most of the cafés are open late into the night and thus popular meeting places after dinner, concerts or theatre.

Tipping tends to be informal. If you want to and if you find the service good you can leave a tip. The tip usually amounts to around 5% of the cost and is simply left on the table. This applies to cafés as well if you were served at the table. In some restaurants a cover charge of 10 % is added to the bill.

Tips

Recommended restaurants

❶ etc. ▶plan p. 112–113

PRICE CATEGORIES
for a main dish
€€€€ more than €22
€€€ €15 – €22
€€ €10 – €15
€ from €9

❶ BSJ – Jorgo
San Jacopo **€€€€**
Borgo San Jacopo 62 r
tel. 055 28 16 61
www.lungarnocollection.com
This excellent restaurant on the banks of the Arn reflects the elegant style of Ferragamo, the famous Florentine footwear label,

Florentine Cooking

Anyone who values regional cooking should try the typical Florentine dishes: from tasty antipasti to the grape cake Schiacciata con l' uva.

Antipasti: Meals can begin with affettati tipici, like spicy Tuscan ham, peppery salami and finocchiona, a soft sausage spiced with fennel seed. Antipasti also include crostini, small slices of toasted bread covered with chicken liver paste, or with pastes made of pureed olives and artichokes.

Pappardelle alla lepre: of course there are a few pasta dishes in Tuscany as well, especially pappardelle, wide ribbon noodles made with an egg dough, which are often served with a sauce of stewed rabbit meat. Tuscans are passionate hunters. But pappardelle can also be served with duck or rabbit sauce.

Trippa alla fiorentina: Veal tripe that the butcher has already cleaned and pre-cooked are simmered in a sauce of tomatoes, garlic, celery, carrots, bay leaves and white wine and covered with lots of grated Parmesan cheese before serving. This is the Florentine way of preparing tripe.

Fritto misto: An especially popular way of preparing vegetables is to fry them. Cut up zucchini, eggplant, chard stalks into short strips, separate small artichokes and cauliflower into small pieces, look for zucchini and pumpkin blossoms, dip the pieces into an egg and flour batter and fry them in hot oil. Small pieces of chicken and rabbit meat can also be fried like this.

Ribollita: The classic Tuscan bread soup made of old bread, kale, savoy cabbage or chard, small white beans. It got its name because this thick soup is heated to boiling again before serving – ribollita – so that the flavours blend even better and the soup becomes smoother. Don't leave off the shot of cold olive oil at the end.

Castagnaccio: In late fall when sweet chestnut flour appears in the markets, Florentine bakeries sell this flat cake made of chestnut flour – the Apennine forests above Lucca, Pistoia and the Mugello are full of chestnut trees – spiced with raisins, pine nuts and rosemary.

Schiacciata con l'uva: When the grape harvest is being brought in this simple cake made with yeast and the very sweet and juicy grape variety Canaiolo. A simple delight that gives the bakeries a delightful aroma in late summer.

Fagioli all'uccelletto: Small white beans of the cannellini variety – but other ones can be used too – are sauteed in olive oil and garlic and cooked until soft with a little tomato and lots of sage. In Florence they are often eaten with bistecca alla fiorentina.

Gelato artigianale

What in English is merely called »ice cream« is a work of art for Italians. While they may not be able to claim to have invented the »handcrafted freezes« no one disputes that they are masters of the craft. Check it out in Florence!

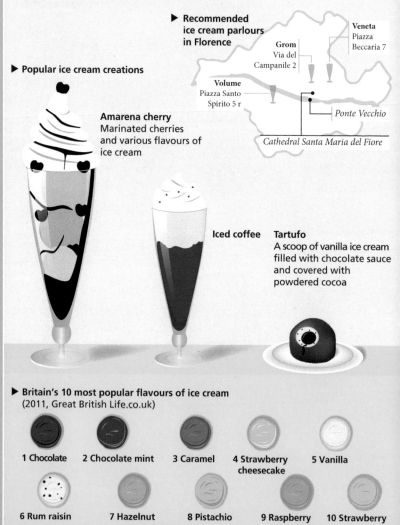

▶ **Recommended ice cream parlours in Florence**

Veneta Piazza Beccaria 7

Grom Via del Campanile 2

Volume Piazza Santo Spirito 5 r

Ponte Vecchio

Cathedral Santa Maria del Fiore

▶ **Popular ice cream creations**

Amarena cherry Marinated cherries and various flavours of ice cream

Iced coffee

Tartufo A scoop of vanilla ice cream filled with chocolate sauce and covered with powdered cocoa

▶ **Britain's 10 most popular flavours of ice cream** (2011, Great British Life.co.uk)

1 Chocolate

2 Chocolate mint

3 Caramel

4 Strawberry cheesecake

5 Vanilla

6 Rum raisin

7 Hazelnut

8 Pistachio

9 Raspberry

10 Strawberry

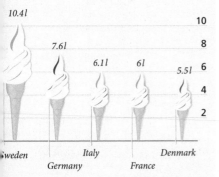

urope's top 5 ice cream consumers
er capita consumption 2011, in litres

10.4l

7.6l

6.1l

6l

5.5l

10	8	6	4	2

weden   Italy   Denmark
Germany   France

► **The story of ice cream**

Antiquity
An ice cold »snow-white delicacy«
(xuebaite) is supposed to have been
consumed in China around 1000 BC
already. In Greek antiquity real ice
was flavoured with honey, nectar,
fruits and spices. These recipes were
lost at the end of the Roman Empire.

Middle ages
Marco Polo brought a recipe back
from China for a partially frozen
water ice that was cooled using saltpetre.

16th century
In Italy the art of freezing liquids using
a saltpetre solution was perfected.
Italian ice cream makers worked in
the courts of European nobility.

Around 1790
The first ice cream making machine
was invented in America. Today's
machines still work on the same principle.

From 1870
Italian immigrants introduced the sale
of ice cream on the streets to the
rest of Europe. Italo Marchioni
(1868 – 1954) invented the ice
cream waffled cone.

aghetti ice cream
nilla ice cream covering
ore of frozen whipped
am, covered with
awberry sauce. Invented
1969 – in Mannheim,
rmany.

Banana Split
The classic dish
with a split banana

**he right ice cream
ishes**

**Long,
slender glass**
for iced coffee
and similar, and
for fruit sundaes

Sundae dish
the classic ice cream dish
for creations with lots of
fruit, whipped cream
and liqueur

Long-stemmed, broad dish
For handmade ice cream
and decorations

Boat
for banana splits
and similar creations

Bread without Salt

Tuscan bread – »pane sciocco«, as the Florentines call it – is made without salt and seems a bit tasteless at first. And yet a meal without this seemingly boring bread simply cannot be imagined.

A loaf of Tuscan bread is made of light wheat flour, has a crunchy crust and the crumbs are soft and loose. Some bakeries still bake it in a wood-burning oven. It keeps for several days and is cut into slices.

Why is it impossible to do without it? And why doesn't it have any salt in it? It is said that Pisa, Florence's archenemy, is to blame. In the Middle Ages Pisa had the **monopoly on salt** because it had a port. In the 12th/13th century, when the animosity between the two cities had reached its peak Pisa raised the price on salt so much that it became unaffordable. That made the proud Florentines reduce their consumption of salt drastically. This became a tradition with bread, maybe because the Florentines discovered that the neutral taste of the bread suited their cooking very well.

A very simple but convincing example is the fettunta, a fresh and warm slice of bread is sprinkled with olive oil. Bruschetta is also a toasted slice of bread with oil, garlic and finely chopped fresh tomatoes. Pane sciocco is the ideal complement to the spices of sliced porchetta, pork roast, or Tuscan ham and to the aromatic sheep cheese called pecorino.

When the bread is dry and old it is not thrown away, that would go against the frugal Tuscan grain. Rather using it up has inspired a row of tasty soup recipes, beginning with ribollita made of old bread, kale and white beans. Or pappa al pomodoro, a thick tomato soup made with fresh tomatoes, old bread and basil.

In the summer the hard bread is softened; chopped cucumber, tomatoes, celery, basil and olive oil are added to make the delicious cold panzanella. Nothing bland and boring about it – on menus in Tuscany and Florence the bread without salt definitely spices up the kitchen.

which also owns hotels. The food lives up to this level of sophistication, as does the location, like the few tables on the balcony over the river for that very special evening.

❷ Il Cibreo €€€€
Via del Verrocchio 8 r
Via dei Macci 122 r
tel. 0 55 2 34 11 00
www.cibreo.com
Closed Mon
In this gourmet restaurant near Sant' Ambrogio market the best Tuscan cuisine can be enjoyed, which chef Fabio Picchi has been celebrating and modernising for years. Reservations are necessary; the prices in the attached trattoria Cibreino are more reasonable; a café and a culinary Teatro del Sale are also part of the Cibreo empire.

Insider Tip

❸ Alle Murate €€€€
Via del Proconsolo 16 r
tel. 0 55 24 06 18
www.allemurate.it
Closed Mon
This chic restaurant in a noble 14th cent. palazzo decorated with frescos, not far from the cathedral serves, thanks to the creativity of the chef Giovanna Iorio an exciting combination of selected regional Italian ingredients, and is one of the best places to eat in the city centre. the midday menu is less expensive (**€€**).

❹ Enoteca Pinchiorri €€€€
Via Ghibellina 87
tel. 0 55 24 27 77
Closed at midday on Sun, Mon
www.enotecapinchiorri.com

This elegant restaurant in a 16th-century palazzo with a very beautiful courtyard promises a top-quality culinary experience, but at a price; the wine cellar is famous for stocking the best wines from all over the world.

REGIONAL COOKING
❺ Gargani €€€
Via del Moro 48/r
tel. 0 55 21 13 96
www.garganitrattoria.com
Closed Mon
The walls of this unique, up-market trattoria in a small old city street between Santa Maria Novella and the Arno show a great love for art and painting. They suit the fruits and leaves that decorate the Florentine specialties served here. Cooking courses offered as well.

❻ Targa €€€
Lungarno Cristoforo Colombo 7
tel. 055 67 73 77
www.targabistrot.net
Closed Sun
The meticulous and original cooking of this bistro, including lots of fish, and the excellent wines can be enjoyed in the summer on a terrace over the Arno.

❼ Antico Ristoro del Cambi €€
Via Sant' Onofrio 1r
Tel.055 21 71 34
Closed Sun
www.anticoristorodicambi.it
The hams hang from the vaulted ceiling, huge steaks wait in the chilled display at the entrance. This traditional trattoria in the San Frediano quarter on the left-hand side of the Arno is the address for

Restaurants, hotels and places to go out

Where to eat

1. Borgo San Jacopo
2. Cibreo
3. Alle Murate
4. Pinchiorri
5. Gargani
6. Targa
7. Antico Ristoro del Cambi
8. Dino
9. Filipepe
10. Il Latini
11. Io Osteria Personale
12. Pane e Vino
13. Pepo
14. Santo Bevitore
15. Zà Zà
16. Il Desco
17. Mario
18. Pallotino
19. Il Santino
20. Il Sasso di Dante
21. Toscanella
22. Trattoria del Carmine
23. Cantinetta de Verazzano

Where to stay

1. Brunelleschi
2. Four Seasons
3. Helvetia & Bristol
4. Regency
5. Villa Mangiacane
6. Principe
7. Torre di Bellosguardo
8. Westin Excelsior
9. Gallery Hotel Art
10. Loggiato dei Serviti
11. Guadagni
12. Villa Carlotta
13. Alessandra
14. Annalena
15. Beacci Tornabuoni
16. Casci
17. Classic
18. Crocini
19. Il Guelfo Bianco
20. Liana
21. Palazzo del Borgo
22. La Scaletta
23. Johanna & Johlea
24. Orti di Cambue
25. In Centro
26. Le Stanze del Duomo
27. La Medicea
28. Ostello Archi Rossi
29. Ciao
30. Florence Youth Hostel

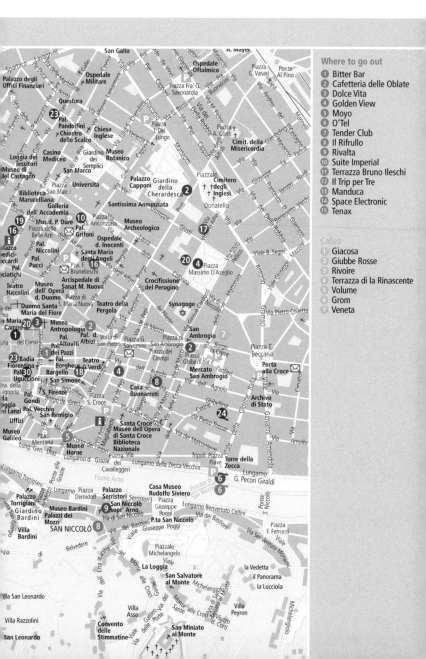

classic bistecca alla fiorentina from real Chianina cattle. In the summer seating is outdoors on the piazzetta.

MODERATE

❽ Dino €€ – €€€
Via Ghibellina 51 r
tel. 0 55 24 13 78
www.ristorantedino.it
Closed Sun
Elegant restaurant with an exceptionally pleasant atmosphere in the historic centre near the church Santa Croce; the cooking is based on historical recipes; try the roast wild boar spiced with raisins, almonds, giner and cinnamon! Large selection of wine.

❾ Filipepe €€
Via San Niccolò 39 r
tel. 055 2 00 13 97
www.filipepe.com
Closed noon
Something different: good Mediterranean cooking in a charming creative atmosphere in Oltrarno, on the southern side of the Arno.

❿ Il Latini €€
Via dei Palchetti 6
tel. 0 55 21 09 16
www.illatini.com
Closed Mon
The classic trattoria on the southern side of the Arno that attracts tourists but also locals. Ham hangs from the ceiling, terra cotta tiles on the floor and on the plates lies the famous bistecca fiorentina, a thick slice of loin that is seasoned only with a dash of olive oil; but there are also lighter dishes. If that isn't enough try the freshly made tiramisu.

⓫ Io Osteria Personale €€ – €€€
Borgo San Frediano 167 r
tel. 055 9 33 13 41
Closed Sun and noon
www.io-osteriapersonale.it
In the San Frediano quarter on the left-hand side of the Arno there are surprisingly many eateries like this one: modern urban ambience under rustic beams, far off from tourist folklore, where the young and successful Florentines meet. So the cooking with fresh ingredients – including fish – enjoyable and delightful.

⓬ Pane e Vino €€ – €€€
Piazza di Cestello 3
tel. 055 2 47 69 56,
www.ristorantepaneevino.it
Closed Sun
The elegant restaurant owned by the Pierazzuoli brothers on the southern side of the Arno in unconventional, just like the meticulous cooking that is based on tradition but always coming up with something new. Try the gnudi, hot balls of spinach, ricotta and sage, or the excellent desserts.

⓭ Pepò €€
Via Rosina 4/6 r
tel. 055 28 32 59, tgl. geöffnet
www.pepo.it
Near the Piazza del Mercato Centrale this especially attractive osteria is the place to try specialties like fritto misto, fried fingerfood mafe of vegetables, chicken and rabbit, or peposo, a kind of beef gulash with lots of pepper.

⓮ Il Santo Bevitore €€
Via Santo Spirito 64 – 66 r

tel. 055 21 12 64
www.ilsantobevitore.com
Closed sun noon
Good Italian cooking with a little
imagination, nice setting in rustic-
elegant ambience, friendly service,
good value, and everyone is happy, both tourists and Florentines:
a popular evergreen not far from
Piazza Santo Spirito. Make reservations!

⑮ Zà Zà €€
Piazza del Mercato Centrale 26 r
tel. 0 55 21 54 11
www.trattoriazaza.it
Open daily
Among the many trattorias on the
lively Piazza del Mercato Centrale
this one stands out for its colourful interior and tasty cooking. Its
bistro-café right next door serves
snacks and delicious speritifs. Reservations a must!

⑯ Il Desco €–€€
Via Cavour 55 r
tel. 055 28 83 30
www.ildescofirenze.it
Closed Sun and evenings
Between the many touristy snack-
bars not far from Piazza San Marco this little bistro in the Hotel Il
Guelfo Bianco surprises with sea-
sonal salads, imaginative vegetable dishes, delicate meat dishes
and a friendly atmospher.

⑰ Trattoria Mario
Via Rosina 2 r
tel. 0 55 21 85 50
Mon – Sat 12.30pm – 3pm
http//:trattoria-mario.com
This tiny typical Florentine trattoria
near Mercato Centrale is family
run and very popular – where else

would the customers wait outside
for a table until the padrone invites them in?

Insider Tip

⑱ Pallottino €
Via Isola delle Stinche 1 r
tel. 055 28 95 73
www.trattoriapallottino.com
Closed Sun
In this solid, more than one hundred year old trattoria in the laby-
rinthine alleys between the cathedral and Santa Croce there are
simple wooden tables and white
tiled walls. Enjoy the good home-
cooking. Popular not only among
tourists but also locals.

⑲ Il Santino €
Via Santo Spirito 60 r
tel. 055 2 30 28 20
Daily 12.30pm – 11pm
Restaurant Il Santo Bevitore right
next door runs this small bistro
and serves cheeses and hams of
excellent quality.

⑳ Il Sasso di Dante €–€€
Piazza delle Pallottole 6 r
tel. 055 28 21 13
www.sassodidante.it
Closed Sun evening
Very close to the cathedral, where
good restaurants are rare, this
comfortable and simple restaurant
serves tasty traditional food. Try
the thick Tuscan spaghetti, called
pici, or the ricotta-spinach balls
gnudi. In the summer the tables
are outdoors in the quiet square.

㉑ Toscanella €–€€
Via Toscanella 32 r
tel. 055 28 54 88, tgl. geöffnet
www.toscanellaosteria.com
Accomplished modern design un-

der the high vaulted ceilings of an old palazzo near Palazzo Pitti, fresh and delicious traditional cooking and an inexpensive lunch menu – makes for a relaxing break.

㉒ Trattoria del Carmine

€–€€

Piazza del Carmine

Insider Tip

tel. 0 55 21 86 01

Closed Sun noon

A stop in this comfortable trattoria, a Florentine classic with exactly the same kind of cooking, rounds off a visit to the famous Cappella Brancacci in Chiesa del Carmine. In the summer seating is on the pretty piazza.

㉓ Cantinetta

del Verrazzano **€–€€**

Via dei Tavolini 18 r

tel. 055 26 85 90

www.verrazzano.com

Closed Sun evening

Though situated in the most touristic area between Piazza della Repubblica and Piazza della Signoria, Focaccie, Crostini, cheese and ham are nevertheless of good quality.

CAFÉS, ICE CREAM PARLOURS

❶ etc. ▶plan p. 112/113

❶ Giacosa

Via della Spada 10 r

tel. 055 2 77 63 28

www.caffegiacosa.it

Thanks to the restyling by Florentine fashion designer Roberto Cavalli, and located in his luxury boutique in Via Tornabuoni, this traditional café with the finest

chocolaterie has entered the 21st century. The famous cocktail Negroni, made with gin, Campari and Martini, was created here.

Gilli

▶MARCO POLO Tip p. 255

❷ Giubbe Rosse

Piazza della Repubblica 13/14 r

tel. 055 22 21 80

Its exhibitions and cultural events makes this beautiful, traditional artist and literary café attractive not only for tourists, but also for Florentine until today.

Gucci-Café

▶MARCO POLO Tip p. 260

❸ Rivoire

Piazza della Signoria 5 r

tel. 055 21 44 12

www.rivoire.it

Expensive, but right on the fabulous square. The hot chocolate with whipped cream is especially delicious.

❹ La Terrazza di La Rinascente

Piazza della Repubblica 1

tel. 055 28 36 12

The rooftop café of the up-market department store Rinascente on the Piazza della Repubblica offers a wonderful close-up view of the cathedral and the roofs of the old city. It serves cappuccino, cocktails and light meals.

❺ Volume

Piazza Santo Spirito 5 r

tel. 055 2 38 14 60

www.volumefirenze.it

This especially charming café

shows the beauty of craftsmanship: old tools and wooden models decorate the walls of this former hatmaker's workshop, today a popular meeting place for artists to enjoy music, readings, wine and tasty snacks.

❻ Grom

Via del Campanile 2
tel. 055 21 61 58
First class ingredients – like fresh eggs and fruits, the best nuts etc.

– are what make the ice cream here so delicious.

❼ Veneta

Piazza Beccaria 7
tel. 055 2 34 33 70
Veneta is famous for its homemade ice cream, which can be enjoyed outdoors with a view of the old city wall.

Vivoli

►MARCO POLO Tip p. 224

Museums

The City – One Big Museum

Florence has more than 60 museums – the whole city is one big museum! The idea of places where the variety of human creativity in the arts and sciences could be presented and admired was already consciously cultivated by the Medici.

Along with the large collections of art and archaeology there are countless galleries of private collectors and art historians, museums dedicated to individual geniuses like Michelangelo, Leonardo da Vinci, Dante or famous fashion designers like Gucci, Ferragamo and Capucci. In addition there are cycles of frescos and portrayals of the Last Supper so typical of Florence and much more – hardly a museum not worth visiting.

Museum scene

The **Firenze Card** is valid for three days and costs €72; with it you can walk past all of the queues at the museums and go right in, as well as use all of the public transportation (www.firenzecard.it). For EU citizens up to the age of 18 admission to public and community museums is free; from 18 to 25 years and from 65 years it is reduced. The state-owned museums are also free every year in April for one week during the culture week (settimana della cultura) and again on the last weekend in September for the European Culture Days (www.beniculturali.it).

Admission

The municipal museums are also free of charge on February 18, the anniversary of the death of the last Medici heiress and art patron Anna Maria Luisa de' Medici (▶MARCO POLO Insight p. 77). Moreover many museums have free admission and are open late on Notte Bianca in mid-April. A visit to the Brancacci chapel is by appointment only (tel. 055 2 76 82 24). As to exhibits: in order to make the many treasures in their storerooms accessible to the public the Uffizi have exhibits every year around Christmas entitled »I Mai Visti« (»The Never-Seen«) .

Museums in Florence

Ordering Tickets and Information
tel. 055 2 65 43 21
www.firenzemusei.it
Special ticket counters right at

the Uffizi and in Palazzo Pitti
www.polomuseale.firenze.it
http://museicivicifiorentini.
comune.fi.it
www.firenzeturismo.it

Uffizi Gallery, one of the most important art museums in the world

HISTORY

Museo Ebraico
▶Synagoga e Museo Ebraico

Museo Galileo
▶Galleria degli Uffizi

Museo di Preistoria (Prehistoric Museum)
Via San Egidio 21
Mon 3.30pm – 6.30pm,
Tue, Thu 9.30am – 12.30pm,
Fri, Sat 9.30am – 12.30pm
www.museofiorentinopreistoria.it
Exhibits from prehistoric times

Museo Nationale della Fotografia Fratelli Alinari
▶Santa Maria Novella

ART AND ARCHAEOLOGY

Casa Buonarroti
▶ p. 155

Galleria dell' Accademia
▶ p. 182

Galleria del Costume
▶Giardino di Boboli

Galleria dello Ospedale degli Innocenti
▶Ospedale degli Innocenti

Galleria Strozzina
▶Palazzo Strozzi

Galleria degli Uffizi
▶ p. 185

Museo Archeologico Naz.
▶ p. 212

Museo Stefano Bardini
▶ p. 215

Museo del Bigallo
▶ Piazza del Duomo, Loggia del Bigallo

Museo della Fondazione Horne
▶ Santa Croce

Museo Marino Marini
▶ p. 217

Museo Nazionale del Bargello
▶ p. 219

Museo dell' Opera del Duomo
▶ p. 225

Michelangelo's Pietà in the Museo dell' Opera del Duomo

Museo dell'Opera di Santa Croce
▶Santa Croce

Museo di Palazzo Davanzati
▶Loggia di Mercato Nuovo

Museo di San Marco
▶San Marco

Museo Santa Croce
▶Santa Croce

Museo di Santa Maria Novella
▶Santa Maria Novella

CRAFTS
Museo Roberto Capucci
▶Giardino di Boboli

Museo Gucci
▶Piazza della Signoria

Museo delle Porcellane
▶Giardino di Boboli

Museo Salvatore Ferragamo
▶Santa Trinità, Palazzo Spini-Ferroni

Museo Stibbert
▶ p. 229

Museo degli Strumenti Musicali Antichi
▶Palazzo Pitti

Opificio e Museo delle Pietre Dure
▶Galleria dell'Accademia

LITERATURE
Casa di Dante
▶Museo Nazionale del Bargello, Casa di Dante

NATURE AND SCIENCE

Museo Botanico
▶"San Marco, Orto Botanico

Museo di Geologia e Paleontologia
Via G. La Pira 4
www.msn.unifi.it
Mon, Tue, Thu, Fri 9am – 1pm,
Sat, Sun 9am – 5pm
Summer Tue, Thu also at
4pm – 7pm,
Sat, Sun 10am – 6pm
Along with an extensive collection of fossils, prehistoric animals and plants mainly from Italy are on display.

Museo Galileo
▶Galleria di Uffizi

Museo Leonardo
▶MARCO POLO Tip p. 53

Museo di Mineralogia e Litologia (Museum of Minerology)
Via G. La Pira 4
Opening hours like the Geological Museum
The museum has a large collection of minerals and objects made of semi-precious stone.

Museo Zoologica »La Specola«
▶Palazzo Pitti, Museo Zoologica

ANTHROPOLOGY
Museo Nazionale di Antropologia ed Etnologia
▶ p. 218

Nightlife · Going Out

Bars and More

Of course the many tourists and foreign students influence nightlife as well as the cultural programme in the city. The selection runs from pubs to lounge and cocktail bars to opera and concerts for the discerning.

In the evenings whole streets are transformed into one long party mile, as in Santa Croce quarter the Via de' Benci and Via Verdi or the alleys around Piazza dei Ciompi, which are popular among young people and foreign students. On the left bank of the Arno a more alternative crowd meets in the bars on Piazza Santo Spirito, and the local congregate San Niccolò between Ponte delle Grazie and Ponte San Niccolò bridges. In the summer months a beach is created in the river banks (Lungarno Serristori), where there are music and cocktails in the evenings. *Party streets*

In the summer there are more venues for bars, live music, dancing and theatre performances, like the Limonaia der Villa Strozzi (**Estate nella Limonaia**, www.officinecreative.fi.it) or the atmospheric inner courtyard of the Museo Bargello (**Estate al Bargello**, www.firenze-today.it). Summer events are also held in the large park Le Cascine on the Arno in western Florence or in Fortezza da Basso. Many evening events, parties and music sessions are organized during the glamorous fashion days of Pitti Uomo and Pitti Immagine Woman in the first half of January. Afterwards people flock to the discos around midnight to continue celebrating. *Events*

The city has many venues for theatre, opera, concerts and dance performances. The brand new Nuovo Teatro dell' Opera at the park Le Cascine has replaced the Teatro Comunale as the showplace for the renowned concert and opera festivals Maggio Musicale Fiorentino (►p. 98). The summer events of this festival like concerts and dance are held outdoors in the courtyard Cortile dell' Ammanati of Palazzo Pitti. *Classics*

The excellent Tuscan regional orchestra (ORT) has its Florentine loaction and performances at Teatro Verdi – where music revues and operettas are also performed – and in the summer they also perform on squares and in churches. In the **Flog Auditorium** Italian and international pop groups perform. A special venue is the Teatro Romano, the Roman amphitheatre in Fiesole, where theatre and concert performances take place as part of the **Estate Fiesolana** (►MARCO

Rock concert with the cathedral as backdrop: what an experience!

POLO Tip p. 181). The daily newspapers La Nazione and La Repubblica carry the local cultural events. Kiosks also have the detailed event calendar Firenze Spettacolo (available in English).

Cinema Films are shown outdoors in many locations in the summer, e.g. at the Nelson Mandela Forum (Viale P. Paoli 3; www.mandelaforum.it) and in Arena Estiva Poggetto of the Flog.

Where to go in the evening

❶ etc. ▶map p. 112-113

BARS AND CLUBS
❶ Bitter Bar
Via de' Pandolfini 39 r
mobile 38 89 75 90 74
www.bitterbarfirenze.it
Every evening around 7.30pm this eclectically charming cocktail bar opens its doors at the Art Hotel Borghese Palace in the middle of the city centre, not far from the cathedral. The news of the quality of its delicious drinks has already got around.

❷ Caffetteria delle Oblate
Via dell' Oriuolo 26
tel. 055 2 63 96 85
www.lospaziochesperavi.it/
caffetteriadelleoblate
In the centre near the cathedral this simple café of the city library Biblioteca delle Oblate in the upper arcade of the former convent stays open in the evenings too. You can get your drink, enjoy the view of the cathedral and sometimes a concert – a real oasis.

❸ Dolce Vita   Insider
Piazza del Carmine 12   Tip
tel. 0 55 28 45 95
www.dolcevitaflorence.com
Stylish venue with a well-heeled

crowd; the excellent cocktails taste even better on the beautiful terrace facing the piazza.

❹ Golden View
Via dei Bardi 54/58 r
tel. 055 21 45 02
www.goldenviewopenbar.com
Café, aperitif bar and restaurant: modern rooms, all with a fantastic view of the Arno and the Ponte Vecchio, good service and often live jazz.

❺ Moyo
Via de' Benci 23 r
tel. 055 2 47 97 38
www.moyo.it
Popular among the younger crowd, this cocktail bar is located in Santa-Croce, where things are lively during aperitif times between 7pm and 10.30pm; Friday and Saturday eves with DJ set.

❻ O' Tel
Via Generale della Chiesa 9
tel. 055 65 07 91
www.otelvariete.com
Restaurant with variety shows, cocktail lounge and aperitif buffet

❼ Tender Club
Via Luigi Alamanni 4
www.tenderclub.it

The street becomes a bar in the summer

In the winter this club near the main railway station opens its doors on Thu, Fri and Sat for live concerts of various kinds, like alternative rock and New Folk music. The discerning programme makes it the best music club in town.

❽ Il Rifrullo

Via San Niccolò 55 r
tel. 055 2 34 26 21
In the summer guests sit in the garden at the Porta San Niccolò. People come here to eat, for an aperitif, for after dinner drinks and for Sunday brunch – an institution!

❾ Rivalta

Lungarno Corsini 14 r
tel. 055 28 98 10
www.rivaltacafe.it
On Sundays guests come to the modern eatery for brunch. But things get really lively around evening first with aperitifs with excellent fingerfood buffet and late in the evening with top class DJ sets.

Se.sto on Arno
▶MARCO POLO Tip p. 230

❿ La Suite Imperiale

Via Baracca 4 r
tel. 33 95 47 14 12

www.lasuiteimperiale.com
Chic, elegant bar with one of the
best aperitif buffets in the city;
music and cocktails

⑪ Terrazza Brunelleschi
Piazza Unità Italiana 6
tel. 055 2 35 80
www.hotelbaglioni.it
In the summer months the roof
terraces of the luxurious Grand
Hotel Baglioni refreshing aperitifs
with imaginative vegetable and
fruit snacks are served, which can
be enjoyed along with the fabulous panorama.

⑫ Il Trip per Tre
Via Borgo Ognissanti 144 r
Daily from 7pm
Harley Davidsons park in front of
this popular pub in the city centre;
the wood-panelled walls are covered with pictures of motorcycles
and rock musicians, the music fits
the ambience and the beer is
fresh.

DISCOTHEQUES
⑬ Manduca
Via San Biagio a Petriolo 2
tel. 055 66 45 41
At the northwestern edge of Le
Cascine Park this elegant disco-
theque opens in the summer Thu,

Fri and Sat. Dine before dancing
under a starry sky and sip cocktails by the pool. Reservations recommended.

⑭ Space Electronic
Via Palazzuolo 37
tel. 055 29 30 82
www.spaceelectronic.net
Large, open all-year discotheque
in the centre. Dance and hip-hop
music. The civil prices are aimed at
young people and students.

Tenax
Insider Tip
Via Pratese 47
tel. 0 55 30 81 60
Tenax is a discotheque, a classic
of Italian nightlife, that has gone
through a complete overhaul and
is back up to speed, the dinner
parties on Friday evening are
especially popular.

CINEMAS
Fulgor
Via Maso Finiguerra 22 r
tel. 055 2 38 18 81
Thursday films in English

Odeon
Piazza Strozzi
tel. 055 21 40 68
Monday films in English resp.
original version

Concerts, Opera, Theatre

TICKET SALES
Box Office
Via delle Vecchie Carceri 1
tel. 055 21 08 04
www.boxofficetoscana.it
Mon – Fri 9.30am – 7pm,
Sat 9.30am – 2pm

Teatro del Maggio Musicale Fiorentino
Box Office
Corso Italia 16
tel. 055 2 77 93 50
www.maggiofiorentino.it

Teatro della Pergola is the oldest stage in Italy still in use

CONCERTS, OPERA
Nuovo Teatro dell Opera
Venue of Maggio Musicale Fiorentino
Viale Fratelli Rosseli 1

Teatro Comunale
Corso Italia 16
tel. 055 2 77 93 50

Auditorium Flog
Via Mercati 24 b
tel. 055 48 51 45
www.flog.it

Orchestra della Toscana (ORT)
Via Verdi 5
tel. 055 2 34 27 22

www.orchestradellatoscana.it
Tickets at Teatro Verdi (see below)

THEATRE
Teatro della Pergola
Via della Pergola 18/32
tel. 055 2 26 43 53
www.fondazioneteatrodellapergola.com
Theatre on the oldest still functioning stage (1656) in Italy; summer programme in the Bargello Museum

REVUE THEATRE
Teatro Verdi
Via Ghibellina 91 r – 101 r
tel. 055 21 23 20
www.teatroverdionline.it

Shopping

Not Just Fashion

Florence's city centre is one huge shopper's paradise and there is no limits to what's available. Along with the many gift shops as can be found in every tourist city there are many worthwhile things to discover.

When strolling through the narrow streets boutiques and shops with beautiful, unusual and original wares surprise again and again. Thanks to many well-heeled tourists from all over the world all of the **large Italian and international fashion and jewellery labels** can be found here – from Armani, Gucci, Prada and Bulgari to French, American and Japanese labels. Their shops with russian, Japanese and Chinese speaking sales women can be found in the middle of the old city, in the palazzi on Via Tornabuoni, Piazza della Trinità and Via della Vigna Nuova. The heart of fashion-conscious Italy doesn't just beat in Milan or Rome, but just as strongly in Florence. The first haute couture show for Made in Italy was stages here in 1951; Gucci, Ferragamo, Enrico Coveri, Roberto Cavalli, Emilio Pucci and Patrizia Pepe come from here. It can be felt every year, too, when the big fashion trade shows Pitti Immagine take place in January and June, when the shows are opened in Palazzo Pitti, in Fortezza da Basso, in Stazione Leopolda and fashion and design events and parties take off everywhere in the city. But along with the big names you will find small boutiques where fashion tailors and jewelery designers present their own personal style.

Fashion centre

Via Calzaiuoli is one of the main shopping streets, running between Piazza Duomo and Piazza della Signoria. Its name »cobblers« refers to an important branch of traditional Florentine products. Hardly anywhere else have as many shops selling shoes, bags and leather jackets been opened as in Florence, concentrated in and around the Mercato di San Lorenzo and around Piazza Santa Croce.

Masses of leather goods

Classical souvenirs from Florence are pretty paper products, notebooks, albums, boxes and much more with peacock feather and marble patterns.
Anyone who wants to take something home that is truly unique should try bespoke **perfume** that has been uniquely blended. Outstanding master perfumers like Paolo Vranjes (Via San Gallo 63 r and Via della Spada 9 r, www.drvranjes.it) or Lorenzo Villoresi (on appointment by telephone: 055 2 34 11 87, Via de' Bardi 14, www.lorenzovilloresi.it).

Souvenirs

Mercato Centrale is the place for food

Or how about one of those attractive, typically Florentine **straw hats**, which women in the rest of Europe were mad over in the 18th century already? An especially supple and at the same time resilient type of straw comes from the Arno Valley. The Grevi family has been making their especially delightful models for four generations already (Via della Spada 11 – 13 r, www.grevi.com).

Crafts   For that matter, a sense of beauty that has been schooled for centuries can be seen the rich tradition of crafts (▶MARCO POLO Insight p. 132). Today the botteghe, the traditional workshops have to fight to survive. But at the same time they are the ground for innovation, for modern jewellery and hat makers, ceramic artists as well as designers who you will discover as you explore the side streets. The many antique shops that have collected on the northern banks of the Arno and on the southern side around Piazza Pitti, e. g. in Via Maggio, also show this ingrained sense of beauty.

Markets   Florence is also a city of markets, with the overflowing Mercato di San Lorenzo (closed Sun/Mon) near the Basilica San Lorenzo leading the way. Souvenirs can also be found at Mercato Nuovo under the Loggia del Porcellino. Two large market halls are reserved for groceries: Mercato Centrale and Mercato Sant'Ambrogio, and every 3rd sunday of the month an organic food market La Fierucolina is held on Piazza Santo Spirito. An attractive flea market on Piazza dei Ciompi invites browsing.

Bargains   Inexpensive clothing is sold every Tuesday morning in the large city park at the Mercato delle Cascine. The outlet centre Barberino di Mugello only 35km/21mi north of Florence (motorway A1) is a kind of modern market village. More than 90 shops sell well-known fashion labels, sporting goods, high quality kitchen appliances, porcelain at good prices.

Selected shops

ACCESSORIES
Aprosio & Co.
Via della Spada 38 r
www.aprosio.it
In the studio behind the shop the designer Ornella Aprosio designs wonderful fashion jewellery with colourful Murano glass beads and Bohemian crystal; she also applies them to bags and shawls, uncom-
monly stylish sparkling accessories.

Ammentos
Via dello Studio 30 r
http://ammentosfirenze.muzy.com
These premium accessories like belts, brooches, armbands, bags and wall decorations, that were inspired by Sardinia, show their

precise craftsmanship. Everything is made in the workshop behind the shop.

CERAMICS · PORCELAIN
Richard-Ginori
Via dei Rondinelli 17 r
Well-known manufacturer of exclusive porcelain in traditional Florentine style.

Mario Luca Giusti
Via della Vigna Nuova 88 r
www.mariolucagiusti.com
Of course Florence stands for the fine porcelain by Ginori, but there are also designers who would like to try something different. The plates, bowls, glasses and pitchers by Giusti are all made of synthetic materials and practically glow in wonderful colours; even the white lace tablecloths are made of plastic.

DEPARTMENT STORES
Rinascente
Piazza della Repubblica 1 r
www.rinascente.it
The top Italian department store has large fashion departments with cosmetics, beachwear, chic housewares and food. don't miss taking a well-earned break in the rooftop café with a spectacular view.

GOURMET FOODS
Pegna
Via dello Studio 8
www.pegnafirenze.com
In this gourmet food shop, which opened near the cathedral in 1860, the Florentines shop for their most festive meals. Along with first class meat, sausage,

Typical Tuscan vase

ham and excellent cheese, with the best varieties of Pecorino leading off, they also sell olive oil, all the varieties of beans and vegetables necessary for Tuscan soups and freshly ground coffee from the Florentine coffee roaster Manaresi. There are also biscuits and pralines from the best bakers and chocolate-makers in Tuscany, dressings and sauces as well as a giant selection of Tuscan wines.

HOSIERY
Emilio Cavallini
Via della Vigna Nuova 24r
www.emiliocavallini.com
The Tuscan designer's geometric patterns and strong colours have become a distinctive style for stocking creations in demand all over the world, for women and men.

Love of Beauty

Florence has always been famous for the artistic production of useful articles. The Renaissance high culture brought several crafts to flourish, and especially added value to anything that had to do with daily living and that beautified church façades, floors and furnishings.

The outstanding example is the art of **pietre dure**, mosaics made of small stones. The puzzle pieces were cut out of coloured stone like marble, crystal and semi-precious stones and made the most intricate pictures with them: flower gardens with birds, geometric and heraldic patterns, cityscapes – for tables, as wall and floor decorations and for altars. The stones came from Tuscany, but the Medici were able to acquire the more unusual stone colours from distant parts of the world through their trade connections. The founding of the Florentine workshop Opificio delle Pietre Dure goes back to this highly specialized and expensive technique; today it is a museum and restoration centre for this art form (▶p. 20). It may be hard to believe, but there are people who still master this craft; they can be seen, for example, in the Bottega I Mosaici di Lastrucci in Santa Croce-Viertel (Via dei Macci 9, www.imosaicidilastrucci.it) or in the workshop connected to the shop Scarpelli Mosaici (Via Ricasoli 59 r, www.scarpellimosaici.it) not far from the cathedral.

The younger generation are at bat now, just like with Pietra di Luna, where the son and daughter are following in the footsteps of the master Bianco Bianchi. They practice the no less difficult art of **scagliola**, a stucco technique in which plaster is coloured with different colours and artistically formed into delicate patterns (Via Maggio 4 – 6 r, www.biancobianchi.com). It can be seen in many churches and villas. Simone Fiordelisi unites stucco work and marble intarsia in his table tops (Arte Decorativa, Via de' Barbadori 41 r, www.tavolidimarmo.it).

For the interior furnishings of palazzi, churches and convents craftsmen who mastered the production of bronze fittings, the bronzisti, but also glass blowers, jewellers, silver, gold and metal smiths, gilders, painters, silk and tapestry weavers, carpenters, pottery makers and of course restorers. Before World War II the left bank of the Arno in Oltrarno around Piazza Santo Spirito was full of workshops; today these elaborate and accordingly expensive crafts have trouble surviving. Many of the craftsmen only restore what already exists.

The **jewellery shops on the Ponte Vecchio** form a regular »cluster« in terms of the art jewellery making. This picturesque conglomeration of buildings on the bridge was built for the butchers in the 15th century so that they could throw their waste directly into the river, at that time a step forward in hygiene. But in order to add value to the ducal corridor, which the Medici had built across the bridge in

Wonderful table in pietre dure technique

the 16th cent., the butchers were quickly replaced by goldsmiths. Alessandro Dari is an example of outstanding modern jewellery making; he has a studio and museum in Palazzo Nasi-Quaratesi (Via Santo Niccolò 115 r, www.alessandrodari.com).

Antico Setificio Fiorentino is an address rich in tradition that continues the silk fabric production of the 14th and 15th cent., which formed the basis of the wealth of some Florentine noble families. This setificio still produces wonderful brocade and damask fabrics for the interior decoration of luxury hotels and luxury residences all over the world, but also for costumes for the large Tuscan festivals, especially the Palio of Siena (Via Bartolini 4, www.anticosetificio.com).

Ask in the tourist offices for material and tours of the botteghe artigiane. There is a large trade and sales fair every year around late April/early May in the Fortezza da Basso, called the Mostra Internazionale dell'Artigianato, where craftsmen from Florence, Italy and also other countries present their skills and wares (www.mostraartigianato.it). A wonderful setting for the best craftsmen of the city is the Palazzo Corsini and its Italian formal park right in the city centre for the annual event Artigianato e Palazzo in late May (Via della Scala 115, www.artigianatoepalazzo.it).

JEWELLERY
Giuggiù di Angela Caputi
Via Santo Spirito 58 r
Borgo Santi Apostoli 44/46
www.angelacaputi.com
The designer uses materials like plastic and artificial resin for her modern fashion jewellery creations, unusual but still light and easy to wear, which makes her line very successful.

LEATHER GOODS
Braccialini
Scandicci
Via della Vigna Nuova 32 r
Via di Casellina 61 d
www.braccialini.it
This Florence firm has conquered the world with its colourful, modern and quirky bags and wallets. Of course its flagship store is located on Via della Vigna Nuova in the city. But anyone who does not want to spend as much on leather goods should go to the factory store in the suburb of Scandicci.

Cellerini   Insider Tip
Via del Sole 37 r
www.cellerini.it
In this family-run business – which is bravely holding its own against the handbag competitors from the Far East – everything is still done by hand, every cut, every seam. The fine leathers come from Italy and France. The styles of bags, belts and wallets can hardly be matched in their classical elegance and meticulous craftsmanship.

San Lorenzo
▶tip p. 267

LINGERIE · FABRICS
Loretta Caponi
Piazza Antinori 4 r
www.lorettacaponi.com
Discerning Florentine upper class families international celebrities order their trousseau, baptismal gowns or baby clothes from Loretta Caponi, who sold here first needlework when she was nine years old, and from her daughter Lucia. A visit to the traditional shop with attached tailoring workshop is worthwhile alone for the ceiling paintings and stucco work.

MARKETS
Flea Market
Piazza dei Ciompi
Mon – Sat 9am – 7pm
The market invites browsing among dusty and unusual oddities.

Mercato Centrale
Piazza del Mercato Centrale
Via dell' Ariento
Mon–Fri 7am–2pm, Sat 7am–5pm
The main floor of the market hall – one of the best in Italy – is devoted to fish, meat, cheese and numerous delicacies; fruit and vegetables are on the upper floor.

Mercato San Ambrogio
Piazza Ghiberti
Mon – Sat 7am – 2pm
Fresh regional groceries, but also clothing and shoes.

PAPER PRODUCTS
Pineider
Piazza della Signoria 13 r
Via Tornabuoni 76 r

Pineider has premium leather bags and writing tools of all kinds

This traditional business located in a former guild hall sells handmade paper, also in marbled Tuscan style, and very beautiful writing instruments; Lord Byron and Stendhal shopped here.

PERFUME
Aqua Flor
Borgo Santa Croce 6
The perfumer Sileno Cheloni from Lucca has opened a wonderful shop in Florence with his precious perfumes, essences, bath products and oils. Like his famous Florentine colleagues Vranjes and Villoresi he will also create a scent especially for you, unique and at a price.

Farmacia Santissima Annunziata dal 1561
Insider Tip
Via dei Servi 80 r

www.farmaciassannunziata1561.it
Not only the legendary Officina Profumo Farmaceutica di Santa Maria Novella (▶Tip p. 289) stands for the old Florentine tradition of the medicinal use of herbs, as it was done in many monasteries and for which Cosimo I had the botanical garden Giardino dei Semplici made. There are also fine scents and beauty treatments. A whole row of these pharmacies have survived over the centuries, like the Farmacia Santissima Annunziata from the 16th century with its 17th/18th century shelves laden with modern products: wonderful scents, skin creams and soaps from their modern laboratory.

Tours and Guides

Discover Florence

For first-time visitors to Florence there are doubledecker sightseeing buses that will give you an overview of the city on both banks of the Arno.

Tourist offices have many flyers on guided city tours, excursions and museum tours, including the famous Vasari corridor, which can only be seen as part of a private tour. The tourist office also has pdf brochures with suggestions on interesting walking tours through the city (www.firenzeturismo.it).

Information

Two sightseeing bus lines with open upper decks run every day. Both start from the main railway station: the blue Line A around the city centre and up to Piazzale Michelangelo and the red Line B, which also runs through the left side of the Arno and then back through the centre and up to Fiesole. The lines have 19 or 25 stops respectively, where you can always get off and on again. Audioguides are available. The bus tickets (starting at €20 for adults and €10 for children age 5 to 15 years), which can be bought in the bus, in hotels and in tourist offices, are valid for 48 hours and can also be used on the busses and trains of the municipal transport system ATAF.

Sightseeing busses

Many agencies also organize bus tours of the Tuscan countryside, to Pisa, Lucca, Siena and wine tours of Chianti. Food & wine tours through Florence, the markets and tours on culinary specialties, are listed for example, at the Internet address www.florencetasting.com (tel. 055 2 39 88 55) or at http://florenceforfoodies.com. Most of these tours are led by Americans of English people living in Florence.

Bus tours

Guided sightseeing tours by bicycle or Segway are very popular; usually quite good bikes and helmets are included. The increasing traffic restrictions in the centre and the growing number of bicycle paths, e. g. along the Arno, as well as nice and competent guides – mostly in English – make these excursions whorthwhile and fun. Generally a three-hour tour costs about €35. Segway tours begin at €75.

Guided Segway and bike tours

Individually guided walks and museum visits are offered by official city guides, art historians who know the city and the language and who live in or near Florence. Offers can be found e.g. online at www.florenceguides.com.

Individually guided tours

Sightseeing busses give a good first impression of Florence

Rickshas will also get you around

Adresses

Sightseeing busses
www.firenze.city-sightseeing.it

CAF Tours & Travel
Via degli Alfani 151 r
tel. 055 28 32 00
www.caftours.com
Respected old agency with a rich
selection of tours through Florence, Tuscany, by bus, Segways,
bikes, Vespa etc.

Città nascosta
Lungarno B. Cellini 25
tel. 055 6 80 25 90
www.cittanascosta.it

Well-versed city guides offer interesting theme walks in English.

Florence Town
Via de' Lamberti 1
tel. 055 0 12 39 94
www.florencetown.com
www.ibikeflorence.com
Bike tours through Florence as
well as Segway and Vespa tours

I Bike Florence
Via de' Lamberti 1
tel. 055 0 12 39 94
www.ibikeflorence.com
Guided bike tours in English

Italy Segway Tours

Via dei Cimatori 9 r
tel. 055 2 39 88 55
www.segwayfirenze.com
Segway, bike tours as well as wine excursions and much more.

My Tours

Viale Giovanni Milton 49
tel. *800 28 99 77
Handy 0039 338 3 97 41 58
www.mytours.it
This agency organizes all sorts of excursions, also Vespa tours, through the Chianti hills and Segway tours through Florence.

I Renaioli

Dock at the Ponte alle Grazie bridge
Piazza Mentana
Handy 0039 34 77 98 23 56
www.renaioli.it
The rowing club I Renaioli has restored old typical Arno rowboats (barchetti) with room for 12 people at the most and offers rowing excursions from March to September with a wonderful view of the city along the river.

TOURS

You don't know the way? These tour suggestions cover all of the city's highlights and will help you plan your visit.

Tours Through Florence

Four walks – the fleet of foot can manage them quickly. But it is better to take your time, especially in large museums like the Uffizi.

Tour 1   **Absolute Highlights**
This walk goes to the most important sights of the brilliant city of art.
►page 144

Tour 2   **In Michelangelo's Footsteps**
Encounters with Michelangelo and his works in the Sagrestia Nuova of San Lorenzo and the Galleria dell' Accademia.
►page 145

Tour 3   **On Monte alle Croce**
The climb up Monte alle Croce is rewarded with a spectacular view.
►page 146

Tour 4   **Everyday Florence**
See a different side of the city on the Arno.
►page 147

Close-up view from the Campanile to the dome of the cathedral

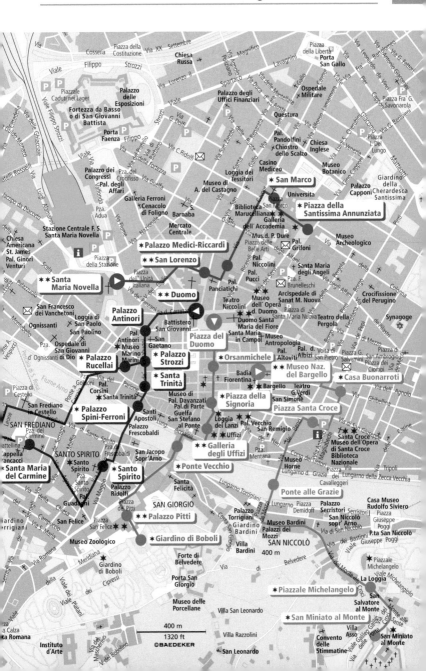

Getting Around in Florence

Overwhelming treasury of art

Of course, it is possible to visit Florence for just a few hours, but a short trip will only give a first impression of this overwhelming city of art. It is better to take several days. A full week discovering the immeasurable artistic wealth of Florence is time well spent. The Uffizi alone, one of the most important art galleries in the world, will take several hours or even a whole day.

City of short walks

We do not recommend visiting Florence by car. The city centre is a pedestrian zone, and parking spaces are rare anywhere in the city. Moreover, the most important sights are very close together, so a car is not even necessary. Highlights that are a bit further away can be reached by bus. On foot it is possible to stroll through the narrow streets, where there are inviting cafés and ice cream parlours on every corner.

Tour 1 Absolute Highlights

Start and finish: From the cathedral to the Giardino di Boboli
Duration: 2 days

Tour 1 includes the Piazza del Duomo and the Piazza della Signoria, two central squares in Florence that lie close to each other, where art treasures are concentrated on a small space. This tour is a must in every sightseeing programme. Since both the Uffizi Gallery and the Palazzo Pitti require several hours each to do justice to their excellent art collections, this tour takes two days to complete.

The tour begins at the ❶ **Piazza del Duomo**, which is dominated by the impressive ****Duomo Santa Maria del Fiore** with its majestic dome and the beautiful freestanding campanile. The greatest treasure of the ****Battistero San Giovanni** next to it are the Paradise Doors, copies of which are still in place. Since the originals are in the ****Museo del Opera del Duomo,** plan to visit this museum as well. It also houses other important pieces from the cathedral, including the moving Pietà, a masterpiece by Michelangelo. Now walk along Via Calzaiuoli, one of Florence's main shopping streets, southwards to the church of ❷ ***Orsanmichele** with its important sculptures. Continue on Via Calzaiuoli to the historic ❸ ***Piazza della Signoria.** Along with the Piazza del Duomo this is the heart of tourist Florence. The ****Palazzo Vecchio** played an important role in the city's history.

The beautiful Gothic ***Loggia dei Lanzi** holds important sculptures. Before turning to the ④****Galleria degli Uffizi**, one of the most famous art galleries in the world, for which you should plan at least several hours, take a break in Café Rivoire and try the famous hot chocolate. The next destination is the nearby picturesque ⑤*** Ponte Vecchio**, where goldsmiths display their goods. After crossing the bridge with its jewellery shops pass the church of Santa Felicità, probably the oldest in the city, and continue a short distance to ⑥****Palazzo Pitti**, whose art gallery is also of great value. After viewing the numerous art treasures the ⑦***Giardino di Boboli** offers a chance to take a break from art. There is a beautiful view of the city from the higher part of the park.

In Michelangelo's Footsteps   Tour 2

Start and finish: From Santa Maria Novella to the Museo Archeologico
Duration: 1–2 days

The highlights of this tour through the northern part of the city centre are masterpieces of sculpture by Michelangelo: the New Sacristy of San Lorenzo with its outstanding statuary and the original figure of David, which can be seen in the Galleria dell' Accademia.

Tour 2 begins at ❶****Santa Maria Novella**, one of Florence's major churches. The church of ❷****San Lorenzo** further to the east is artistically even more important. Here Michelangelo's world-famous

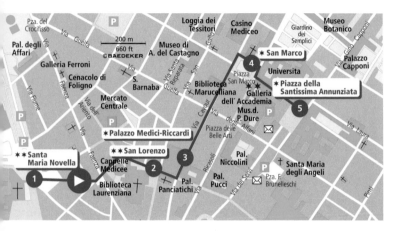

Sagrestia Nuova houses unique works of sculpture. ❸*Palazzo Medici Riccardi** diagonally opposite demonstrates the power of the Medici family, which once ruled the city. Now follow Via Cavour to the north to the monastery of ❹*San Marco**, where wonderfully expressive frescoes by Fra Angelico await. The nearby **Galleria dell' Accademia** attracts crowds of visitors who come to see Michelangelo's statue of David. Continue south-eastwards to ❺*Piazza della Santissima Annunziata**, a unique architectural ensemble. The church of ❻*Santissima Annunziata**, an architectural masterpiece, and the *Ospedale degli Innocenti** with the beautiful loggia are especially worth seeing here.

Tour 3 **On Monte alle Croce**

Start and finish: From Museo Bargello to San Miniato al Monte
Duration: 1 day

This unusual tour goes from Museo Bargello with its masterpieces of sculpture and up the hill to the church of San Miniato al Monte with its beautiful view of the city.

The tour begins at the ❶**Museo Nazionale del Bargello**, in which excellent 14th to 16th-century sculptures can be seen. Then follow Via Ghibellina eastwards to ❷*Casa Buonarroti**, where two original works by Michelangelo are the main attraction. The expansive ❸Piazza Santa Croce** to the south is dominated by the church of **Santa Croce**. With its tombs and important works of art the church is one of the most impressive in Italy. After viewing the church a walk up to Piazzale Michelangelo is worthwhile. Those who do not enjoy the climb can take bus no. 13. To go up on foot, first cross the bridge ❹ **Ponte alle Grazie**. Past Museo Bardini turn into Via San Niccolò and walk to the 12th-century church of San Niccolò sopr' Arno. From here Via San Miniato passes through the city gate of the same name (1258), and then Via del Monte alla Croci leads to ❺ * **Piazzale Michelangelo**, where there is a wonderful view of the city with its imposing buildings. From the square walk a little higher to the historic church of ❻ * **San Miniato al Monte,** which has an impressive site. From here there is another wonderful view of the complete city panorama.

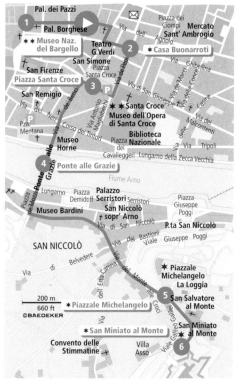

Everyday Florence   Tour 4

Start and finish: Cathedral
Duration: 1 day

The tour in the district of Santo Spirito, on the opposite side of the Arno from the city centre, focuses on a different side of Florence, where craftsmen work and small restaurants serve local cuisine.

The tour begins at the centrally located ❶ ** **cathedral** (▶Tour 1). Walk along Via de Cerretani to the west past Santa **Maria Maggiore**, one of the city's oldest churches. At the nearby ❷ **Palazzo Antinori**, where the cantinetta of the same name serves Tuscan cuisine and

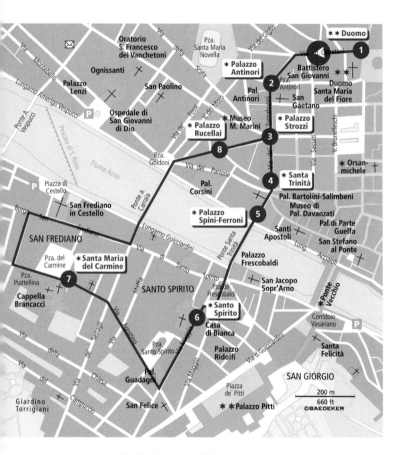

wines, **Via de' Tornabuoni** begins. Expensive international designer fashion and valuable jewellery are sold in this elegant shopping street. Pass by the church of San Gaetano with its beautiful 17th-century façade to ❸*Palazzo Strozzi, which is considered to be the most beautiful of Florence's Renaissance palaces. Then comes Florence's first Gothic church, ❹*Santa Trínita on Piazza Santa Trínita. The nearby ❺*Palazzo Spini-Ferroni at the end of Via de' Tornabuoni houses the shoe museum of the famous shoe designer Ferragamo. After crossing the Santa Trinità bridge walk along Via Maggio past various palaces and Casa di Bianca Cappello (no. 26); a short distance to the west is the Renaissance church of ❻*Santo Spirito, designed by the famous architect Brunelleschi. The church lies at the centre of the Santo Spirito neighbourhood, with its small shops, trattoria and above all craft workshops. After visiting the church, take a break on the idyllic tree-shaded piazza. Via Sant' Agostino runs north-west to another important church, ❼ ***Santa Maria del Carmine** with the Brancacci Chapel. Return via the Baroque church of San Frediano in Cestello and the Ponte alla Carraia. ❽ ***Palazzo Rucellai** in the exclusive shopping street Via della Vigna Nuova is a beautiful example of a Renaissance city palace. Anyone interested in modern art should make a side trip to the **Museo Marino Marini**, one of the few museums for modern art in Florence. Finish the tour in one of the many cafés at the nearby **Piazza della Repubblica** to the east.

SIGHTS FROM
A TO Z

The »Beauty on the Arno« is a city of culture through and through,
where artists of genius created priceless works.

** Bargello

▶Museo Nazionale del Bargello

** Battistero San Giovanni

———————————— ✴ H 6/b III

Location: Piazza S. Giovanni
Bus lines: C 1, C 2, C 14, C23
❶ Mon – Sat 11.15am – 7pm, 1st Sat in the month 8.30am – 2pm,
Sun 8.30am – 2pm; admission: €5, www.opera duomo.firenze.it

The Baptistery owes its fame to its three monumental bronze doors, an unsurpassed achievement of Gothic and Renaissance sculpture.

Model for architecture
The octagonal Baptistery of St John was completed in 1128 after 70 years of construction. Various builders worked on it and gave the Baptistery, which was first used in 1128, its fine proportions and its variety of colours – white and green marble – forms and figures. The Romanesque central structure was considered to be a model for similar architecture in northern Italy. Three outstanding and artistic bronze doors were added in the 14th and 15th centuries.

*South door
The oldest door, in Gothic style, is on the south side; it was designed by **Andrea Pisano** and cast by Leonardo d' Avanzano in the years between 1330 and 1336. It is divided into 28 squares with quatrefoils. 20 relief panels in the style of goldsmith work show scenes from the life of John the Baptist, the patron saint of the church. The remaining eight fields contain allegorical scenes of Christian and secular virtues. Each of the figures is exemplary in its representation of facial features, the folds of the garments and its expressive pose, and all of them are different. The decoration of the frames was designed by Vittorio Ghiberti, the son of Lorenzo; their leaves, animals and fruits are an early indication of the wealth of forms used in the Renaissance.

*North door
A competition for the north door was held in 1401 and won by **Lorenzo Ghiberti** against six competitors, including Brunelleschi. Ghiberti and his assistants (including Donatello) executed the doors from 1403 to 1424, closely following the plan of Andrea Pisano's south door in assigning the subjects: 28 squares with 28 quatrefoils, including twenty scenes from the New Testament and eight figures (four evangelists, four fathers of the Latin church). Ghiberti's work far surpasses Pisano's in the elegance of the figures and their lively

expressions. The artist's new style can be seen especially in tl
of the Resurrection (right door, top row on the left), the Bap
the Temptation of Christ (left door, 4th row from the top
right), the Birth of Christ (left door, 5th row from the top, r
the Dispute with the Teachers of the Law (right door, 5th
the top, right). In other parts Ghiberti followed a more traditional
style. Little heads look out at the points where the frames intersect.

154

Ghiberti broke completely with tradition when he created the east   ****East door**
door, his main work. Michelangelo thought that it was worthy to   **(Porta del**
       Paradiso)

Porta del Paradiso: look and be amazed

ı.ıstero San Giovanni

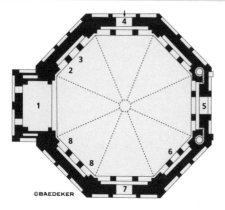

1 Tribuna with mosaics
  by Jacopo
2 Stone coffin of
  Bishop Ranieri
3 Tomb of John XXIII
4 North doors (entrance)
5 East doors
  (Porta del Paradiso)
6 Marble baptismal font
7 South doors
8 Roman sarcophagi

©BAEDEKER

decorate the gates of paradise, which is why it is called Porta del Paradiso, and Ghiberti himself praised it next to his signature on the right door as »mira arte fabricatum« (»created with admirable skill«). The Porta del Paradiso was replaced by a copy in 1990 in gilded bronze; the original panels can be seen in the Museo dell' Opera del Duomo. The door, which was created between 1425 and 1452, was the most perfect expression of art in bronze relief until Rodin.

The ten panels are surrounded by prophets, sibyls and other biblical and pagan figures; in each one several scenes have been combined masterfully. The beauty and perfection of perspective, the delicate lines, the varying depths in the levels of depiction, the realism of the figures and scenic composition of the groups all contribute to the **perfect overall impression** of this work. From top left to bottom right the panels depict Adam and Eve (creation, the original sin, expulsion from paradise); Cain and Abel (the sacrifices of Cain and Abel, the murder of Abel, Cain's punishment); Noah (his offering, leaving the ark, his drunkenness); Abraham and Isaac (angels with Abraham, sacrifice of Isaac); Jacob and Esau (birth of Esau and Jacob, selling the birthright, Esau's hunt, Rebecca, deceiving Isaac); Joseph (the sale of Joseph, Benjamin, Joseph and his brothers); Moses (Moses receives the tablets with the commandments on Mount Sinai); Joshua (the Jews before Jericho, tent camp, trumpet miracle); and finally Saul and David (battle against the Philistines, slaying Goliath; and finally Solomon and the Queen of Sheba).

Interior   The interior of the Baptistery, unlike the clear structure of the exterior, surprises with its solemn and mystical darkness. Its octagonal, double-skinned dome (diameter 26m/85ft) is completely covered by a ****Mosaic** 13th-century mosaic. It is one of the major works with Byzantine influence and stands out equally for its thematic depictions and its rich ornamentation. Above the choir chapel Christ conducts the Last Judgement as the judge of the world; the figure of Christ alone measures 8m/26ft. Grouped around him in various zones are the saved and the condemned, angels, apostles, prophets and saints with Mary and John the Baptist, with the realm of Satan opposite them devouring the damned. Other series of images show moving, expressive scenes of the Creation and the lives of Jesus Christ, Mary, Joseph and John the Baptist. Further interesting features are the **tomb of the antipope John XXIII** (deposed by the Council of Constance in 1415), a masterpiece by Donatello; the marble floor with coloured stone inlay work (signs of the zodiac and ornaments); the marble baptismal font; the sarcophagus of Bishop Ranieri; and the main altar with an angel holding a candelabra.

AROUND THE BATTISTERO SAN GIOVANNI

Santa Maria Maggiore

One of the oldest churches in Florence is located in Via de' Cerretani, not far from the Baptistery. It was built before the 11th century and renovated in the late 13th century. The old **bell tower** shows that the Romanesque church was low-lying. A late Romanesque bust, named Berta, is set into the upper part of the tower. There is a copy of a 14th-century *Madonna with Child* of the Pisan school above the church door.

Of the beautiful paintings and statues inside – a three-aisled Gothic hall with columns – the colourful, gilded wooden relief and a *Madonna Enthroned with Child* in the left side aisle. The large, colourful and precious gilded panel painting is dominated by a central figure of solemnly pensive Mary sculpted in wood and stucco. Long ascribed to the Florentine Coppo di Marcovaldo (1261), now it is presumed to be the work of local and Byzantine artists.

⋆ Casa Buonarroti

✦ J 6/c III

Location: Via Ghibellina 70
Bus: C 1, C 2, C 3, 14
❶ Mon, Wed – Sun 10am – 5pm; admission: €6.50, www.casabuonarroti.it

The world-famous painter and sculptor Michelangelo Buonarroti bought this house for his nephew Leonardo di Buonarroti; the artist himself never lived in it.

Michelangelo

Michelangelo, the son of Leonardo Buonarroti, decorated the house and established a memorial to the great artist whose namesake he was. It was in bad condition for a long time, but it was restored completely in 1964. **Two original works by Michelangelo** deserve note: the Battle of the Centaurs, a marble relief that Michelangelo made when he was 17 years old, already shows traces of the genius of later years, for example in the movement and fullness of the figures; the relief *Madonna with Child* – also called *Madonna della Scala* – was his first work, which he finished at the age of 16. His mastery can already be seen in the spatial composition, the movement and countermovement on the steps on the left – hence the name *Madonna at the Steps* – the rich profile expression and the flowing robe. The wooden crucifix for Santo Spirito of 1494 was Michelangelo's first work for a church. Christ is depicted here not as the man of sorrows but as a gentle, beautiful youth. Models or copies of other works by Michelangelo are also on display, as well as mementoes of his life. There are also sculptures and paintings by other masters. Casa Buonarroti also hosts good temporary exhibitions.

❶ Mon, Wed–Sun 9.30am–2pm

AROUND CASA BUONARROTI

Le Murate   A few steps further along Via Ghibellina to the east is the large complex Le Murate, built in the 14th cent. as a convent and used as a prison from 1845 to 1985. Today Le Murate is an accomplished example of modern reconstruction and remodelling, which even the star Architect Renzo Piano contributed to, into a residence with 45 council flats, social meeting rooms and cultural centre and café with concerts and exhibitions.

❶ Via Ghibellina 2 – 16; www.lemurate.it

Loggia del Pesce   Just like Loggia di Mercato Nuovo, Loggia del Pesce, the fish market north-east of Casa Buonarroti, is not part of a building but a separate structure of its own. Vasari (1567) designed the loggia, which was originally part of the old market on today's Piazza della Repubblica; it was moved to Piazza dei Ciompi in the late 19th century. An antique and flea market has taken place every day on this rustic and placid piazza since the 1950s. Go a short distance to the east to the large market hall Mercato di Sant' Ambrogio on Piazza Ghiberti, next to Mercato Centrale near San Lorenzo the second largest food market in the centre of Florence.

Certaldo

Location: 40km/25mi south   level
Province: Firenze (FI)   **Population:** 16,000
Elevation: 130m/430ft above sea

The town of Certaldo lies in hilly country between wheat fields and olive groves. The upper town, Certaldo Alto, where the poet Boccaccio (▶Famous People) lived at the end of his life, is small and extremely charming.

WHAT TO SEE IN CERTALDO

Its position high up on the hill, its largely intact wall that encircles the town completely and red brick houses give the upper part of Certaldo an impressively harmonious appearance but also an almost fortress-like character. It does not take much time to see it. A cobbled main street, named Via Boccaccio after the town's most famous son, leads straight up to the highest point of Certaldo Alto, which is crowned by Palazzo Pretorio. The little road up to Certaldo Alto is closed to cars, but the **cable car** that runs every fifteen minutes from the main piazza of the lower city is an alternative to the steep steps. ***Certaldo Alto**

> **!** *Mercantia*   **Insider Tip**
>
> MARCO POLO TIP
>
> ... is the name for the most important event of the year in Certaldo. It is a combination of theatre festival, music festival and medieval market. The old walls and buildings of the town are a superb stage set for the annual spectacle, which takes place in the third week of July.
> www.mercantiacertaldo.it

Below Palazzo Pretorio, in Casa del Boccaccio (house no. 18), the great Renaissance poet is supposed to have lived. A museum with a library attached has information on Giovanni Boccaccio (▶Famous People), who is buried in the former monastery church Chiesa dei Santi Jacopo e Filippo nearby. **Casa del Boccaccio**
❶ April–Oct daily 9.30am–1.30pm, 2.30pm–7pm; Nov–Mar Mon, Wed–Sun 9.30am–1.30pm, 2.30pm–4.30pm; admission: with Palazzo Pretorio: €4; www.casadelboccaccio.it

In the convent of a former monastery a few steps higher is the Museo del Arte Sacra, a worthwhile collection of altar panels, sculptures and church implements. **Museo del Arte Sacra**
❶ June–Sep 9.30am–1.30pm, 2.30pm–7pm; Oct–May Tue–Sun 9.30am–1.30pm, 2.30pm–4.30pm; admission: €6, www.museoartesacra.net

Certaldo

INFORMATION
Pro Loco
Via Boccaccio 16
tel. 0571 65 27 30
www.prolococertaldo.it

WHERE TO EAT
Taverna l' Antica Fonte €€
Certaldo Alto
Via Valdracca 25
tel. 0571 65 22 25
www.tavernaanticafonte.it
The terrace of this attractive eatery in the old city is wonderful when the weather is nice; let your gaze roam over the hills and silhouette of San Gimignano while enjoying tasty Tuscan food.

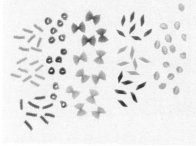

Osteria di Casa Chianti €€ **Insider Tip**
Fiano, Case Nuove 77
tel. 0571 66 96 88
www.osteriadicasachianti.it
7 km to the north-east in the hills, equally popular with locals and tourists, this trattoria is known for its ribollita, home-made pici pasta, excellent meat and for its terrace with a wonderful view. There are three nice rooms upstairs (Internet: www.casachianti.it, €) for overnight guests.

WHERE TO STAY
Agriturismo Il Paluffo €€€
Certaldo, Via Citerna 144
Mobile 3355 39 52 73
www.paluffo.com
4 rooms, 4 apartments
This picturesque old country house estate in the hills 8 km north of Certaldo is the Tuscan dream. Solar power, natural water regeneration in the pool as well as organic farming in the surrounding olive groves and vineyards make this paradise perfect. The holiday flats are roomy and tasteful; there are rooms with one common kitchen for self-caterers.

*Palazzo Pretorio Via Boccaccio terminates impressively at the massive medieval palace with its rich decoration of coats of arms on the façade. The Counts Alberti, and later administrators from Florence, lived in the building, which dates from the late 12th century. From 1530 court judgments and new laws were proclaimed from the front loggia. In the former offices, which are used for exhibitions today, there are several frescoes to admire, including a Pietà (1484) that is attributed to Pier Francesco Fiorentino as well as a fresco *Doubting Thomas* (1490), thought to be a work of Benozzo Gozzoli. On the walls of the 13th-century St Thomas Chapel fresco fragments depict the 24 Florentine podestà. Be sure not to miss the enchanting view from the tower.

❶ Opening times and admission like Casa del Bocaccio

* Certosa del Galluzzo

Location: 5km/3mi south of the city centre, Via della Certosa 1
Bus: 37
❶ Visit only with a monk as guide, Tue – Sat 9am, 10am, 11am, 3pm, 4pm,
Sun 3pm, 4pm, in the summer also at 5pm;
www.cistercensi.info, admission: free will donation

**The former Carthusian monastery of Galluzzo has interesting
architecture and famous works of art. It rises high above the
Ema Valley.**

Certosa (»chartreuse«) lies near the road from Florence to Siena; at
the southern outskirts of Galluzzo follow the signs. When the last
Carthusian monks left the monastery in 1956, it was then taken over
by Cistercians. Niccolò Acciaiuoli, a Florentine statesman and friend
of Petrarch and Boccaccio, had the fortress-like monastery built in
1341 for the Carthusians, an order that was founded in the 11th century by St Bruno of Cologne.

Donated by a Florentine statesman

It consisted of cell-like huts and common rooms for prayer and wor-
ship. The complex was expanded and converted several times in the
following centuries. The complex is still characterized by the Carthusian way of life, which tries to balance monastic fellowship with the
lifestyle of a hermit. The monastery once had precious works of art
but **Napoleon** robbed the order of about 500 works, of which only a
few were given back.

The church of San Lorenzo on its broad piazza is worth a visit. The
tomb of the founder, Niccolò Acciaiuoli († 1365), is in the Cappella
di San Tobia (left of the main altar), as are three other gravestones of
the Acciaiuoli family – including one for Lorenzo di Niccolò. The famous tomb of Cardinal Agnolo II Acciaiuoli, which is attributed to
Francesco da Sangallo, is in the Cappella di Sant' Andrea. The other
chapels also hold valuable works of art.

San Lorenzo

The tour continues through the monastery buildings, which include
a parlatorium, the Middle Cloister, the chapter house, the impressive
Great Cloister (1498–1516), the refectory and the Little Cloister. The
buildings were not residences but meeting rooms. The monks lived
in the **cell huts** that were part of the complex. One of these huts,
which consists of three rooms, a loggia and a small garden, can be
viewed. Palazzo degli Studi, which Acciaiuoli commissioned Jacopo
Passavanti and Jacopo Talenti to build, but which was only finished
in the 16th century, houses the **picture gallery**. It includes examples
of what was once an immense treasury of art, such as lunette frescoes

Monastery buildings

(1523–25) by Pontormo to designs by Albrecht Dürer and a *Madonna with Child* by Lucas Cranach. There is a **shop** where the cordials produced by the monks can be sampled and bought.

✴✴ Chianti

south of Florence

Provinces: Florence/Firenze (FI), Siena (SI)
Altitude: 230 – 400m/400 – 1300 ft

Everyone who has seen Florence, done the full programme of culture and now longs for a rural scene, should go to Chianti, which welcomes visitors with gently rolling hills, olive groves, forests and vineyards.

Famous wine region

The **Strada Chianti classico** (www.stradachianticlassico.it) runs 70km/45mi through the famous wine region, past vineyards, farms and majestic castles and through pretty little towns and medieval villages. Chianti Classico is offered for direct sale from many wine estates (»vendita diretta«), including a wine tasting and tour of the fattoria. Of course, every village in Chianti holds its wine festival in September or October.

STRADA CHIANTI CLASSICO

*Impruneta

The south-east road out of Florence (city side of the river) towards Pontassieve leads straight to the feeder road for the Bologna/Roma autostrada. Just before the autostrada approach ramp (A 1), turn off towards Grassina, the first town on the Strada Chianti Classico (SS 222). Follow the SS 222 almost 10km/6mi to Pitigliolo, where there is a turn-off toward Impruneta (5km/3mi). The town, which is enchantingly sited amongst vineyards, is a **centre of pottery**. Here the traditional handmade terracotta is still popular. The planters are especially popular. The roof tiles for the cathedral in Florence were fired in the terracotta ovens of Impruneta.

*Castelli

Framed in cypresses, **Castello Vicchiomaggio** occupies a hill commanding a wonderful view just about 4km/2.5mi before Greve. Its oldest parts – tower and enclosure wall – date from the 13th century. In the nearby **Castello di Verrazzano** the production of Chianti has a very long history, going back to the 12th century. The wine cellars, as well as the castle and the garden of Verrazzano are open to the public. Rooms for overnight guests at the inn Foresteria Casanova.
Castello di Verrazzano: reservations tel. 055 85 42 43; www.verrazzano.com

Chianti

INFORMATION
Castellina in Chianti
(open seasonally)
Via Ferrucchio 40
tel. 05 77 74 13 92

Greve in Chianti
(all year)
Piazza Matteotti 11
tel. 055 8 54 62 99
www.chianti.com
www.tuscanyaccomodation.com
www.terresiena.it

WHERE TO EAT
Albergaccio €€€
Castellina in Chianti
Via Fiorentina 63
tel. 05 77 74 10 42
Sonia Visman und Francesco Cacciatori
swear by the top quality ingredients
from Chianti for their creative, refined
cuisine in this elegant country restaurant.

Bottega € – €€
Volpaia
Piazza della Torre
tel. 0577 73 80 01
www.labottegadivolpaia.it
Closed Tue
Inviting place to stop on an excursion
with tasty Tuscan cooking and a wonderful view of the Chianti hills.

Oltre il Giardino € – €€ *Insider Tip*
Greve in Chianti – Panzano
Piazza Bucciarelli 42
Tel./fax 05 58 28 28, closed Thu
The homemade pasta and the selected
cheese taste especially good. Seating on
the pleasant terrace with a wonderful
view of the Chianti hills in the summer.

ACCOMMODATION
Relais Fattoria Vignale €€€
Radda in Chianti
Via Pianigiani 9
tel. 05 77 73 83 00
www.vignale.it, 42 rooms
One of the best addresses in Chianti – in
a historic building of course. The hotel is
also the seat of the wine consortium
Chianti Classico; gourmets should try
the restaurant.

Belvedere di San Leonino €€ – €€€
Castellina in Chianti
Loc. San Leonino
tel. 05 77 74 08 87
www.hotelsanleonino.com, 29 rooms
In the hills, but nevertheless on the route
to Siena; a hotel in Tuscan country-
house style with beautifully furnished
rooms and a well-tended garden with
pool.

*Greve in Chianti The small town of Greve is the wine centre of Chianti. On the beautiful triangular Piazza Matteotti is a statue of **Giovanni Verrazzano**, whose home is not far away (see above). Comfortable trattorias in houses with flower-decorated loggias, cafés and one of the best sausage shops in all Tuscany (►MARCO POLO Tip p.162) line the square, which is transformed into an outdoor enoteca during the one-week wine festival (Rassegna del Chianti Classico) in mid-September.

!

MARCO ◉ POLO TIP

Sausages! **Insider Tip**

Sausage and nothing but sausage is available in Antica Macelleria Falorni on the marketplace of Greve. The aroma that welcomes you into this sausage paradise would make anyone hungry. Of course the Tuscan speciality, salami made from wild boar, is available but also fennel salami. Piazza G. Matteotti 71 www.falorni.it

*Monte-fioralle An excursion absolutely to be recommended (2km/just over a mile above Greve, extreme inclines but a **wonderful panoramic view**) is to the castle village of Montefioralle, where excellent olive oil is produced. Park in the parking lot behind the village (signposted, but with hardly any shade), since only residents may drive into Montefioralle. The amateur painters in the steep streets decorated with flowers show that Montefioralle is no longer an insider's tip. To enjoy the view for a while, choose between the terrace of the local restaurant and the shady square under the Chiesa Santo Stefano, where a rest on a park bench might lead to a conversation with local residents.

*Castellina in Chianti The closer to Castellina, the more mountainous and forested the country. In the main street of the medieval town centre, Via Ferruccio, there are several proud palazzi and many small gourmet and wine shops. A **castle** with an exhibition an the Etruscans crowns the highest point of the village; there is also an observation platform. There is a confined feeling by contrast in **Via delle Volte** on the east side of the town wall, which has been completely covered by other buildings. But almost every visitor strolls through the old street, as it has been carefully restored and is filled with chic galleries and shops with original souvenirs.

*Radda in Chianti A country road leads from Castellina via Radda (13km/8mi) to the southern slopes of the Chianti hills. In the sunny valleys of the Mon-

Quiet evening atmosphere in Greve in Chianti

ti del Chianti the best **DOCG wines** of the region ripen. The medieval town gets many visitors and offers beautiful views from the crown of a hill. Park along the old city wall, which is also an observation platform (parking limited to one hour). In the centre, on Via Roma, stands the **Palazzo del Podestà** (15th century), which is richly decorated with coats of arms and today houses the town hall and tourist information office Pro Loco (tel. 0577 73 84 94). The **Franciscan monastery of Santa Maria al Prato** (11th to 17th centuries) has been converted to a cultural and wine museum.

*Volpaia Volpaia, one of the **prettiest villages in southern Chianti**, 5km/3mi north of Radda, has less than 50 residents. The **castle** was already mentioned in 1172. Every year in Sepember the castle is transformed into an art gallery with exhibitions on the subject of wine and art.

*Badia a Coltibuono There is a beautiful view about 5km/3mi to the north (signposted) at the Abbey of Coltibuono, which was consecrated in 1049. The monastery building was taken over in 1402 by Benedictine monks from Vallombrosa, who renovated the cloister and refectory. Today it is possible to visit the Romanesque church and eat afterwards with a beautiful view of the Arno valley.

➊ Tours: Apr – Oct daily hourly 2pm – 5pm, www.coltibuono.com

Gaiole in Chianti The neighbouring town of Gaiole in Chianti (13km/8mi from Volpaia) is surrounded by vineyards famous for their excellent quality, most of which also sell directly (vendita diretta). Gaiole is situated in a valley, rather than on a hill, and has no special charms, not even in the marketplace with renovated houses.

Chianti Sculpture Park Beyond Gaiole there is a choice between two branches of the Via Chiantigiana, both of which can be recommended for the beautiful scenery. On the western route (no. 408) the small detour to the Chianti Sculpture Park near Pievasciata, one of the newest attractions an the Chiantigiana, is worthwhile. The last section of about 4km/2.5mi is unpaved. The charm of the park lies above all in the close symbiosis between the landscape and modern sculptures by **contemporary artists from all over the world**.

➊ April – Oct Tue – Sun 10am until sunset; www.chiantisculpturepark.it

Castello di Meleto The eastern route (SP 484) of the Chiantigiana is called the **Strada dei Castelli dei Chianti**, »Chianti castle route«. The first castle appears about 4km/2.5mi south of Gaiole in Meleto. Round corner towers from the 11th century crown the castle of Meleto, which the Firidolfi family made the strongest fortification of the Chianti Liga during the 13th century. It defied all sieges until 1498.

*Castello di Brolio A further 8km/5mi south-east, the imposing Castello di Brolio looms an a mountain ridge 530m/1739ft high. The history of the mighty bastion is connected closely with the Ricasoli family, who ruled the region from the 13th century. After repeated destruction, the last time in 1529 by the Sienese, it was thoroughly renovated in the 16th century. **Bettino Ricasoli** (1809–90), who developed the classic style of full-bodied Chianti in 1841 through his blending of grapes, had the castle remodelled around 1860 in neo-Gothic style. The interior is not open to the public, but the garden, bastions, walkways and chapel, where members of the Ricasoli family are buried, as well as the baron's magnificent **wine cellar**, can be visited. The **Collezione Ricasoli** in one of the castle towers shows a collection of weapons and informs on the history of the fortress. The osteria (tel. 0577 74 72 77) in the park serves food with the good wines.

Garden: Mid March – mid Oct daily 10am – 7pm; 1st half of March, mid Oct – Dec Sat, Sun 10.30am – 4.30pm

Collezione Ricasoli: daily 10.30am – 12.30pm, 2.30pm – 5.30pm; www. ricasoli.it, admission: €8

** Duomo Santa Maria del Fiore

✦ **J 6/b III**

Location: Piazza del Duomo
Bus: C1, C2, 14, 23
Church: Mon – Wed, Fri 10am – 5pm Thu, 1st Sat in the month 10am – 4.30pm
Sat 10am – 4.45pm, Sun 1.30pm – 4.45pm, www.operaduomo firenze.it
Dome: Mon – Fri 8.30am – 7pm, Sat 8.30am – 5.40pm, admission: €8
Crypt: Sun, Sat 10am – 4.30pm, admission: €3
Campanile: daily 8.30am – 7.30pm, admission: €6

The cathedral of Florence is more than just a city landmark. Together with the Campanile and the Baptistery (▶Battistero San Giovanni) it is one of the greatest ensembles of church architecture in Europe.

For the people of Florence, life is not worth living without the view of their cathedral; when Michelangelo created the dome of St Peter's Basilica, it seems he wanted to move Brunelleschi's masterpiece from his hometown of Florence to Rome. In the late 13th century the citizens of Florence, conscious of the city's growing power, planned to build a new church, larger and more beautiful than all of the other churches in the city, on the site of the church of Santa Reparata.

Famous architects, first **Arnolfo di Cambio** (from 1296), then **Giotto, Andrea Pisano, Francesco Talenti and Giovanni Ghini,** despite interruptions, brought the building work so far that **Filippo Brunelleschi** was able to crown it between 1420 and 1434 with a sensational and daring feat of architecture. In 1436 the cathedral and bishop's seat was dedicated to Mary, the Holy Virgin and Mother of God, and from the lily on the Florentine coat of arms it got its second name, »del Fiore«. The present, richly decorated façade was added only between 1875 and 1887, to a design by Emilio de Fabris. The incomplete first façade was removed in 1587. The cathedral's size is

Incomparable building ensemble (▶MARCO POLO Insight p. 170, 172)

Unusual view of the cathedral and campanile

impressive: its length is 161m/528ft, its width 43m/141ft in the nave and 91m/299ft in the transept, and the height of the façade is 50m/164ft. The dome is 107m/351ft high and 46m/151ft in diameter. The church holds about 25,000 people. It is the **third-largest church in Italy** after St Peter's in Rome and the cathedral in Milan.

Exterior   The cathedral exterior is elaborately decorated with **different kinds of marble**: white from Carrara, green from Prato and red from the Maremma. Marble is the dominating building material: on the Gothic-style façade, the flanks of the aisles and the nave, the buttresses, the smaller half-domes and the massive main dome. The varying colours embody severity and beauty, the two basic principles of Florentine art. When walking around the cathedral, take special note of the four doors. On the right-hand side by the Campanile is the **Porta del Campanile** with a *Beatific Christ* in the gable and a *Madonna with Child* in the lunette, both from the school of Andrea Pisano. Then comes the **Porta dei Canonici**, with a *Virgin and Child* by Lorenzo di Giovanni d'Ambrogio above it. The monuments to the two architects Arnolfo di Cambio and Brunelleschi, as well as a stone with the inscription »Sasso di Dante« at the place from where the poet is supposed to have watched the building work on the cathedral, are not far away.

On the left-hand side: **Porta della Balla** (14th century) with a colourful *Madonna with Child* and two angels; lions support the turned columns at the sides; the **Porta della Mandorla**, the most beautiful of the church doors, was created by Giovanni d' Ambrogio and Nanni di Banco and completed by various artists including Donatello, Niccolò di Pietro Lamberti and Ghirlandaio. The mandorla relief (1414 – 1421) *Assumption of Mary* is the work of Nanni di Banco.

In the double-shelled ****dome** Brunelleschi constructed a daring masterpiece of engineering – wisely and modestly he commended the building of the dome to the protection of the Virgin – that appears both massive and beautiful (►MARCO POLO Insight p. 170). The white ribs that extend into the lantern give clear contours to the red roof of the dome. The streets behind the apse give an impressive view of the marble mass of the cathedral with Brunelleschi's dome. The gallery on this part of the dome's drum was built in the time of Michelangelo, who criticized it severely. There is a marble plaque in the pavement in front of the apse: on 17 January 1600, the gilded globe on the dome was struck by lightning, fell to the ground here and burst. It was replaced by a larger one under the cross. The **lantern** has also often been struck by lightning, but always repaired again. Today it is protected by a modern lightning rod. The dome is open to the public; the entrance is at the Porta dei Canonici. The lantern offers a wonderful view to those who are not put off by the 463 steps.

The cathedral interior is characterized by severity and beauty. Its **Interior** Gothic forms, soaring arches and pillars are impressive and the open space is not spoiled by ostentatious decoration. Later additions were removed during restoration. The austere impression is increased by the earthy colour of the stone. The ground plan is a Latin cross; the short transepts and the apse are bound together by the massive dome. Despite the generally plain impression, there are some valuable adornments.

The three **windows** over the west entrance with *St Stephen* (left), the *Assumption of the Virgin* into heaven (middle) and *St Lawrence* (right) were designed by Lorenzo Ghiberti and made by the glass artist Niccolò di Piero. To the left of the main door is the Gothic **tomb**

Duomo Santa Maria del Fiore

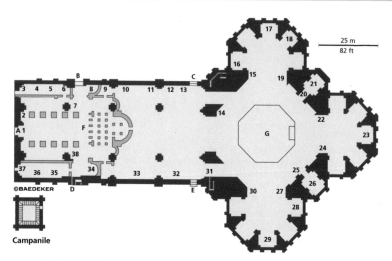

Campanile

A Portale Maggiore with relief »Maria in Gloria« by A. Passaglia

B Porta dei Cornacchini

C Porta della Mandorla by d'Ambrogio and di Banco
Above the door is the Madonna by di Banco carried by angels

D Porta del Campanile with Annunciation group

E Porta dei Canonici, above is »Madonna with Child« by d'Ambrogio

F Crypt of Santa Reparata

G Dome of Brunelleschi with fresco of the Last Judgement by Vasari and valuable glass paintings

1 Window designed by Ghiberti, mosaic by Gaddi

2 Tomb of Antonio d'Orso

3 Window by Ghiberti

4 Bust of Emilio De Fabis by Consani

5 Statue of Joshua (the head was made by Donatello)

6 Bust of Arnolfo di Cambio by Cambi

7 Niche with San Zanobi by G. dei Biondo

8 Bust of the organist Squarcialupi by Benedetto da Maiano (1490)

9 Painted equestrian portrait of Niccoló da Tolentino by dei Castagno (1456)

10 Painted equestrian portrait of Giovanni Acuto (John Hawkwood) by P. Ucello

11 Window from 1395. Under it in the marble niche a statue of King David by Ciuffagni

12 »SS Cosmas and Damian« by Bicci di Lorenzo (15th century)

13 Window from the 14th century, under it »Dante and the Divine Comedy« by di Michelino

14 Statue »San Giacomo Maggiore« by Sansovino

15 Statue »San Tomasso« by De' Rossi

16 Painting »San Giuseppe« by di Credi

17 Marble altar (Buggiano)

18 »Madonna with Saints«, altar covering from the school of Bonaguida

19 Statue »San Andrea« by A. Ferrucci

20 In the lunette over the door the terracotta »Resurrection« by Luca della Robbia
Bronze door also by della Robbia in cooperation with Michelozzo and Maso di Bartolomeo

21 New Sacristy

22 Statue »San Pietro« by Bandinell

23 Above the altar two angels bearing candles (by L. della Robbia)

24 Under the altar the reliquary of San Zanobi by Ghiberti

25 Statue »San Giovanni« by da Rovezzano
In the lunette Ascension of Christ made of enamelled terracotta by L. della Robbia

26 Old Sacristy

27 Statue »San Giacomo Minore« by Bandini

28 Fragment of the fresco »Madonna dei Popolo« from the school of Giotto

29 Altar by Michelozzo

30 Statue »San Filippo« by Bandini

31 Access to the dome

32 Bust of Marsilio Ficino by A. Ferrucci

33 In the marble niche a figure of Isaiah by Ciuffagni

34 »San Bartolomeo« by di Jacopo Franchi

35 Medaillon by da Maiano, depicting Giotto at work

36 Bust of Brunelleschi by A. Cavalcanti

37 Window »San Lorenzo e Angeli« after Ghiberti

38 Steps to crypt of Santa Reparata

of Bishop Antonio d'Orso (†1321), created by Tino da Camaino. It is incomplete, and various parts are in the Museo Nazionale del Bargello.

In the first marble niche on the **left aisle** there is a **statue of Joshua** (early 15th century), by Bernardo Ciuffagni, Donatello and Nanni di Bartoli. Opposite the second pillar there is a painting of a fresco by Niccolò da Tolentino (1456). To its right is a large **equestrian portrait by Paolo Uccello** (1436), which looks like a sculpted monument; it depicts the commander of the Florentine mercenary army, John Hawkwood (in Italian Giovanni Acuto). The next marble niche holds a **statue of King David** (1434), which was made by Bernardo Ciuffagni for the façade. Under the window there is a painting of Dante by Domenico di Michelino (1465), a late rehabilitation of the poet who was exiled from the city.

The short **left transept**, which is called »tribuna« like the right transept, is divided into five chapels. The windows are based on designs by Ghiberti. In the fourth chapel there is a **two-sided altar back panel** from the school of Pacino di Bonaguida, with *Madonna with Saints* and *Annunciation to the Virgin with Saints*. A metal plaque in the floor of the transept has been used for astronomical measurements since 1468: on 21 June at noon a sunbeam strikes it through a conical opening in the dome lantern and shows the exact moment of the summer solstice.

On the underside of the **dome**, which is double-skinned and creates a impressive spatial effect, there is a magnificent fresco of the *Last Judgement* by Giorgio Vasari, which was begun in 1572 and completed by Federico Zuccari in 1579. The round windows in the drum have **stained glass** designed by Ghiberti, Paolo Uccello and Andrea del Castagno.

There are eight **statues of apostles** on the pillars of the drum, of which St James the Elder is by Jacopo Sansovino and St Thomas by Vincenzo de Rossi (1st pillar on the left), St Andrew by Andrea Ferrucci and St Peter by Baccio Bandinelli (2nd pillar on the left). On the other side Benedetto da Rovezzano created the figure of St John and Giovanni Bandini those of St James the Younger (third pillar on the right) and St Philip, and Vincenzo de Rossi that of St Matthew (4th pillar on the right).

The **choir** with the high altar is directly under the dome. The octagonal marble balustrade was designed by Baccio d'Agnolo; the 88 reliefs on it are by Baccio and Giovanni Bandinelli. The high altar by Baccio Bandinelli and the crucifix by Benedetto da Maiano (1495–97) are also remarkable.

It is also worth visiting the sacristies. In the lunette above the door of the **New Sacristy** there is a glazed terracotta by Luca della Robbia depicting the *Resurrection of Christ* (1444). The **bronze door** is also

Brunelleschi's Legacy

The dome of Florence's cathedral is the first structure of this kind with a double-skinned construction and the legacy of Filippo Brunelleschi.

He was the first to use herringbone (a spinapesce) brickwork on an octagonal layout where the bricks were wedged together at increasing angles the higher the construction went.

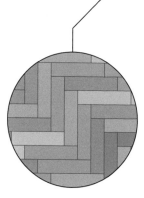

▶ **Facts and figures on the cathedral dome**

Constructor/engineer	Filippo Brunelleschi
Commission date	1420
Closure of the dome	1436
Frescoes (Vasari, Zuccari)	4000 sq m/43,060 sq ft
Diameter	42m/137ft
Height of vault	84m/275ft
Höhe einschl. Laterne	114m/374ft
Weight	37,000 t

▶ **Building materials:**
Marble, stone, natural stone, tuff stone, brick, oak wood, chestnut wood, glass (windows), stone chains, iron chains

▶ **Famous domed structures in comparison**

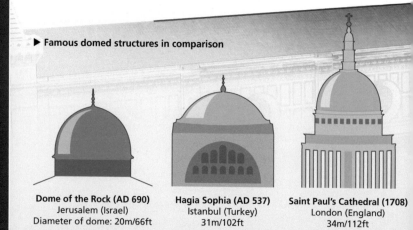

Dome of the Rock (AD 690)
Jerusalem (Israel)
Diameter of dome: 20m/66ft

Hagia Sophia (AD 537)
Istanbul (Turkey)
31m/102ft

Saint Paul's Cathedral (1708)
London (England)
34m/112ft

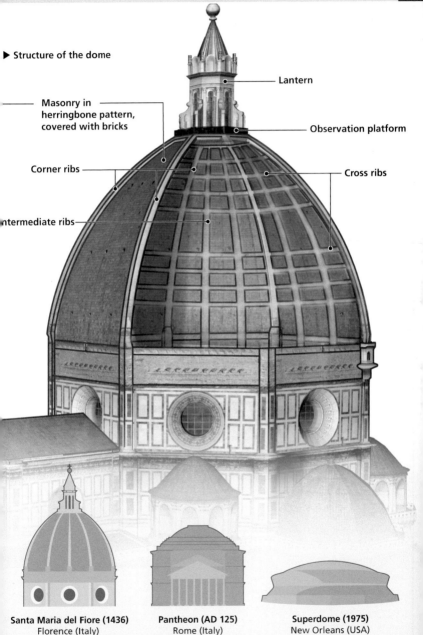

▶ Structure of the dome

Lantern

Masonry in
herringbone pattern,
covered with bricks

Observation platform

Corner ribs

Cross ribs

Intermediate ribs

Santa Maria del Fiore (1436)
Florence (Italy)
42m/137ft

Pantheon (AD 125)
Rome (Italy)
43m/142ft

Superdome (1975)
New Orleans (USA)
207m/683ft

** *Duomo Santa Maria del Fiore*

The cathedral is a gem of Gothic architecture with richly decorated doors and an expansive interior. The double-skinned dome by Brunelleschi, the first one in modern times, makes the building one of a kind.

❶ Façade

The façade is richly decorated with figures: God the Father in the gable; in the fields below famous Florentine artists; under a massive rosette »Mary with Child« and statues of apostles; under them in the four pillar niches bishops of Florence and Pope Eugene IV, who dedicated the church in 1436. The bronze doors have reliefs of Mary and allegorical figures of Christian virtues.

❷ Dome

Almost all of the master builders failed to conceive a dome that would cover the huge crossing. Neither a wooden construction was possible nor would the suggestion to build a giant earth mound and construct the dome around it work. Brunelleschi finally built it between 1420 and 1430 as a double-skinned parabolic construction – a feat of engineering that broke ground for the Baroque period.

❸ Inner entry wall

Above the main entrance there is beautiful mosaic of the Coronation of Mary (around 1300) by Gaddo Gaddi as well as the famous clock with heads of the prophets in the corners by Paolo Uccello (1443) and hands that move counter clockwise.

❹ New Sacristy

Outstanding works of art are the »Resurrection of Christ«, a terracotta by Luca della Robbia, and the bronze door by the same artist. Lorenzo the Magnificent hid in the sacristy in 1478 when conspirators hired by the Pazzi family attacked him and his brother during a mass. He saved himself but his brother was killed.

❺ Campanile

Giotto was the master builder of this 82m/264ft high, architecturally outstanding Campanile; after his death Andrea Pisano continued the work on the original plans. The climb up the 414 steps is rewarded by a wonderful view of the city panorama.

The campanile offers a unique view of the massive cathedral dome

a masterpiece by della Robbia (together with Michelozzo): the Virgin with child, John the Baptist, evangelists and church fathers are depicted in ten panels. The room itself is furnished with a wall fountain and wooden cabinets. In the eastern **apse** in the Cappella di San Zenobio (»chapel of St Zenobius«) there is a beautiful **bronze urn**, a work of Lorenzo Ghiberti, which holds relics of the saint.

In **Sagrestia Vecchia** (Old Sacristy) or dei Canonici (»of the Canons«) above the door on the outside there is a **terracotta relief of the Ascension of Christ** by Luca della Robbia; inside there is a **wall fountain** by Buggiano, *Archangel Michael* by Lorenzo di Credi and two terracotta angels holding candles, also by della Robbia. The **right-hand transept** is also divided into five chapels. In the first chapel beyond the Sagrestia Vecchia there is a **fresco by Giotto** that should not be missed: *Madonna del Popolo*.

In the **right-hand aisle** there is a **bust of Marsilio Ficino** (1521), the great Renaissance philosopher (under the glass window), as well as a **medallion with a portrait of Giotto** by Benedetto da Maiano (1490; opposite the last pillar). Next to it in a wooden niche stands a **statue of the prophet Isaiah** by Nanni di Banco (1408) and a **medallion with a portrait of Brunelleschi**. It is by Andrea Cavalcanti, called Buggiano, who was Brunelleschi's favourite pupil and heir.

Right by the entrance to the cathedral, steps leads down into the **crypt of Santa Reparata** to the **tomb of Brunelleschi**, which was only discovered in 1972, and the remains of the previous church of Santa Reparata, which was built in the 4th–5th century and enlarged in the 8th and 11th centuries. The cathedral was first built around the older church, which was not torn down until 1375. However, the crypt of Santa Reparata was preserved in part; it was excavated later and now serves as a museum.

MARCO ⊕ POLO **TIP**

! *Insight into sculpture* **Insider Tip**

The narrow street Via dello Studio runs along the south side of the cathedral; in the small old building with house number 23 A is the sculpture workshop of the cathedral (Bottega dell' Opera del Duomo). Along with traditional tools as have been used for centuries to work on stone the most modern computer techniques are also applied to restore and conserve the masonry decorations on the cathedral.

Campanile **Giotto's Campanile, the cathedral's 82m/260ft-high bell tower, had a decisive effect on the appearance of Florence. Construction began in 1334. After Giotto died in 1337 **Andrea Pisano** continued the work according to the original plans. His successor **Francesco Talenti** departed from Giotto's plans. The tower was completed in 1387. It is characterized by the harmony of its dimensions, the solidity of the octagonal pillars, the delicate structuring of the intermediate walls and the skilful variation of colours in the marble. The lower

Inside the grand spatial effect of
the double-skinned dome is also
impressive.

Filippo Brunelleschi was the inventor of this unique type of construction, which he worked on for 16 years. His epoch-making scientific achievement was the discovery of central perspective projection.

The Campanile is also an architectural milestone.

part is decorated with **hexagonal reliefs**, for the most part by Andrea Pisano, who made them according to plans by Giotto, and by Luca della Robbia. They depict the world of labour and thought. The lozenge-shaped reliefs above them depict allegories of planets, virtues, free arts and sacraments. The niches above used to contain statues of saints, prophets and sibyls, created before 1341 by Florentine sculptors. Between 1420 and 1435 Donatello added more statues. They are now on display in the ▶Museo dell'Opera del Duomo; some of the niches hold copies. The effort of climbing the 414 steps to the top of the Campanile is rewarded with a **fantastic panoramic view** of the city.

▶p. 152

Battistero
San Giovanni

AROUND THE CATHEDRAL

San Michele (Via de' Servi) stands in the shadow of the cathedral; it was the church of the Vicedomini family – hence the name San Michele Visdomini – and had to make way for the cathedral. It was rebuilt in the 14th century just a short distance from its original location and renovated in the 17th century. Inside there is *Sacra Conservazione* (1518) by Pontormo among the 16th and 17th-century altarpieces.

San Michele
Visdomini

The Convento delle Oblate not far to the east of cathedral was once a convent for nuns who cared for the sick in the nearby Ospedale Santa Maria Nuova. Today the convent is a **cultural centre** with an extensive public library, with reading rooms that are open until late evening and it is a place for concerts, events and exhibits.
On the third level of the cloister there is a café that stays open until late evening and attracts many young people, the **Caffetteria delle Oblate** (Via dell' Oriuolo 26); it offers a fantastic view of the cathedral dome.

Convento
delle Oblate

The Ospedale Santa Maria Nuova opposite the convent, whose oblates cared for the patients, was founded in 1287, which makes it the **oldest hospital in the city**. It was rebuilt in the late 14th century and named Santa Maria Nuova (New Saint Mary's). From 1611 to 1618 it was enlarged considerably by Giulio Parigi, and in 1708 the upper story was added. The clearly structured design of the loggias on Piazza Santa Maria Nuova is remarkable. The **church of Sant' Egidio** was built inside the hospital. The most significant interior art works have been moved to the Uffizi Gallery. Of the remaining decorations the marble tabernacle (1449/1450) to the left of the main altar is worth noting; it is by Bernardo Rossellino.

Ospedale
Santa Maria
Nuova

✴ Fiesole

✦ G 10

Province: Florence/Firenze (FI)
Elevation: 295m/1000ft
Population: 14,000
www.comune.fiesole.fi.it

When the summer gets hot and humid, the people of Florence like to get away to Fiesole, a pretty town where the wealthy have built their stately villas. Fiesole is only 8km/5mi away, nestled between two hills above its larger neighbour. An excursion is worthwhile not only for the magnificent view of Florence, but also for the local attractions.

»Mother of
Florence«
Fiesole was founded by the Etruscans in the 7th century BC and was named Faesulae. It got its nickname »Mother of Florence« because the Etruscans were traders before Florence was even founded. Toward the end of the 1st century BC a Roman city was founded on this site with a capitol, forum, temple, theatre and

Fiesole

INFORMATION
Via Portigiani 3 – 5
tel. 055 5 96 13 11
www.fiesolefor you.it

WHERE TO EAT
❶ *Le Cave di Maiano* €€
Via Cave di Maiano 16
tel. 055 5 91 33
www.trattorialecavedimaianofirenze.it
Open every day
In this classic trattoria on the south-eastern edge of town the Tuscan specialties taste especially good, from pappa al pomodoro to tender, juicy Chianina steak. In the summer guests sit on a quiet garden terrace.

❷ *Vinandro* € – €€
Piazza Mino da Fiesole 33
tel. 055 5 91 21

www.vinandrofiesole.com
Closed Mon
Cosy little wine room with tasty food, on the main piazza.

ACCOMMODATION
❶ *Bencista* €€–€€€
Via Benedetto da Maiano 4
tel. 05 559 1 63
www.bencista.com, 42 rooms
Pleasantly located country inn in the middle of olive groves, located below Fiesole with a spectacular view of Florence.

Insider Tip

❷ *Le Canelli* €–€€
Via Gramsci 52
tel. 05 55 97 83 36
www.lecannelle.com, 4 rooms
Charming inn only 200m/660ft from the central piazza.

baths; it declined after the fall of the Western Roman Empire and was later completely dominated by nearby Florence. Fiesole has been the seat of a bishop since 492. Today some of the villas function as the residences of cultural foundations, which can be visited on guided tours. From Florence (Piazza San Marco) bus no. 7 runs to Fiesole

WHAT TO SEE IN FIESOLE

The centre of this likeable town is the broad Piazza Mino da Fiesole, named after the sculptor Mino da Fiesole (around 1430–84), which occupies the site of the ancient forum. The monument unveiled on the piazza in 1906 is named Incontro di Teano. The two bronze equestrian figures represent King Victor Emanuel II and Garibaldi. In the many street cafés the motto is »see and be seen«.

Piazza Mino da Fiesole

On the north side of the square is the ***Duomo San Romolo**, which was begun in 1024, extended in the 13th and 14th centuries and remodelled in the 19th century. The 42m/138ft-high **bell tower**, completed in 1213 and fortified with battlements, towers over

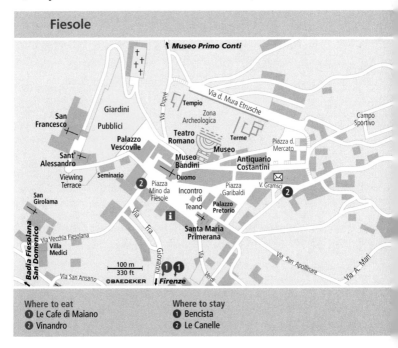

Fiesole

↑ *Museo Primo Conti*

Via d. Mura Etrusche

San Francesco

Giardini Pubblici

Tempio
Zona Archeologica

Campo Sportivo

Palazzo Vescovile

Teatro Romano

Terme

Piazza d. Mercato

Sant' Alessandro

Museo Bandini

Museo

Antiquario Costantini

Viewing Terrace

Seminario

Duomo

San Girolama

❷ Piazza Mino da Fiesole

Incontro di Teano

Piazza Garibaldi

V. Gramsci

❷

Palazzo Pretorio

ℹ

Badia Fiesolana San Domenico

Via Vecchia Fiesolana

Santa Maria Primerana

Villa Medici

Via San Ansano

100 m
330 ft

Via Fra Giovanni

Via Verdi

Via San Apollinare

Via A. Mari

©BAEDEKER

↓ *Firenze*

❶❶

Where to eat
❶ Le Cafe di Maiano
❷ Vinandro

Where to stay
❶ Bencista
❷ Le Canelle

the whole town. The church contains several notable works. The tomb of Bishop Leonardo Salutati in the Cappella Salutati was created by Mino da Fiesole around 1465. The **terracotta statue of its patron saint San Romolo** is by Giovanni della Robbia. Adjacent to the cathedral in the north is the **Museo Bandini**, devoted to works of sacred art collected in the 18th century by Canon Angiolo Maria Bandini, scientist and librarian of the Biblioteca Medicea Laurenziana in Florence. After his death the collection was turned over to the cathedral chapter of Fiesole. It includes altar panels, majolica work and furniture.

The north-western side of Piazza Mino da Fiesole is taken up by the stately buildings of the **Seminario** (1697) as well as the **Palazzo Vescovile** (bishop's palace), which dates from the 11th century. On the south-west side of the piazza are the 14th-century **Palazzo Pretorio** – the entry and loggia were added in the 15th century – and the medieval **Oratorium Santa Maria Primerana** with a 16th-century gate.

Museo Bandini: March/Oct Fri, Sat, Sun 10am – 6pm; April – Sep Fri, Sat, Sun 10am – 7pm; Nov – Feb, Fri, Sat, Sun 10am – 2pm, admission: €5

*Zona Archeologica

Behind the cathedral to the north-east the excavation site, Zona Archeologica, is dominated by a **Roman theatre** that was rediscovered in the early 19th century. It was constructed in the early imperial period (1st century BC) and enlarged under emperors Claudius and Sepimius Severus. The semicircle has a diameter of 34m/37yd and seats about 3000 spectators.

Not far from the theatre are the **Roman baths**, which were also built during the imperial period and expanded under Emperor Hadrian. Even though the arches, which were carried by massive columns, were always visible, the site was not recognized as a bath and excavated until the end of the 19th century. In the eastern part the water was heated by means of furnaces and hypocausts; the three central rooms were for cold baths (frigidarium), lukewarm baths (tepidarium) and warm baths (caldarium); the larger pools in the western part served as swimming pools and reservoirs. In the north-west corner of the excavation site are the remains of a Roman and an **Etruscan temple** (1st and 3rd century BC respectively). Towards the north the site is bordered by a section of the massive **Etruscan city wall** from the 3rd century BC.

Archaeological museum

The small **archaeological museum** to the south and above the Roman theatre exhibits finds from the Etruscan and Roman periods, including remains of a marble frieze for the stage decoration of the Roman theatre, a grave stele (470–460 BC; with funeral ban-

The Roman theatre is an unusual venue for concerts, theatre and ballet

quet, dance and animal battle), a copy of the head of Emperor Claudius (41–54) and a Dionysius statue (Roman copy of a Greek original).

❶ April–Sep daily 10am–7pm; Oct–March daily 10am–6pm; Nov–Feb Mon, Wed–Sun 10am–2pm; admission: €10

Antiquarium Costantini
Not far to the east of the entrance to the Zona Archeologica is the Antiquarium Costantini; the admission ticket for the excavation site is also valid for this collection of Greek, Etruscan and Italian ceramics.

Museo Primo Conti
North-west of the excavation site in Via Dupré 18 is the foundation and a small museum for the Tuscan painter Primo Conti (1900–88). Conti first painted in Futurist and Cubist styles but after the Second World War he developed his own style with wild colours. In addition to works by Conti, documents on Italian Futurism are also exhibited.

❶ Mon–Fri 9am–2pm, admission: €3, www.fondazioneprimoconti.org

*Observation platform
Between the bishop's palace and the seminary building a path leads steeply uphill to two small churches and a tree-shaded observation platform, from which there is an outstanding view of Florence. In the small park a monument honours the soldiers who fell in the First World War; another honours three carabinieri who were killed by the Nazi SS in 1944.

Sant' Alessandro
Above the observation platform is a church that was probably founded in the 3rd century and dedicated to the bishop of Fiesole, Alessandro. It stands above an Etruscan temple that was later replaced by a Roman temple to Bacchus. In the 6th century Theodoric the Great is supposed to have converted the building to a Christian church, which was remodelled several times over the centuries.

San Francesco
Diagonally opposite is the monastery church of San Francesco, established by Augustinian monks in 1330. In 1407 it passed to the Franciscan order, was later remodelled and in 1905 renovated extensively. The main altar is particularly worthy of note: The Annunciation is by Raffaellino del Garbo, the Adoration of the Magi by Cosimo Rosselli.

The **Museo Missionario Francescano** presents the history of Franciscan missionary work. The little **monastery cloister** is idyllic.

In front of the monastery a path leads to the **municipal park**, and through it to the centre of town.

❶ San Francesco: April–Sep Tue–Sun 9.30am–12noon, 3pm–7pm, Sun 11am–12noon closed, Oct–March Tue–Sun 9.30am–12noon, 3pm–5pm

AROUND FIESOLE

A good 1km/0.5mi to the south-west of Fiesole and right on the Florence city limits (with a panoramic view) lies a group of houses called San Domenico di Fiesole. The church of San Domenico here is worth viewing. It was built between 1406 and 1435 for Barnaba degli Agli and extended in the 17th century, and is richly decorated inside. On the altar in the first chapel on the left note the beautiful **triptych** (around 1430) by **Fra Angelico**, who also painted the Crucifixion and an image of the Virgin in the chapter house of the monastery. The son of a wealthy farmer from the Mugello Valley, he entered the Dominican monastery at the age of twenty. His reputation as an outstanding painter spread quickly and when the Dominican monastery of San Marco in Florence was remodelled in 1436, Fra Angelico received the commission to paint the cells with themes from the passion of Christ. Fra Angelico's realism had an unusual effect: it is said that his fellow monks fainted at the sight of his crucifixion scene because of the amount of blood depicted.

*San Domenico di Fiesole

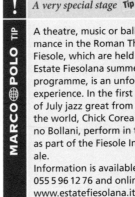

MARCO POLO TIP

Insider Tip

A very special stage

A theatre, music or ballet performance in the Roman Theatre in Fiesole, which are held during the Estate Fiesolana summer culture programme, is an unforgettable experience. In the first two weeks of July jazz great from all over the world, Chick Corea and Stefano Bollani, perform in the theatre as part of the Fiesole Internationale.
Information is available at tel. 055 5 96 12 76 and online at www.estatefiesolana.it.

North-west below San Domenico lies Badia Fiesolana. The cathedral church of Fiesole stood here until 1028, when it was replaced by the duomo. After Camaldolese monks had rebuilt the church with a monastery (»badia« means »abbey«), it was handed over to the Benedictine order. During the Renaissance the monastery and church were remodelled again; Romanesque parts from the 12th century are still preserved on the façade. In 1778 the church and monastery were dissolved. Since 1976 Badia Fiesolana has housed the **international institute Università Europea**.

Badia Fiesolana

Via Vecchia Fiesolana, which runs south-west down from Fiesole, leads to Villa Medici, which the architect Michelozzo built in 1458–61 for **Cosimo the Elder**.
The Pazzi conspirators at first planned to murder the brothers Lorenzo and Giuliano de Medici here in 1478, before they decided that the Duomo Santa Maria del Fiore in Florence would be a better site. The villa can be visited only as part of an organized tour; inquire at tourist information.

Villa Medici

★★ Galleria dell' Accademia

⊹ J 6/b II

Location: Via Ricasoli 60
Bus: C1, 7, 10, 25, 31, 32, 33
❶ Tue – Sun 8.15am – 6.50pm; admission: €6
www.polomuseale.firenze.it, reserve tickets ▶p.119

The Galleria dell' Accademia has special position among the museums of Florence due to its outstanding collection of works by Michelangelo, especially the world-famous statue of David.

One of Florence's best collections

The academy is housed in the expansive rooms of the hospital of San Matteo; it was founded in 1784 by Grand Duke Pietro Leopoldo I as a school of art. As a supplement to the other famous art collections of Florence, the Uffizi Gallery and the Palazzo Pitti, it holds important works of the Florentine school from the 13th to the 16th century. The gallery acquired its Michelangelo collection in the late 19th and in the first decades of the 20th century.

Salone del Colosso

The Salone del Colosso has Florentine art from the early 16th century, including works by **Perugino and Filippino Lippi**. The chest with a painted wedding procession from around 1450 is a showpiece. There is also an original plaster cast of the *Rape of the Sabine Woman* by Giambologna. The original is in the Loggia dei Lanzi on the Piazza della Signoria.

Galleria del David

Nowhere else can one get as close to **the sculptor Michelangelo**'s creative process as in the Accademia. In the Galleria del David are the four incomplete ★**Slaves** which Michelangelo began for the tomb of Pope Julius II in Rome. He probably created them around 1519. After the artist's death his nephew Leonardo gave them to the Grand Duke Cosimo I, who put them in the Giardino di Boboli. The figures were given to the academy in 1909: they are named *Waking Slave*, *Bearded Slave*, *Youth* and *Atlas*. The statues are at different stages of completion. Michelangelo worked on the front and removed layer after layer. The slaves are trying to free themselves from the stone, according to the Platonic idea that the body is the prison of the soul. Two of the prisoners are trying to remove chains. Thus they are aspiring to freedom, but are not successful.

The figure of the apostle **Matthew**, which Michelangelo worked on in 1505 and 1506, is also incomplete. It was intended for the cathedral of Florence, as were eleven other figures which were never made. The

Galleria dell' Accademia

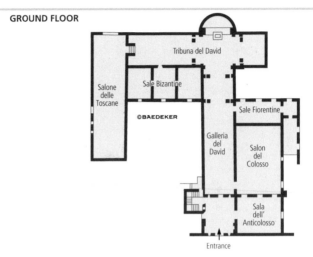

GROUND FLOOR

Tribuna del David

Salone delle Toscane

Sale Bizantine

©BAEDEKER

Sale Fiorentine

Galleria del David

Salon del Colosso

Sala dell' Anticolosso

Entrance

block chosen for the figure obviously had less depth than the ones for the slaves: the statue was meant to be viewed from the front. The origins of the **Pietà of Palestrina** on display here have been contested recently. Some imbalance in the figure makes it unlikely that it was done by Michelangelo; it was probably made by one of his successors.

The world-famous ****David has pride of place among all Michelangelo's sculptures** (▶MARCO POLO Insight p.184). It was removed from its original location on the Piazza della Signoria in 1873 already because of the effects of weather, replaced with a copy and displayed in the Accademia in 1887. In 1991 a visitor destroyed one of its toes, which was then reconstructed. In 2004 the statue, which weighs five and a half tons and is almost 5m/16ft tall, was given a thorough cleaning that caused controversy among specialists. Damp paper was stuck onto the statue to absorb the dirt.

On David's right is a bronze portrait of Michelangelo by Daniele da Volterra. Just like the walls of the Galleria, those of the Tribuna del David used to be covered with valuable 16th-century tapestries. Because they were in such poor condition they were removed when the museum was given a thorough renovation in the 1980s and replaced with **16th-century Florentine paintings** including works by Alessandro Allori, Stefano Pieri and Santi di Tito.

Tribuna del David

Hero of Faith and Nude Model

As the epitome of an ideal of masculinity, Michelangelo's over-life-sized David has fascinated countless visitors to the city for half a millennium. The original has been in the Galleria dell'Accademia since 1877. There are copies in front of the Palazzo Vecchio and on Piazzale Michelangelo.

While Florence's trademark has now been reduced to a symbol of Eros, it originally gained fame as a righteous hero of the faith and a symbol of the Florentine republic. In the 15th century Florence had its work cut out defending its independence against the power-hungry dukes of Milan and Naples. It was only when the greatest enemy of the republic, the duke of Milan, died suddenly in 1402 at the city gates that the Florentines could relax. They took courage by identifying themselves with a biblical hero who had shown strength from a position of weakness: David, who killed the giant Goliath and later became king.

In this way the just fight was given a religious and political purpose. For the 26-year-old **Michelangelo** the commission from the cathedral office of works was not simple, for in 1464 Agostino di Duccio, a pupil of Donatello, had already acquired the 5.5m/16.5ft-high block of marble for a statue for one of the cathedral's buttresses. He did not get far with it and had only completed the opening between the legs. The fact that the block was not very deep forced Michelangelo to make a statue that was primarily to be viewed from the front. The monumental statue that he made between 1501 and 1504 was thus conceived not as a freestanding figure but as a niche figure to be seen at a great height. For this reason, Michelangelo's solution is highly unusual.

First Modern Nude

He created the first over-life-sized nude figure of modern times with strong influence from antiquity. The mark of the marble David is the contrapposto (opposite) pose, whereby the free leg, unlike the leg that bears the weight, is angled, which leads to asymmetry and a slight shifting of the body's axis. This is balanced out by one shoulder that is lowered and pushed back while the other is raised and pushed forward; the result is harmony between rest and movement, relaxation and tension. The tense muscles are clearly defined and point to the sculptor's knowledge of human anatomy. David's facial features, however, show little individuality, even though the eyes under the furrowed brow appear to pierce the viewer. Compared to Donatello and Verrocchio, who depicted David after the deed in a victorious pose, Michelangelo showed David in the moment of concentration between rest and motion, immediately before releasing the deadly stone in his slingshot against the giant Goliath. In the pose and movement of the body Michelan-

Copy of the sculpture of David on the Piazza della Signoria

gelo's David reflects his own state of mind in this superhuman feat, in which he suppresses his fear and entrusts himself to God in doing the work.

Model of Knightly Virtue

From the Middle Ages, David's victory against Goliath was seen as an Old Testament precursor of Christ's victory over Satan. But in general David, as a young hero, was also seen as a model of knightly virtue. His battle for justice and freedom was useful once more at the beginning of the 16th century as **Florence's self-portrayal** in its battle for civic autonomy against ducal rule. After the exile of the Medici in 1494, the republic returned in 1502 with a new constitution under Pie-

ro Soderini as gonfaloniere della giustizia for life. He got his support mainly from the middle and lower classes, which antagonized the patrician families and in the end led to the downfall of his republic in 1512. During his rule it was decided that the figure of David, which was originally intended for the outer façade of the cathedral, would be put in front of the Palazzo Vecchio. It is an irony of history that the statue's left arm was broken in 1527 during the unrest that led to the next exile of the Medici. The young artist Giorgio Vasari collected the pieces with his friends, and in 1543 the figure was restored without much permanent damage. Despite a few scars David, a magnificent work of sculpture, still embodies an admirable, powerful and sensual masculinity.

Much admired and often copied: Michelangelo's David

Sale Bizantine

The Sale Bizantine (Byzantine Rooms), the Sala di Giotto e della sua scuola, Sala del Duecento e del primo Trecento and the Sala degli Orcagna display the oldest paintings of the Accademia collection; they date from the late 13th and the 14th century. The first room has works from artists like Taddeo Gaddi, one of the most important Gothic painters of the 14th cent. One of the greatest works in the museum, the *Tree of Life* by Pacino di Bonaguida (around 1310) is in the second room. It depicts the crucifixion of Christ on a tree with twelve branches, including Genesis and the creation of man up to the expulsion from the Garden of Eden. The upper part shows the hosts of heaven, saints, Christ and the Virgin Mary.

Salone dell' Ottocento

The Salone dell' Ottocento has **works by members of the Accademia delle Belle Arti** of the 19th century as well as plaster casts by the sculptors Lorenzo Bartolini and Luigi Pampaloni. The marble sculptures were copied from these models.

The ground floor also houses the Dipartimento degli Strumenti Musicali, the valuable collection of stringed instruments of the grand dukes of Tuscany including violins by Stradivari.

Instrument collection

The collection of **Florentine art** continues on the upper floor. The large main room Pittura a Firenze 1370 – 1420 II exhibits a series of wonderful alater panels from Florentine churches including ones by Niccolò di Pietro Gerini, Lorenzo di Niccolò, Giovanni del Biondo, Spinello Aretino and Lorenzo Monaco.

Upper floor

In the small adjacent room Pittura a Firenze 1370 – 1420 I the panel picture *Cristo morto sorretto dalla Vergine e da San Giovanni Evangelista* stands out and a Pietà, which Giovanni da Milano painted for the Florentine convent San Girolamo alla Costa in 1365. In the Sala del Gotico Internazionale works by Lorenzo Monaco (1370 – 1425) as the outstanding representative of the forms and colours of Gothic art are displayed.

AROUND THE GALLERIA DELL' ACCADEMIA

Behind the Accademia is the Opificio e Museo delle Pietre Dure, (Workshop and Museum for Stone Inlay Work, Via degli Alfani 78). The art form known as **Florentine mosaic**, intricate inlay work of precious stones in stone, has a long and unique tradition. This Florentine speciality is still practised today, mainly in restorations. The workshop has an interesting **museum** with examples of this unusual craft. Tools and valuable stone as well as gemstones are on display.

Opificio e Museo delle Pietre Dure

❶ Mon – Sat 8.15am – 2pm, www.opificiodellepietredure.it, admission: €4

✶✶ Galleria degli Uffizi

──────────────── ✦ H/J 7/b IV

Location: Piazzale degli Uffizi
Bus: C1, C2, 23
❶ Tue – Sun 8.15am – 6.50pm, www.uffizi.firenze.it, admission: €6.50
Reserving tickets: tel. 055 29 48 83, www.firenzemusei.it, www.b-ticket.com;
Welcome desk for information: Piazzale degli Uffizi, entrance no. 2, Tue – Sat 10am – 5pm, tel. 055 28 56 10

The Uffizi Gallery houses one of the most important and famous collections of paintings in the world. It includes not only Florentine and Italian masterpieces, but also a large number of paintings from other countries and valuable ancient sculptures. The Uffizi should be part of every visit to Florence.

Palazzo degli Uffizi   Around 1540 Cosimo I de'Medici, Duke of Florence, from 1569 Grand Duke (Granduca) of Tuscany, moved out of his family palace, the Palazzo Medici-Riccardi, into the Palazzo Vecchio, which then became the Palazzo Ducale (»ducal palace«). The Florentine magistracies and courts slowly had to make way for the ducal family's requirements. A separate building was planned for the judicial Uffizi, the offices, which was to be attached to the Palazzo Ducale. Groundbreaking took place in 1560. In 1565 a corridor was quickly built – in less than half a year – that connected the Palazzo Vecchio via the Palazzo degli Uffizi and the Ponte Vecchio with the Palazzo Pitti. The work was overseen by Vasari, Buontalenti and Parigi and completed in 1580.

The Palazzo degli Uffizi incorporated the old customs house, the Zecca, where the famous Florentine coins, »florins«, were minted, and the Romanesque church San Piero Scheraggio. At the same time artists' studios and workshops as well as rooms for experiments in the natural sciences and alchemy were constructed. Room was even found for a theatre in 1585–86, where **the first operas in musical history** were performed. Today the palace is the seat of the Galleria degli Uffizi and the state archives. In 1993 a bomb exploded behind the Uffizi, killing five people and damaging or destroying more than 200 paintings and sculptures.

The museum complex has been undergoing comprehensive renovations for years, called Nuovi Uffizi. Along with new entry and stair areas the exhibition areas are being reorganized and expanded so that more of the treasures in the large depots may be made accessible to the public. In 2012 La Tribuna was reopened, the octagonal room with the Medici's favourite works. Room 35 has been showing a presentation of Michelangelo's works since 2013. New exhibition areas were opened in the second floor, eight blue rooms for foreign artists and nine red rooms for masterpieces of Florentine Mannerism.

Form   The Palazzo degli Uffizi is U-shaped and encloses the elongated Piazzale degli Uffizi, stretching from Palazzo Vecchio down to the Arno and back to Loggia dei Lanzi. Its architecture is characterized by its various functions: on the ground floor colonnades with alternating columns and pillars make room for market stalls and have been always enlivened by the comings and goings of Florentine citizens and visitors. The upper floors accommodate offices and exhibition rooms. The regular façades hide an irregular interior that came into being when buildings from the 14th and 16th–17th centuries were joined. Incidentally, this is the first building in Europe for which cement and iron bracings were used.

Collections (►MARCO POLO Insight p. 192)   The collections were originally the Medici dukes' private property. The last Medici heiress, Elector Princess Anna Maria Luisa (d. 1743),

The U-shaped palazzo encloses the Piazzalle degli Uffizi

left them to the city of Florence. The Uffizi Gallery is admired not just for its paintings, but also because of the charming interiors. The corridors are decorated with grotesque paintings, ancient sculptures and valuable tapestries. The numerous ancient statues of Roman and Greek origin, which the Medici collected, showed the strong interest of the Renaissance period in the ideals of antiquity.

The largest treasure is most certainly the **unique collection of Florentine Renaissance painting**, one of the great achievements of European art that this city brought forth. Since Florentine painting between about 1300 and 1500 set the course for all Western painting, a representative selection with interpretation follows here. The explanations present the pictures chronologically based on the time when they were painted, so that a visitor beginning in room 2 on the second floor of the Uffizi Gallery can easily follow the orientation line that runs through the rooms. From the so-called Tribuna (room 18), an octagonal room, the chronological order is changed to one that follows individual schools, regions and countries – for example German, Dutch, north Italian etc. – from about 1500 to 1700. This continues in the newly opened second floor with the Sale Blu with Spanish, French, Dutch painting of the 17th and 18th cent., as well as the Sale Rosse of the 16th cent. with masterpieces of Florentine Mannerism, but also by Raphael and Caravaggio.

SECOND FLOOR

Room 2
Tuscan painting around 1300

Room 2 of the gallery brings together three large-scale Madonnas from around 1300, which show the beginnings of Tuscan painting and one of its first highlights: *Santa Trinita Madonna* by **Cimabue** (around 1275) is still the traditional Byzantine-style Madonna. She looks like a statue, far from reality and surrounded by symmetrically arranged angels. In a room like a crypt below her are four prophets. The Madonna's gesture towards the child Jesus is just as traditional as his sign of blessing. There are no signs of tender feelings between mother and child. Cimabue's Jesus is dressed like an ancient Roman military commander, and the Madonna is covered with a cloak that, in typical Byzantine style, falls in numerous thin folds.

Giotto's depiction is the most human. His *Madonna Enthroned* (around 1310) shows a throne that is almost tangible, figures with physical characteristics that look at each other and at the viewer. Moreover, all of the figures are standing on the ground, i.e. in real space. Giotto's Madonna is the first one not to be portrayed as a disembodied queen of heaven, but as a human woman who can be physically perceived. The figures around her are also lifelike and have different facial expressions. Giotto makes the whole scene livelier by using new colours, not just the simple earth colours used by the Byzantine-style painters but also more brilliant and differentiated colours. However, the simple gold background is traditional and intended to emphasize the solemnity of the scene. Giotto's epoch-making feat is the composition of the picture. He was the first painter to compose a picture in a set, **real space**, which also allowed for the viewer's perspective. The white robes of the angels and the Madonna form the corners in colour and geometry of a sophisticated triangular composition, which is extended upwards by the triangular gable over the throne. Giotto's triangular compo-

Galleria degli Uffizi

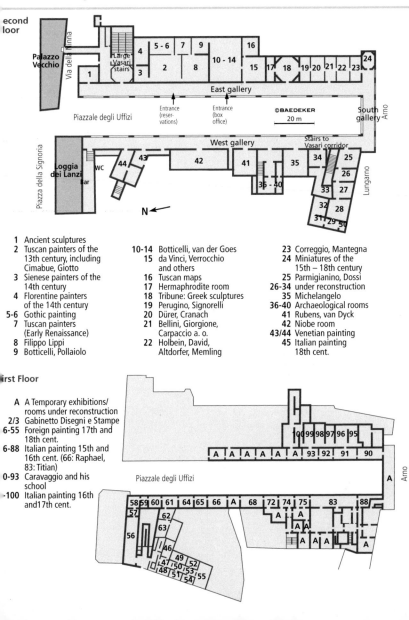

Second floor

1 Ancient sculptures
2 Tuscan painters of the 13th century, including Cimabue, Giotto
3 Sienese painters of the 14th century
4 Florentine painters of the 14th century
5-6 Gothic painting
7 Tuscan painters (Early Renaissance)
8 Filippo Lippi
9 Botticelli, Pollaiolo

10-14 Botticelli, van der Goes
15 da Vinci, Verrocchio and others
16 Tuscan maps
17 Hermaphrodite room
18 Tribune: Greek sculptures
19 Perugino, Signorelli
20 Dürer, Cranach
21 Bellini, Giorgione, Carpaccio a. o.
22 Holbein, David, Altdorfer, Memling

23 Correggio, Mantegna
24 Miniatures of the 15th – 18th century
25 Parmigianino, Dossi
26-34 under reconstruction
35 Michelangelo
36-40 Archaeological rooms
41 Rubens, van Dyck
42 Niobe room
43/44 Venetian painting
45 Italian painting 18th cent.

First Floor

A A Temporary exhibitions/ rooms under reconstruction
2/3 Gabinetto Disegni e Stampe
6-55 Foreign painting 17th and 18th cent.
6-88 Italian painting 15th and 16th cent. (66: Raphael, 83: Titian)
90-93 Caravaggio and his school
96-100 Italian painting 16th and 17th cent.

Art Instead of Archives

Where the clerks of the Tuscan dukes once started and maintained files, one of the most important collections of paintings in the world is now at home. While other large art galleries get significantly more visitors no where else can such wonderful Florentine works of Renaissance painting be seen.

Uffizi Gallery, Florence
1560 – 1580

Visitors 2013: 👫 1.9 mil.

▶ **Famous works in the Uffizi Gallery**

SANDRO BOTTICELLI				
LEONARDO DA VINCI				
MICHELANGELO				
GIOTTO	**Maesta** around 1310			
TITIAN				
RAPHAEL			**Madonna of the Goldfinch** 1505/1506	
LUCAS CRANACH THE ELDER				
ALBRECHT DÜRER				
ARTEMISIA GENTILESCHI				
1250	1300	1350	1400	1450

Louvre, Paris
1793

Visitors 2013:  9.3 mil.

National Gallery, London
1824

Visitors 2013: 6 mil.

Eremitage, St. Petersburg
1764

Visitors 2013: 2.9 mil

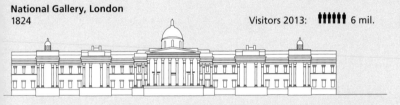

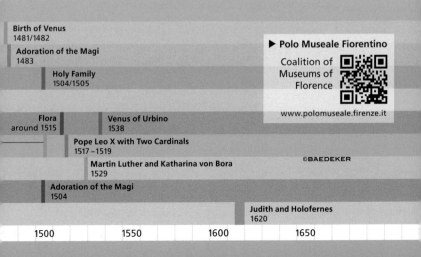

Birth of Venus
1481/1482

Adoration of the Magi
1483

Holy Family
1504/1505

Flora
around 1515

Venus of Urbino
1538

Pope Leo X with Two Cardinals
1517–1519

Martin Luther and Katharina von Bora
1529

Adoration of the Magi
1504

Judith and Holofernes
1620

▶ **Polo Museale Fiorentino**

Coalition of
Museums of
Florence

www.polomuseale.firenze.it

©BAEDEKER

1500   1550   1600   1650

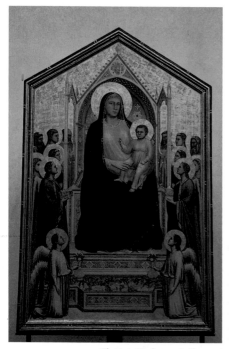

Giotto's Madonna Enthroned

sition was used for centuries as a model for other pictures. Compared to the Byzantine perception of art, Giotto's more personal, individual and above all more realistic way of viewing and painting led to a true Renaissance in painting.

In the following years the Gothic style dominated painting, and early 15th-century works by **Lorenzo Monaco**, *The Adoration of the Magi* (1420) and *The Coronation of the Virgin* (1413), still show the forms and colours typical of international Gothic. **Gentile da Fabriano's** *Adoration of the Magi* (1423) also shows the artist's Gothic ideal of beauty. This picture was created during the transition from Gothic to Renaissance art. Its extravagant use of detail shows the expensive tastes of the patron who commissioned it, the wealthy Palla Strozzi. But still there is no sign of a radical break with tradition: instead of revealing consciousness of Renaissance influences through interest in the characteristic and individual, Gentile indulges in fairytale-like fantasies.

Room 7: Early Renaissance

His contemporary **Masaccio**, however, (room 7) took a different course. *The Madonna with Child, St Anne and Angels* (around 1420), which Masaccio made together with Masolino, is an early work in which he introduced perspective, the depiction of a three-dimensional space on a flat surface, into painting. Together with the architect Brunelleschi and the sculptor Donatello, he paved the way for the Renaissance. Based on exact observation of nature this work aimed to lead to a new experience of reality. Masaccio's altar panel can be recognized as the work of a true artistic pioneer in its energetic drawing and relief-like modelling of the sovereign, stern and realistic natural beauty of the faces and figures.

A picture by one of Masaccio's contemporaries hangs nearby: the *Coronation of the Virgin* (around 1430–35) by **Fra Angelico**, who is Masaccio's opposite in his deeply religious, mystic and traditional approach to art. Fra Angelico, a Dominican monk, is unjustly characterized as conservative or old-fashioned. Even though the gold background dominates his work and the figures appear to be disembodied, their shape determined by their clothing, Fra Angelico used a rich palette of colours and with the help of circular and semicircular arrangements of figures he achieved an impressive composition that unites the surface and space of the picture. Fra Angelico's painting certainly appears to be traditional when compared with that of an impassioned perspectivist like **Paolo Uccello**. *The Battle of San Romano* was painted around 1456 by Uccello as a memorial to a battle that took place in 1432, when the Florentines defeated the united forces of Siena and Milan. The fact that the picture was hung high up on the wall-panelling

Masaccio: Madonna with Child, St Anne and Angels

of a room in the Medici palace explains the exaggerated perspective from below. Uccello did not paint a bloody battle scene, but rather a tournament in an arena in which the characters look almost like marionettes. The extreme foreshortening of the broken lances, for instance, or the fallen riders and horses, and the forms of the fighters that have been reduced to pure volume reflect Uccello's strong interest in problems of perspective. All in all his style is rather anti-natural, abstract and almost modern in view of the red and blue horses.

The **portrait** was another focal point of early Renaissance painting. It developed from studying ancient medallions and was especially popular in the form of profile portraits.

The **Portraits of the Duke and Duchess of Urbino* by **Piero della Francesca**, painted around 1465, are a good example of this. The heads of Federico da Montefeltro and his wife Battista Sforza are also shown in profile. The duke faces left because he lost his right eye in a tournament as a young man. Apart from this concession Piero left

Room 8: Piero della Francesca, Filippo Lippi

out none of the smallest irregularities in the faces of his subjects in any of his paintings. He conscientiously painted the duke's hawk nose, every wrinkle, the thin lips, hard look and the heavy body of the ruler, whom he respected greatly. Nor did the artist miss the worn, pale face of the duchess. Along with the realistic and detailed characterization of the ducal couple, the background is also interesting as a rare example of early Renaissance landscape painting. It is intended to exalt the ruling couple. It documents the duke's claim to the duchy of Urbino with its mountain and port cities.

The *Madonna with Child and Two Angels* (around 1465) by Filippo Lippi is another example of Florentine portrait painting. Lippi's late work was for the most part devoted to secular themes, and this portrait depicts a maidenly young woman in noble attire. The half profile shows a high, smooth forehead that was shaved, as was the fashion at that time. A veil is skilfully woven into the flaxen hair. The Madonna is sitting on a richly decorated chair at an open window, and two angels smiling with pleasure are lifting the child Jesus up to her. The scenes exudes happiness and charm, even if the child looks a bit serious. Since the background is a rocky landscape, it can be assumed because of the earnest expression on his face that the hill is Golgotha and points ahead to Jesus' death on the cross. However, the intimate relationship between mother and child, the gentle touch and the meeting of the eyes are more important to the painter. In the late 15th century religious subjects became more and more worldly and served to portray human relationships. The woman's role as mother, the raising of children and family happiness are important themes that were topics of conversation for contemporaries and which artists depicted in paintings.

Lippi's other works, the predella panels (around 1437), the *Enthroned Madonna with Saints* (around 1445), the *Coronation of the Virgin and the Adoration in the Forest with St Romuald and the Young John the Baptist*, connect the three-dimensional and monumental approach to figures of Masaccio with architecture and landscape that are bathed in light, and elegant, flowing lines.

Room 9:
Pollaiolo,
Botticelli's
early works

The pictures and small statues of the brothers **Antonio and Piero Pollaiolo** stand out for their depictions of powerful bodies full of movement, which were the results of detailed anatomical studies. This is especially clear in the small **Hercules panels** (*Wrestling with Antaeus* and *Death of the Hydra*).

Sandro Botticelli's early work is of particular interest; his paintings of the Madonna are still reminiscent of his teacher Filippo Lippi. *Courage* (1470) is one of his first works.

Rooms 10–14:
Botticelli

Botticelli painted the *Adoration of the Magi* (▶ill. p. 30) altarpiece around 1475 at the age of thirty, during the rule of Lorenzo the Magnificent, who was four years younger. This was the golden age of Florence. Art historians debate whether Botticelli's painting of the Three Magi was commissioned by the Medici themselves or by their friend Giovanni del Lama for the Dominican church of Santa Maria Novella in Florence. Whatever is the case, the upper class of Florence had themselves painted as part of the assembly of the worshippers by Botticelli. The painter used a classical triangular composition with the holy family at the top, the kings, in this case Medici family members, below them but still central and in socio-political order of rank – father Cosimo the Elder, ruler of Florence with his sons Giovanni and Piero de Medici – in the middle of the picture. At the edge of the triangle are the younger Medici, Cosimo's grandson, the pensive Lorenzo the Magnificent with dark hair and clothing and his proud, high-spirited brother Giuliano, dressed in bright colours. They are framed by groups of humanists, aristocratic and middle-class friends and artists with a backdrop of antique-style architecture and landscape. The actual biblical theme of the picture fades into the background and becomes a mere excuse for an ostentatious representation of the Medici and their followers. The Florentine patriciate was also interested in ancient literature and philosophy. The following works by Sandro Botticelli should be interpreted with this in mind: *Birth of Venus* (Nascita di Venere) and *Spring* (Primavera). Both works were commissioned by Lorenzo di Pierfrancesco de Medici, a cousin of Lorenzo the Magnificent.

The **Birth of Venus** was painted in 1482–83. Here Botticelli connects ancient and Christian thought in Renaissance style, as the rebirth of the spirit from ancient mythology and Christian theology. He painted a female nude modelled on an ancient statue of Venus, the goddess of love, and indirectly incorporated a Christian motif of baptism, as in the baptism of Christ in the Jordan. According to his contemporary, the philosopher Marsilio Ficino, an important teacher at the Platonic Academy that Cosimo de' Medici founded in Florence, Venus is the allegory of heavenly love, embodied in a beautiful woman. Looking at earthly beauty and perfection creates a longing for the origins of beauty, which means in the end going back to God, the creator.

In Botticelli's **Spring** (*Primavera*, 1485–87) lightly-clad virgins dance gracefully on a flowery meadow, the image of the three graces in antiquity. The other figures are also mythological. Venus appears in the centre of the picture with her arrow-shooting son Cupid. Mer-

?

MARCO ◉ POLO INSIGHT

Don't miss

- Madonna panels by Cimabue and Giotto (Room 2)
- Portraits of the Duke and Duchess of Urbino (Room 8)
- Birth of Venus by Botticelli (Room 35)
- Venus of Urbino by Titian (Room 61)
- Pope Leo X with Two Cardinals by Raphael (Room 66)

cury is at the extreme edge of the picture. On the right, in the style of medieval simultaneous pictures, is the transformation of the nymph Chloris – after being raped by Zephyr, the god of the wind – into the flowery goddess Flora. At first glance the painting seems to depict a festival of spring, as the arbitrary title that Vasari gave the picture much later indicates, but the meaning is far more complex. Its im-

Botticelli's *Birth of Venus* attracts all visitors

mediate interpretation comes from ancient literary sources. The three graces are known from ancient sources as the daughters of Atlas or the Hesperides. Another level of interpretation comes from contemporary philosophical thought on ideal love and beauty. The feelings and compulsions of man awaken in spring. Mercury uses his staff to keep the dark clouds of melancholy away so that they can develop unhindered. The group of Zephyr, Chloris and Flora depicts the conflict between sensuality, chastity and beauty. The elegantly dressed figure of Venus posing in the centre with an inviting gesture is reminiscent of a figure of the Virgin Mary. She symbolizes spiritualized, moral, divine love, an example of perfect humanity.

When Botticelli died in 1510, a new generation of artists was already at work. The famous triad at the beginning of the 16th century was Leonardo, Michelangelo and Raphael.

Room 15: Verrocchio, Leonardo da Vinci

Leonardo da Vinci was a pupil of Andrea del Verrocchio. Together with his teacher he painted *Christ's Baptism in the Jordan* (around 1470). Verrocchio started his career as a goldsmith but worked as a sculptor most of his life. The figures of the Saviour and John the Baptist show powerful, even somewhat stern modelling from his work as a sculptor. The kneeling angel facing the front with his hands crossed on his chest might appear to be graceful, but his angular face and the short, curly hair give him an ordinary look. The angel by Leonardo, kneeling sideways, is more winsome with his blond curls falling in waves down his back, his expressive glance and the rich folds of his robe.

Leonardo da Vinci lived at a time of scientific exploration of the world and of man, when the Christian story of salvation was becoming less and less suitable as the sole model to explain the complex relationships of the universe. Leonardo grasped the mood of crisis and depicted it sensitively in the *Adoration of the Magi* of 1481. The Madonna with child in the middle of the unfinished picture is a calming factor. She is surrounded by a restless crowd of old and young people, who confront the birth of the Son of God in part with amazement and in part with doubt and horror.

While the Christmas story was depicted earlier in a fairy tale and folksy manner, Leonardo's version shows a new dimension to the salvation of the world. In a world chaotic and out of control – the ruins, the warriors and wild groups of horsemen in the background make this clear – the worshippers place all their hope in a small child who is supposed to give power and strength. The figures crowd out of the darkness and their faces are almost dazzled by the light of the Saviour. It is left open whether or not their longing for salvation is satisfied.

Room 16: **Tuscan maps** **(currently** **closed)**	The first part of the Uffizi tour, which was dedicated to Florentine and Tuscan painters from about 1300 to 1500, ends in room 16, where **Tuscan maps** from the 16th century are on display. The rooms following the Tribuna show schools of middle and northern Italian as well as German and Flemish Renaissance painting. The next period covers Italian High Renaissance painting with works by Raphael and Michelangelo and begins in room 25.

Room 18:
Tribuna

The architect Bernardo Buontalenti built this octagonal domed room in 1586 for the Grand Duke Francesco I as the treasure chamber of the Medici collection. The walls are covered with red silk; about 6,000 shimmering shells cover the octagonal dome and colourful marble inlay work decorates the floor. The ancient statues suit Renaissance ideals, like the famous *Medici Venus*, probably a late Hellenistic marble statue influenced by the *Aphrodite of Cnidos* by Praxiteles, **Apollino** (after Praxiteles), **Arrotino** (Pergamon school of the 3rd or 2nd century BC), **Wrestlers** (Pergamon school) and **Dancing Faun** (copy from the 3rd century BC).

❶ The room may only be viewed from the door, not entered.

Room 20:
Cranach,
Dürer

Masterpieces by Lucas Cranach are displayed here: portraits of Martin Luther and his wife Katherine von Bora, a self-portrait and an impressive portrait of Melanchthon as well as **Adam and Eve**. Albrecht Dürer's **Madonna with Child** (1526), the **Portrait of his Father** (1490) and the **Adoration of the Magi** (1504), painted just before his second trip to Italy, are also present.

Room 23:
Mantegna

In this room the works of the north Italian master Andrea Mantegna are especially worth noting: a **triptych** (1466) of the Ascension, Adoration of the Magi and Circumcision as well as the **Madonna of the Caves** (1489). His realistic depiction of people and his humanist and religious attitude were a strong influence on Albrecht Dürer.

Rooms 26-34

This group of rooms is being reorganized, but it is still dedicated to some of the great northern Italian painters of the second half of the 15th and 16th cent., especially Lorenzo Lotto, Titian, Tintoretto and Veronese. A temporary selection is currently being shown in **rooms 43 and 44**.

The works of the Venetian painter **Titian** include *Venus of Urbino* (1538), *Ludovico Beccadelli* (1552), *Venus and Cupid* (1560), *Eleonora Gonzaga della Rovere, Francesco Maria, Duke of Urbino* and *La Flora*, one of his most beautiful paintings of a woman. The *Venus of Urbino*, painted for the Duke of Urbino, stands out because of its colour composition. The red tones tie together the separate parts of the picture in their spatial perspective and diagonal positions. **Tintoret-**

The Tribuna is a magnifi:cent setting for antique sculptures

to is represented by the following major works: *Leda with the Swan, Venetian Admiral, Adam and Eve* and various portraits.

One of the most important works in the Uffizi is **Michelangelo's **Holy Family** (1504–05), a tondo that was painted for the wedding of Agnolo Doni and Maddalena Strozzi, has absolutely no religious pathos. The family looks as if it were chiselled from one block of stone and unmistakably shows Michelangelo's interest in sculpture as well as in painting. Its composition and theme are extremely complex. In the foreground a group of figures is built up with a view from below; it is framed in the background by a group of nude youths in a large basin. A small boy looks over the edge in front of them. Recently the background has been interpreted as the act of baptism and the little boy as John the Baptist. The painting may also be a preliminary study for the many nude figures in the frescoes in the Sistine Chapel that Michelangelo painted some years later. The unnaturally light, iridescent colours also foreshadow the Sistine Chapel. The cen-

Room 35: Michelangelo

tre of the red room is dominated by a reclining, Greek marble statue, *Arianna addormentata* (2nd cent AD), after Vasari, who was himself a painter, brilliant architect and great expert on art, a ground-breaking model for artists of his time.

Niobe Room (no. 42)
A room decorated in the classical style is the worthy setting for the **Niobe Group**, a Roman copy of Greek originals of the 5th and 4th century BC, which was found in Rome in 1583. Among the 18th cent. paintings, the famous vedute by **Canaletto** stand out.

Room 45: Italian painting
Here are mainly Venetian painting with works by Guardi, Rosalba Carriera, Longhi and Tiepolo – the 18th cent. was the last time when art flowered in Venice.

Corridoio Vasariano
Between room 25 and room 34 of the Galleria degli Uffizi is the entrance to the Corridoio Vasariano (Vasari Corridor). It is 1km/3,200ft long, begins in the Palazzo Vecchio, runs through the Uffizi, through the Ponte Vecchio to the other side of the Arno and ends at Palazzo Pitti near the grotto by Bernardo Buontalenti in the Giardino Boboli. It got its name from Giorgio Vasari, who built it in 1565 for Cosimo I. The Vasari Corridor made it possible for the Medici to cross from Palazzo Vecchio to Palazzo Pitti without being seen. The Vasari Corridor now holds a rich **collection of portraits by Italian and other European artists**. Most of them are self-portraits, but there are also portraits of others as well as copies of portraits. New works are added regularly, so that along with portraits of Leonardo, Raphael, Michelangelo, Rembrandt or Velázquez there are also self-portraits by modern artists like James Ensor and Carlo Levi. Only open to groups.

❶ In order to see the corridor it is necessary to contact a private agency that organizes tours for small groups at the price of €80 to €90 per person.
www.corridoiovasariano.com,
www.florence-museum.com

FIRST FLOOR

Rooms 2-3: Gabineto Disegni e Stampe
Because of the high value placed on artistic work in the Renaissance a whole new value was placed on the preparatory **sketches** as well, which caused the Medici to lay the foundation for this major collection of more than 150,000 leaves. With the aid of the art historical institute of Florence the process of digitalizing valuable but light-sensitive collection began in 2006 in order to make it more readily available to international research. In the rooms only facsimiles are on display.

The Niobe rooms present the Niobe group

Sale Blu (46-55) The Sale Blu (blue rooms) begin with Room 46 with the Spanish artists, including the famous Mannerist El Greco (16th cent.) as well as the Baroque painters Velazquez (17th cent.) and Goya (18th cent.). **French art** of the 18th cent. is in Room 51 with works by Watteau, Boucher, Liotard and Chardin. The central corridor and side rooms are dedicated to **Dutch painting** from Amsterdam, Delft, Den Haag, Leyden, who in the so-called golden age of the Netherlands (17th – 18th) produced an unusually fruitful amount of work. It reflects the genre of everyday life with landscapes, city views and especially portraits of the economical rise of the gentry. In Room 49 there are three wonderful portraits by **Rembrandt**. These works often go back to the preferences of Grand Duke Cosimo III de'Medici as well as the rich art collection of his daughter Electress Anna Maria Luisa, and her husband, the Elector Johann Wilhelm of Pfalz-Neuburg. Bartholomäus van Douvenpainted her as a great art benefactress in 1722 in the painting *Allegoria degli Elettori Palatini come Protettori delle Arti*, which hands today in the centre corridor of the Blue Rooms (►MARCO POLO Insight p. 77). Rooms 52 and 55 are dedicated to the works of Flemish Baroque painting of the 17th and 18th cent including **Bruegel the Elder, Peter Paul Rubens, Antonis Van Dyck**.

Salle Rosse (56-66): The Sale Rosse (Red Rooms) pick up a typical Medici colour with their carmine red walls. Painting begins in Rooms 57 and 58 with the exhilarating, consummate grace of the Late Renaissance painter **Andrea del Sarto**, who is considered to be a forerunner of Florentine Mannerists like Pontormo and Rosso Fiorentino. Del Sarto left behind masterpieces in churches and monasteries like Santissima Annunziata, in Chiostro dello Scalzo and in San Salvi.

Rooms 60, 61: Florentine Mannerists The year that Raphael died (1520) marks the beginning of Mannerism, the late phase of the Renaissance until about 1600, which is marked by an anti -classical, unnatural feel for form and colour. Deformation of reality and mystically exalted religiosity were supposed to achieve an enhancement of expression.

Rosso Fiorentino (Room 60) was an early Mannerist. His preference for developing figures in areas and for cool, pale colours can be seen in his painting *Moses Defends the Daughters of Jethros* (1523), which refers to an Old Testament story in which Moses drives away the shepherds from a well and lets the herds of the seven daughters of Jethro drink first. In a strict geometric composition two triangles more or less equal in size are constructed on the scene, which meet in Moses' left knee. While the three nudes are portrayed with anatomical accuracy, but which still seem unnatural, almost like jointed dolls. **Jacopo da Pontormo** (Room 61) painted *Christus in Emmaus* (around 1525) for the Carthusian monastery near Florence. The work is characterized by a spiritual-mysterious portrayal of Christ and the disciples while the Carthusian monks are treated naturally by an effective use of light. Pontormo's portrait of Cosimo the Elder (1520) is a fundamental asset to the Medici family pictures.

The two rooms painted by Luigi Ademollo hold mainly small works by additional 16th cent. Mannerist masters, including Alessandro Allori and especially the grand master Giorgio Vasari, including his famous portrait of Lorenzo the Magnificent (1534).

Sale Ademollo (62, 63): Vasari and the 16th cent.

Three important Raphael works are also hanging in this room: a self-portrait (around 1506) showing him at the age of 23, his lovely *Madonna of the Goldfinch* in an effective triangular composition and finally the portrait *Pope Leo X with two Cardinals* (1517 – 1519). The Medici pope shows himself to the viewer as a modern person in the Zeitgeist of the Renaissance. Raphael shows the pope as an individual person, not as an official and also manages to balance ideal form with real appearance by portraying the art- and music-loving pope despite his unattractive appearance as a self-confident, strong-willed, personality marked by his spirituality without giving him an attributed powerful stature. Following the pope's wish Raphael painted two cardinals in the background, close relatives and confidants of the pope who are also his protégées, which in turn gets him accused of nepotism. Raphael carries out the difficult task of a group portrait of people of unequal rank by depicting the pope seated and looking up from studying an opened precious miniature codex with the confidants, Cardinal Luigi Rosso and Giulio de Medici – the later Pope Clemens VII – standing and both of them framing the pope. The contrast between the idealized figures on the one hand and the naturally exact details of the writing, the finely chased bell and the chair knob in which the room is reflected.

Room 66: Raphael

! *Bar with a View* **Insider Tip**

MARCO POLO TIP

After viewing the art in the Uffizi Gallery, enjoy a break there as well. The bar in the Uffizi has a roof terrace and serves drinks, ice cream and cake with a wonderful view of the Piazza della Signoria and the cathedral.

In Florence there were hardly any important representatives of Baroque painting, but it belongs into any art collection. Here it is represented by the contrast-rich paintings of Caravaggio, which influenced other painters as well. Room 81 has his frightening *Head of Medusa*, the *Young Bacchus* and the dramatic *Sacrifice of Isaac*. No less dramatic is *Judith and Holofernes* (1620) by Italy's most famous Baroque woman painter **Artemisia Gentileschi**.

Room 80-84: Caravaggio

AROUND THE GALLERIA DEGLI UFFIZI

Museo Galileo In the austere, fortress-like, medieval Palazzo Castellani (Piazza dei Giudici 1) behind the Uffizi the law courts of the Ruota were housed from 1574 to 1841 – hence the name Piazza dei Giudici (judges). Since 1930 it has housed the Museo di Storia della Scienza (Museum of the History of Science), which was renamed Museo Galileo in 2010. It covers astronomy, physics, mathematics and optics.

The museum collection includes instruments and scientific objects, some of which belonged to the Medici and some to other Florentine institutes, optical and mathematical apparatus including a mechanical writing apparatus, electrical devices, astronomical and cosmographical instruments as well as physical and anatomical models. One room is dedicated to **Galileo Galilei** (▶Famous People and ▶MARCO POLO Insight p. 72), who worked as mathematician for the grand duke from 1610, and his discoveries. Displays include his telescope, compass and the lens with which he discovered the moons of Jupiter, the *pianeti medicei*.

❶ Mon, Wed – Sun 9.30am – 6pm, Tue 9.30am – 1pm, www.museogalileo.it, admission: €9

✳ Giardino di Boboli

✳ H 7

Location: Piazza Pitti
Bus: C2, 11, 36, 37
❶ Jan, Feb, Nov, Dec Tue – Sun 8.15am – 4.30pm, March Tue – Sun 8.15am – 5.30pm, April, May, Sep, Oct Tue – Sun 8.15am – 6.30pm, June – Aug Tue – Sun 8.15am – 7.30pm, 1st and last Monday of the month closed, www.polomuseale.firenze.it, admission: €7, with exhibits €10. Entrances: Piazza Pitti, Via Romana 37
Admission to the park includes the museums in the park and the Giardino Bardini park to the east.

Behind the Palazzo Pitti lies the pretty Boboli Garden, an expansive, sloping park. Anyone looking for green surroundings as a break from viewing the art should find time for a walk through the park.

By the Medici After Duke Cosimo I bought Palazzo Pitti in 1549, the adjacent land which had in part belonged to the Boboli or Bobolini family – hence the name – was also bought. **Niccolò Pericoli**, called »Tribolo« (»the troubled one«), began to redesign the park between 1550 and 1560. **Bernardo Buontalenti** continued (1583 – 1593) and **Alfonso Parigi the Younger** completed it (1628 – 58).

Giardino di Boboli

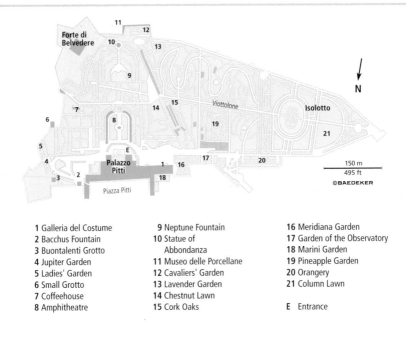

1 Galleria del Costume
2 Bacchus Fountain
3 Buontalenti Grotto
4 Jupiter Garden
5 Ladies' Garden
6 Small Grotto
7 Coffeehouse
8 Amphitheatre

9 Neptune Fountain
10 Statue of
   Abbondanza
11 Museo delle Porcellane
12 Cavaliers' Garden
13 Lavender Garden
14 Chestnut Lawn
15 Cork Oaks

16 Meridiana Garden
17 Garden of the Observatory
18 Marini Garden
19 Pineapple Garden
20 Orangery
21 Column Lawn

E Entrance

On the west side of Palazzo Pitti is Fontana del Bacco (»Bacchus Fountain«), which was created in 1564 by Valerio Dioli. The figure depicts Morgante, the **court dwarf of Cosimo I**, riding on a turtle.

Fontana del Bacco

The grotto near the fountain was built between 1583 and 1593 to designs by Buontalenti. The figures in the niches to the right and left of the entry depict **Ceres** and **Apollo**. Inside the grotto, what appear to be stalagmites turn out to be shepherds and sheep.
Cosimo I had Michelangelo's famous sculptures *Slaves* placed in the corners of the grotto and they were only replaced by copies in 1908. Today the originals of the sculptures are in the ▶Galleria dell' Accademia.

Grotta del Buontalenti (▶ill. p. 58)

The amphitheatre opposite the south-east façade of Palazzo Pitti was built in 1618 by Giulio and Alfonso Parigi and remodelled in 1700. The grand dukes used it as the setting for extravagant festivals. The obelisk is from Egypt, the granite basin from Rome.

Amphitheatre

Not far above the coffee house (currently closed) is the Neptune Fountain, which was created by Stoldo Lorenzi in 1565. Neptune stands on a rock surrounded by tritons and sirens.

Neptune Fountain

A short distance higher at the southern edge of the park is the colossal statue *Abbondanza* (Abundance). It was begun by Giambologna and completed by Pietro Tacca in 1637.

Abbondanza

Only a few steps away is the entrance to the Giardino del Cavaliere. It is a terrace garden above the fortifications. **Silkworms** were once raised and the first potatoes in Italy planted here. It is adorned by a monkey fountain.

Giardino del Cavaliere

The 18th-century Palazzina del Cavaliere in the Giardino del Cavaliere now houses the porcelain museum. It exhibits Italian, French and German porcelain as well as a collection that once belonged to the Lorraine-Habsburg grand dukes of Tuscany.

Museo delle Porcellane

● Opening times: like the Giardino di Boboli

Viottolone, an avenue lined impressively by cypresses, holm oaks and pine trees, runs downwards steeply to Isolotto. In the centre of the oval Isolotto (1618) is a fountain, Fontana dell' Oceano, whose main figure, the **statue of Oceanus**, was created by Giambologna in 1576 (copy; original is in the Museo Nazionale del Bargello). The sculptures at Oceanus' feet represent the rivers Nile, Ganges and Euphrates.

Isolotto

Palazzina della Meridiana next to the Palazzo Pitti houses the Galleria del Costume, a costume collection ranging from the 18th century to the First World War, and the **Collezione Contini Bonacossi**. This collection, which was established by Conte Alessandro Contini Bonacossi, includes priceless works of art, including paintings from Cimabue to Goya. The classical-style palace with a façade facing the garden was begun in 1776; at the beginning of the 19th century it was expanded considerably. The Italian royal family often stayed in the Palazzina della Meridiana until the end of the Italian monarchy. Today the palace has the same furnishings and paintings that it had during the 19th century, but has not been renovated.

Galleria del Costume

● Opening times: like the Giardino di Boboli; enter through the Galleria d' Arte Moderna in Palazzo Pitti

AROUND THE GIARDINO DI BOBOLI

Forte di Belvedere (Costa di San Giorgio), on the north-eastern boundary of the Giardino di Boboli, was built for Grand Duke

Forte di Belvedere

The place to relax after all that art

Ferdinando I de'Medici by the **architect Bernardo Buontalenti** in 1590 to 1595, probably to plans by Giovanni de'Medici. The fort was not intended for defence against foreign enemies but for the protection of the ruling Medici family itself. The fort's cannons are therefore surprisingly pointed at the city, in order to warn his subjects against trying to rebel. A small **palace** inside the fort was also designed by Buontalenti and is used for rotating exhibitions today.

❶ Only accessible during exhibitions

Porta San Giorgio
Porta San Giorgio, a short distance below Forte di Belvedere, was completed in 1260. It is part of a second city wall on the left banks of the Arno; the gates San Niccolò, San Miniato, San Giorgio, Romana and San Frediano today still mark the course of this wall. The fresco of the Madonna inside is by Bicci di Lorenzo; outside there is a relief of St George. Visitors to the bastion have a **wonderful view of the city** from next to Porta San Giorgio.

Giardino Bardini
What few Boboli visitors know: anyone who leaves via the exit at Forte di Belvedere can go to another park along the street Costa di San Giorgio towards the Arno, the Giardino Bardini. This idyllic, terraced villa garden is full of roses and camelias. In the elegant **Villa Bardini** in the park the enchanting gowns and fabric sculptures of the fashion designer **Roberto Capucci** can be admired. The dream view of the city is best enjoyed from the **loggia of the Café Belvedere** with a delicious capuccino.

Porta Romana
Porta Romana (south-western end of the park), **Florence's most massive and best-preserved city gate** marks the road from Florence to Rome, which is how the gate was named. Above the arch inside the fortification, which was built in 1326, there is a 14th-century fresco from the Florentine school: *Madonna with Child and Four Saints* painted by Franciabigio.

* Loggia di Mercato Nuovo

✴ H 6/b III

Location: Via Porta Rossa
Bus: C1, C2

In the Loggia di Mercato Nuovo where once silk, jewellery and other luxury goods were sold, things are simpler today: leather goods, basketry and souvenirs are sold.

If you rub the wild boar's nose on Fontana del Porcellino
you are certain to come back to Florence

The open, columned market was built by **Giovanni Battista del Tasso** between 1547 and 1551, and first used mainly by silk traders and goldsmiths. A marble slab in the middle of the loggia marks the spot where bankrupt traders were publicly beaten and ridiculed.

Market hall

The fountain on the south side of the loggia is affectionately called the Fontana del Porcellino, the »piglet's fountain«, as the **bronze wild boar** (1612) by Pietro Tacca is called locally. The figure is a copy of a Roman marble sculpture in the Uffizi Gallery. Anyone who rubs the boar's nose will return to Florence, they say.

Fontana del Porcellino

AROUND LOGGIA DI MERCATO NUOVO

The Gothic windows and the crenellations on the Palazzo di Parte Guelfa right behind the Loggia date from the 14th century. In the war between the Guelphs and Ghibellines, the parties loyal either to the pope or to the emperor, the Capitani di Parte Guelfa kept the possessions confiscated from the Ghibellines in the 13th century in this house. The palazzo was remodelled in the 15th century by

Palazzo di Parte Guelfa

Brunelleschi and Francesco della Luna. The medieval palace is situated on the square of the same name not far to the east of the museum – and houses various organizations. It has magnificent rooms with harmonious proportions; the decorations on the ceilings and walls are by such artists as Giambologna, Luca della Robbia and Giambologna.

Museo di Palazzo Davanzati

The museum close to the Logia to the east also became known by the name Museo della Casa Fiorentina Antica. It is housed in the Gothic Palazzo Davanzati. On three storeys it displays furniture, drawings, sculptures, carpets, ceramics and household utensils from the Middle Ages, Renaissance and Baroque periods. The austere, five-storey façade of Palazzo Davanzati has three massive gates at the bottom; it is crowned by a loggia, and the middle is decorated by a magnificent Davanzati coat of arms. Valuable tapestries were attached to the iron bars on the windows. The Davizzi family first built an urban villa here in 1300; a family member was gonfaloniere of the republic in 1294. In the 16th century the palace was passed on to the Bartolini family, later (1578) to the Davanzati. In 1906 the art dealer Elia Volpi bought the building and restored it to its former glory. The palace has been the home of the Museo dell' Antica Casa Fiorentina since 1956.

The **Parrot Room** on the first floor, which was named after the decorations, is especially interesting. The walls are painted like tapestries with parrots. Articles from the Bargello, other collections and donations were combined to make up the exhibits. They give an impression of the highly cultured life of Florentine citizens, who furnished their homes with precious works of art and utensils.

❶ Via Porta Rossa 13, daily 8.15am – 1.50pm on the 2nd and 4th Sun, closed 1st 3rd, 5th Mon of the month, 2nd and 3rd floors only open on appointment tel. 055 2 38 86 10, www.uffizi.firenze.i/musei/davanzati, admission: €2

✱ Museo Archeologico Nazionale

✦ J 6/c II

Location: Piazza Santissima Annunziata 9 b
Bus: 6, 31
❶ Tue – Fri 8.30am – 7pm, Mon, Sat, Sun 8.30am – 2pm; admission: €4

The Museo Archeologico, the most important archaeological collection in northern Italy, was established in 1870 and mainly presents finds from Etruscan settlements in Italy, but also prehistoric, Egyptian, Greek and Roman items.

The collections housed in the **Palazzo della Crocetta**, built in 1620 for Grand Duchess Maria Magdalena of Austria, the wife of Cosimo II, were partly initiated by the Medici. The collections consist of the Museo Topografico dell' Etruria (Topographical Museum of Etruria), Museo Egizio (Egyptian Museum) and Antiquario Etrusco-Greco-Romano (Museum for Etruscan, Greek and Roman Antiquity).

Museum in three parts

The Museo Topografico on the first floor, which is considered to be **the largest of its kind after the Villa Giulia in Rome**, displays finds from Etruria; they give an detailed picture of the life of the Etruscans. Room IX holds the **Amazon Sarcophagus** from the 5th century BC; it is remarkable for its depiction of battles between Amazons and Roman soldiers.

*Museo Topografico dell' Etruria

The museum's most famous work is a bronze sculpture of a wounded ****Chimera** (room XIV), an excellent example of Etruscan metal work. According to an inscription, the »holy object« was probably cast in the 4th century BC. It is the figure of a lion with the head of a goat and the tail of a snake.

The Chimera is a masterpiece of Etruscan bronze work

The ***Arringatore** (Orator, 1st cent. BC) in the same room is Aulus Metellus, according to an inscription, wearing the official robes of a Roman senator. It is a rare example of an honorary statue for an Etruscan, on whom Roman citizenship was bestowed in 89 BC, as a visible sign the blending of the Etruscan and Roman upper class.

The bronze statue of **Minerva** in the same room was probably copied from a Greek original of the 4th century BC. The same applies to a Roman copy of a bronze original from late antiquity, the so-called **Idolino** (little idol) in room XIII, an attractive lamp holder from the Augustan period. Only part of the rich collection is on display.

In the garden there are reconstructions of graves and tombs. The **Horse's Head** is also a Greek bronze that was copied in Roman times.

Museo Egizio The Museo Egizio, the **second most important Egyptian museum in Italy** after the one in Turin, was established after a large expedition (1829) and has been open to the public since 1831. On display are statues, busts, ceramics, reliefs, sarcophaguses, mummies, pictures and utensils from various Egyptian dynasties. A well-preserved chariot (15th cent. BC) from a tomb near Thebes is worth noting.

Vase collection The vase collection in the top floor is varied and consists of richly painted Greek and Etruscan objects. The most famous item is the Attic ***François Vase**, by the painter Kleitias and the potter Ergotimo (6th century BC). In 1900 an emotionally disturbed museum guard shattered the vase into hundreds of pieces; it was painstakingly restored. The vase has detailed and lively depictions of Greek myths, including the return of the Athenians from the Minotaur's labyrinth on Crete.

Topographic department Etruscan finds from Tuscany are arranged here by location. Exhibits worth seeing are the so-called **Mater Matua**, a 5th-century BC urn shaped like a woman sitting on a sphinx throne, and the coloured **terracotta sarcophagus of Lathia Scianti** (according to a coin 147 BC at the latest), who is portrayed on the lid as a richly dressed and bejewelled woman.

AROUND MUSEO ARCHEOLOGICO

Santa Maria Maddalena Pazzi Santa Maria Maddalena Pazzi am Borgo Pinti can be reached by walking south-east on Via della Colonna. A member of the famous Florentine Pazzi family, Maria Maddalena, was canonized in 1669. The 13th-century church and Benedictine monastery that was remodelled by Giuliano da Sangallo (1480 – 1492) was enlarged in her honour. Thus the atrium of the church shows the harmonious style of the late 15th century, while other parts of the church and monastery have Baroque elements. The chapels are decorated with valuable paintings by Tuscan artists of the 15th and 16th centuries like Portelli and Giordano. The monastery refectory is part of a carabinieri barracks today, and the cloister by Sangallo is part of the Liceo Michelangelo.

In the **Sala Capitolare**, the chapter house of the monastery, ***frescoes by Perugino** which are among his most beautiful works have been preserved. They were painted between 1493 and 1496, Perugino's most creative period, and depict Christ on the cross and Mary Magdalene, St Bernard and the Virgin, St John and St Benedict, Christ on the cross helping St Bernard. In the background is the Umbrian landscape that was Perugino's home: his name is derived from Perugia.

Sala Capitolare

❶ Access to the Sala Capitolare via the school entrance (Via Colonna 9), Tue, Thu 2.30pm – 5.30pm; July, Aug. closed

Museo Stefano Bardini

✦ J 7

Location: Piazza de' Mozzi 1/Via dei Renai 37
Bus: C1, D, 23
❶ Fri – Mon 11am – 5pm, admission: €6, www.museobardini.org

The Bardini Museum display includes sculptures, paintings, furniture, ceramics, carpets and weapons from antiquity, the Renaissance and the Baroque period mainly from northern Italy.

The art dealer Stefano Bardini left the collection to the city of Florence in 1923. It is housed in his 19th-century palace. The most noteworthy items include a **marmorne Caritas**, an allegory of love, by Tino di Camaino, a **bust of John the Baptist** by Andrea Sansovino, the **Archangel Michael**, a painting by Antonio del Pollaiolo and three reliefs by Donatello. A small stucco by Michelangelo is also significant. The collection is open again after a detailed restoration. The palace garden is also open to visitors.

Collection of an art dealer

AROUND MUSEO BARDINI

Not far from the Piazza de' Mozzi is the complex of the three Mozzi palaces (Via San Niccolò 123–125), which was probably built in the 13th century. In the Middle Ages the Mozzi were Visdomini, the bishop's secular rulers.

Mozzi palaces

San Niccolò sopr' Arno The late Gothic hall church of San Niccolò sopr' Arno is located not far to the east on Via San Niccolò. Its main works of art are the altar tabernacle in the style of Michelozzo with a beautiful fresco of the Assumption of the Virgin and The Virgin Giving her Belt to the Doubting St Thomas (around 1470), possibly by Piero del Pollaiolo, in the sacristy. The church was built in the 12th century, reconstructed in the 14th century and remodelled in the 16th century. After Florence was occupied by imperial and papal troops, **Michelangelo** is supposed to have hidden in the bell tower in 1530 to escape being arrested.

Porta San Niccolò Porta San Niccolò east of the church San Niccolò sopr' Arno was well suited to defend the city and – together with the Zecca tower on the other side of the Arno – to blockade the river. The tower of the bulwark, which was built in 1324, is the eastern end of the city wall on the south side of the Arno.

Insider Tip This neighbourhood along the river with its old palazzi, nice eateries, the bike path along the riverbank is very popular.

Museo del Cenacolo di Andrea del Sarto a San Salvi

✦ L 6

Location: Via di San Salvi 16
Bus: 3, 6, 20, 34
❶ Thu – Sun 8.15am – 1.50pm, admission: free, www.polomuseale.firenze.it

Among the many depictions of the Last Supper, Andrea del Sarto's masterpiece in the refectory of San Salvi deserves special mention. It is one of the most beautiful early 16th cent. frescoes in Florence.

Highlight: Last Supper The former Vallombrosan monastery of San Salvi, which was founded in 1048, was converted into the **Museo del Cenacolo di Andrea del Sarto a San Salvi**. It contains other works by Florentine painters, above all by Andrea del Sarto and his school. The fresco of the *★Last Supper*, which del Sarto created after 1519, is the main attraction; it was inspired by Leonardo's *Last Supper* and stands out for the natural motions of the figures and its harmonious colours. The expanse of the room, which distracts the viewer's eye from the main event, stands out. The monastery kitchen with a large fireplace is also worth visiting.

✱ Museo Marino Marini

✦ H 6/a III

Location: Piazza San Pancrazio
Bus: C3, D, A
❶ Mon, Wed – Sat 10am – 5pm, Aug. closed; www.museomarinomarini.it,
admission: €4

**The former church of San Pancrazio now houses a museum
dedicated to the Tuscan sculptor, painter and graphic artist
Marino Marini (1901–80). He is one of the most important Italian artists of the 20th century.**

The façade of the San Pancrazio church, which has been renovated
several times, dates mainly from the 14th century. Several building
elements reveal **Alberti** as the master builder. He was commissioned
by the Rucellai family between 1457 and 1467 to remodel it and to

San Pancrazio

Modern art found a home in Museo Mario Marini

build the Cappella Rucellai. In the chapel Alberti crated a copy of the Holy Sepulchre in Jerusalem, eloquently designed in white marble with black stone inlays and open again for visitors since 2013. After the church had been used as a tobacco factory and finally as a military depot, the renowned architects Lorenzo Papi and Bruno Sacchi began to remodel it in the early 1980s. The result was a construction in which stairs and balcony are interlaced, and the combination of wood panelling, poured concrete and iron beams create an effective setting for art exhibitions.

Museum The museum exhibits 176 sculptures, paintings, drawings and graphics by Marini, who gave many of his works to the city of Florence before his death. Beginning with the painting *The Virgins* of 1916, they represent all of his creative periods. Of course, various versions of Marino Marini's **equestrian statues** are also present. While the early works mainly show horses in harmony with people, beginning in the late 1940s they show animals rearing up and trying to throw off their riders. Marini's favourite female figure is Pomona, the voluminous portrayal of a goddess of fertility. He also created figures of woman dancers and jugglers. Interesting rotating exhibits of contemporary art are held in the lower floor.

Museo Nazionale di Antropologia e Etnologia

—————————————————— ✦ J 6/b III

Location: Via del Proconsolo 12
Bus: C1, C2
❶ Mon, Tue, Thu, Fri, 9am–5pm, Sat, Sun 9am–1pm, admission: €6, www.firenze-online.com

Museo Nazionale di Antropologia e Etnologia (National Museum of Anthropology and Ethnology) has been housed since 1869 in the Palazzo Nonfinito, which – as its name but not necessarily its appearance indicates – is unfinished.

Oldest museum of its kind in Italy Alessandro Strozzi commissioned Bernardo Buontalenti in 1593 to build a new city residence for his family next to the Palazzo Pazzi, but neither Buontalenti nor his successors were able to complete the large palace. The Museo di Antropologia e Etnologia has large collections on many of many ethnic groups and cultures outside of Europe. Clothing, jewellery and weapons are on display in the ethnographic department while the anthropological department has many significant bone and skeleton finds. For example, wooden objects and amulets from Africa, ceramics and idols from Asia as well as clothing and boats from China and India can be viewed. The musical instrument collection is unique.

AROUND THE MUSEO DI ANTROPOLOGIA

Palazzo dei Pazzi-Quaratesi (Via del Proconsolo 10) opposite the museum was built for **Jacopo de'Pazzi**, who was executed in 1478 after the conspiracy against Lorenzo and Giuliano de' Medici. **Brunelleschi** was first responsible for the construction from 1430. Later Giuliano da Maiano took over the work from 1462 to 1472. His work is known for its careful execution and love of architectural details. The Pazzi family, which had moved from Fiesole to Florence in the Middle Ages, was the embodiment of business sense and striving for power. Since Lorenzo de' Medici escaped the assassination attempt by the Pazzi they were not able to break the power of the Medici. The family was banished, and its palace given first to the Cibo family, later to the Strozzi and the Quaratesi.

Palazzo dei Pazzi-Quaratesi

Palazzo Altoviti is not far to the east on Borgo degli Albizi (no. 18), a street with many beautiful townhouses. It first belonged to the Albizi family, then to the Valori and Guicciardini families and goes back to designs by Benedetto da Rovezzano. In the 16th century it was decorated by Baccio Valori with portraits of famous Florentines (Vespucci, Dante, Petrarch, Boccaccio among others), so that it is disrespectfully called Palazzo dei Visacci (**Mugs Palace**) by local people.

Palazzo Altoviti

** Museo Nazionale del Bargello

⟶ J 6/ b III

Location: Via del Proconsolo 4
Bus: C1, C2
🕐 daily 8.15am – 4.50pm; closed 2nd, 4th Mon of the month
www.polomuseale.firenze.it, admission: €6

Museo Nazionale del Bargello is one of Italy's most important sculpture museums; it is located in the palace of the same name. It has numerous epoch-making works by Tuscan sculptors of the 14th to 16th centuries, especially Donatello, della Robbia and Michelangelo.

Symbol of the citizens' power (▶ill. p.41) Palazzo del Bargello, a massive Gothic fortress that the citizens of Florence had built in 1250 as a symbol of their victory over the nobility, is a landmark on the city skyline with its defensive tower and crenellations. From 1261 the palace was the seat of the podestà, the neutral city officer who was responsible for law and order. From 1502 the ruota (judiciary) and the prison were located here, and from 1574 the palace was the seat of the bargello (chief of police). In 1859 the first Italian national museum was established here.

Ground floor The Gothic courtyard is very impressive. It is bordered on three sides by arcades with octagonal supports and cross vaulting. On the fourth side steps lead to the upper floors. The walls and pillars are decorated with coats of arms of the podestàs, the ruota members, the city quarters and districts. In the centre of the courtyard is an octagonal **fountain**; the scaffold for executions stood nearby in times when the Bargello still served as a prison. Today the arcade is used to display sculptures, including works of Bartolomeo Ammanati and Giambologna.

Michelangelo Room The imposing courtyard leads to rooms with outstanding works by Michelangelo. The unfinished marble bust *Brutus* (around 1540) portrays Lorenzino, the Tuscan Brutus and murderer of the tyrant Alessandro de' Medici. The round relief *Madonna with Child and the Young John the Baptist* (around 1504), which was created for Bartolomeo Pitti, portrays the Mother of God as a pensive visionary. The figure *Apollino* (around 1531) turns on its own axis. The impressive early work **Drunk Bacchus* (around 1497), Michelangelo's first large statue, shows the intoxication of the young god in a highly naturalistic manner.

Other works are by 16th-century artists. Note particularly the statue *Bacchus* by Jacopo Sansovino (around 1520), Michelangelo's bronze bust of Daniele da Volterra as well as the bust of Cosimo I and others by Benvenuto Cellini (1557) including the marble statue *Narcissus* (1540).

Room for medieval sculpture The expressive variety of 14th-century Gothic sculpture is presented in the Florentine sculpture of Tino di Camaino, Arnoldi, Talenti and Cambio. Camaino's *Madonna with Child* is remarkable; it was probably made for the tomb of Bishop Antonio d'Orso.

First floor In the loggia of the first floor are the breathtakingly balanced bronze statue of *Mercury* (1580) and the *Allegory of Architecture* by Giambologna, as well as sculptures by Baccio Bandinelli and Francesco Moschino.

Masterpieces of the great Renaissance sculptor **Donatello** can be seen in the Salone del Consiglio Generale, including the *Marble Da-*

Bargello, the former seat of the podestà, now shows sculptures

vid (1408–09), which he made for the cathedral as a young man. The softly sculpted, boyish ****figures of David**, made around 1435 for Cosimo the Elder, is the first free-standing nude figure made since Antiquity. Note the marble statue of St George (1417), made for the church of Orsanmichele, and the accompanying relief, the first example of the use of central perspective. *Marzocco* (1420), the lion with the Florentine lily coat of arms, is also a masterpiece.

To compare the styles of Ghiberti and Brunelleschi, the competing reliefs for the second door of the Baptistery depicting the sacrifice of Isaac (1402), make good subjects. Moreover the room contains some of **Luca della Robbia's** most beautiful terracottas, like the brilliant *Madonna delle Rose*.

Prisoners who were sentenced to death were taken into the **Maddalena Chapel**, which is decorated with frescoes (around 1335) from Giotto's workshop, before they were executed. The **Ivory Room** has ivory carvings from antiquity up to the Middle Ages. The **Bruzzichel-**

Museo Nazionale del Bargello

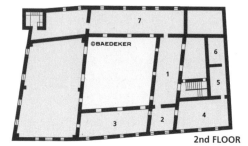

2nd FLOOR

SECOND FLOOR
1 G. della Robbia room
2 A. della Robbia room
3 Room with small bronzes
4 Verrocchio room
5/6 Rooms with Baroque sculptures and medallions
7 Weapons room

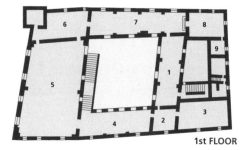

1st FLOOR

FIRST FLOOR
1 Room with ivory work
2 Bruzzichelli room
3 Room with majolica
4 Verone (Loggia)
5 Large Donatello room
6 Islamic room
7 Carrand room
8 Maddalena Chapel
9 Sacristy

Entrance ➡

GROUND FLOOR

GROUND FLOOR
1 Courtyard
2 Michelangelo room
3 Room with medieval sculptures

li **Room** has Tuscan furniture and glass from the 16th and 17th centuries; ceramics from the same period are in the **Majolica Room**.

In the **della Robbia rooms** works of colourfully glazed terracotta by Giovanni and Andrea della Robbia, as well as a portrait bust of Costanza Bonarelli by Bernini, are exhibited. As the name implies, the Verrocchio room holds mainly works by **Andrea del Verrocchio**, Leonardo da Vinci's teacher. His bronze David, which prompts a comparison with the sculpture of David by Donatello on the first floor, is a finely modelled figure of a shepherd boy. The *Lady with a Bouquet* (around 1475–80) shows the influences of antiquity. The relief *Madonna with Child* is one of the artist's early works. The very realistic portrait bust of Pietro Melini (1474) by *Benedetto da Maiano*, the marble bust of Matteo Palmieri (1468) by Antonio Rosselino and the ceramic busts of a youthful warrior (around 1475–1480) by *Antonio Pollaiolo* with a relief of Hercules and the hydra on his breastplate are also outstanding works. Two other rooms hold Baroque sculptures and the famous Medici **medallion collection**, which was begun by Lorenzo de' Medici and to which his descendants contributed regularly. The second floor also houses a collection of **bronze figurines**, **weapons** from the 13th to the 17th century, **tapestries and textiles** from Florentine workshops.

Second floor

AROUND THE MUSEO DEL BARGELLO

The pointed tower of the Badia opposite the Palazzo del Bargello cannot be missed on the city skyline. The Benedictine monastery, once an imperial abbey, was founded in 978 by Willa, the mother of Conte Ugo, Marchese di Toscana, which makes it the oldest Florentine monastery. Every year on 21 December, the day on which Conte Ugo died, a mass is read for his soul. Since then the church has been expanded and remodelled, in the 13th century by Arnolfo di Cambio and in the 17th century by Matteo Segaloni. On the Gothic outer façade note the door by Benedetto da Rovezzano (1495) and the early 16th-century glazed terracotta *Madonna with Child* in the lunette (under the arch) by Benedetto Buglioni.

Badia Fiorentina

Inside the church take time to look at the painting *The Appearance of the Madonna to St Bernard* (left at the entrance), a masterpiece by Filippino Lippi (1485), and the **tomb of Conte Ugo di Toscana** (d. 1001), to the left in the rudimentary transept. The tomb was made between 1469 and 1481 by Mino da Fiesole. The church choir leads to the beautiful, atmospheric **cloister**. Here there is a cycle of frescoes with scenes from the life of St Benedict. It was made immediately after the cloister was completed (presumably 1436–39).

❶ Mon 3pm – 6pm, admission: free

! MARCO ☉ POLO TIP

Craving ice cream **Insider Tip**

Lovers of top-quality ice cream go to Vivoli, just to the east of the Bargello (Via Isola delle Stinche 7 r). There is a choice of 40 different flavours.

Casa di Dante
In Via Dante Alighieri not far to the west of the Bargello are the houses of the Alighieri family. Tradition has it that the city's famous poet, **Dante Alighieri**, was born in one of the houses in 1265. He was not treated well by Florence. Dante opposed the ambitions of Pope Boniface VIII to incorporate Florence and all of Tuscany into the Papal State. When Charles of Valois was sent to Florence by the pope as a mediator, Dante was banned from Florence as one of the leaders of the Ghibellines. He never returned. Some of the rooms display photographs, editions of his main work, the *Divine Comedy*, reproductions of Botticelli drawings for Dante's work and portraits of the greatest Italian poet.

❶ Via Santa Margherita 1, daily 10am – 6pm, admission: €4

San Martino
Opposite Casa di Dante lies the unassuming church of San Martino. It was founded in 986 and acquired in 1442 by the Compagnia dei Buonomini, a charitable brotherhood that took care of the »ashamed poor«. These were formerly wealthy citizens who had lost all of their possessions. The present church dates from the late 15th century. The church is worth visiting for its **frescoes**, which depict the brotherhood's various acts of charity, such as visiting the sick and hosting pilgrims, and thus provide a graphic picture of everyday life in 15th-century Florence.

San Firenze
Not far south of the Bargello, San Firenze takes its character from the Baroque delight in stage sets: it consists of two church façades with a palace between them. There are historical reasons for this remarkable ensemble. In place of an oratory named San Fiorenzo – hence the name Firenze – the church of San Filippo Neri was built from 1645 to 1696. Ferdinando Ruggieri created the façade in 1715. Between 1772 and 1775 another church was built next to this one; it, too, had a façade based on Ruggieri's plans of 1715. At the same time the palace was built between the churches and first used as a monastery. Today San Firenze is the seat of the Tribunale, the law courts.

A **lovely example of a 15th-century Florentine city palace** is Palazzo Gondi (opposite the church), built from 1490 to 1501 by Giuliano da Sangallo but only completed in 1874 by Poggi. The reduction of the rustication higher up on the façade is typical. The **courtyard** is one of the most graceful of the Renaissance. Note the careful choice of materials and the perfection of the craftsmanship – on the capitals, the stairs and the fountain.

Palazzo Gondi

** Museo dell' Opera di Santa Maria del Fiore

—————————— ✦ J 6/b III ——

Location: Piazza del Duomo 9
Bus: C1, C2, 14, 23
❶ Mon – Sat 9am – 7.30pm, Sun 9am – 1.40pm, admission: €6, Reservations at www.operaduomo.firenze.it

Many exhibits from the cathedral, its campanile and baptistery are now in the very attractive cathedral museum, Museo dell' Opera di Santa Maria del Fiore, which makes it one of the leading sculpture collections in Europe.

The cathedral museum presents cathedral statuary attractively

Museo dell' Opera del Duomo

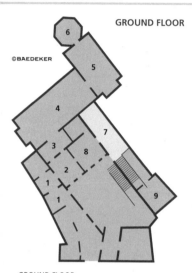

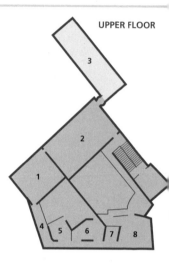

GROUND FLOOR

UPPER FLOOR

©BAEDEKER

GROUND FLOOR
1 Ancient fragments
2 Tino di Camaino room
3 Passage
4 Room of the
   old cathedral façade
5 Painting room
6 Chapel
7 Lapidarium
8 Room of the almond door
9 Michelangelo, Pietà

UPPER FLOOR
1 Room with the panel paintings
   of the Campanile
2 Room of the choir lofts
3 Room of the silver altar
4 Brunelleschi's construction site
5 Gallery room
6-8 Façade rooms
9 Courtyard

Cathedral treasures Many artists created great works of art for the decoration of the cathedral, campanile and baptistery including sculptures, gold and silver utensils, needlework and textiles. These objects could not remain in place on and inside the buildings because of the effects of weather and for security reasons. They were removed long ago and kept in a safe place, from 1891 in the cathedral museum. The cathedral office of works was first accommodated in this building in the 15th century; the artists' studios and craftsmen's workshops were also located here.

Currently the exhibition area is undergoing a considerable expansion, which means that rooms can be closed temporarily. But the main works like the Pietà by Michelangelo or the newly restored Paradise Doors of the Baptistery will always be accessible. The opening of the expanded museum is planned for October 2015, when Pope Francesco I plans to visit Florence.

Above the portal of the museum there is a **bust of Grand Duke Cosimo I** (1572), which was placed there by Giovanni Bandini dell' Opera.

The second small room after the entrance is dedicated to **Tino di Camaino**, who created the sculpture groups above the doors of the Baptistery in 1320–1321; parts of them have been preserved. **Ground floor**

Walk along the passageway with the 14th-century figures of angels to the **room of the old cathedral façade**. It holds statues that were once on the cathedral front, which was torn down in 1587. A drawing of the late 16th century shows the unfinished old façade. Among the most impressive works are a statue of *St Luke by Nanni di Banco and one of *John the Evangelist by Donatello. The figure of Luke, engrossed in reading the gospel, radiates outward peace and inner tension at the same time. The folds of his robe show Gothic influence, and his face that of antiquity. Donatello's figure of John is marked by exhaustion (1415); its expressive face and the effects of light and shade created by the drapery of his robes are fascinating. Michelangelo used it as a model for his famous statue of Moses in Rome. Other outstanding works are *St Matthew* by Bernardo Ciuffagni, who must have known Donatello because of the similarity of this work to the statue of St John, and the seated figure of *Pope Boniface VIII* (13th century) by Arnolfo di Cambio with its aura of exalted sanctity.

The **Painting Room** exhibits paintings from the 13th to the 15th century. The marble bas-reliefs by **Bandinelli the Elder** were once in the cathedral choir; at the base of the figure of God the Father, Bandinelli added his own portrait and the date 1156. Sculptural decoration from the **Mandorla Door** on the cathedral's north side is exhibited in the next room. The door is named after the *Assumption of the Virgin* by **Nanni di Banco** in the lunette, where the Mother of God is surrounded by an almond-shaped halo.

In the mezzanine is **one of the most famous sculptures of Western art**: Michelangelo's *Pietà*, a gripping, unfinished marble group that Michelangelo created when he was 80 years old. The slumped body of Christ, the stark pain in Mary's face, Joseph of Arimathea's tortured expression, actually a self-portrait of Michelangelo, the incomplete state of the entire group – all of these together are the supreme expression of death and human helplessness in the face of it. Michelangelo broke up the sculpture because he was not happy with the quality of the marble, but at the same time was so fascinated by the work that he wanted to be buried beneath it. His pupil Calcagni ****Pietà by Michelangelo (▶ill. p. 120)** put it together again and continued to work on it, except for the figure of Christ. The figure of *Mary Magdalene* was added on the left.

First floor In the **room of the relief panels of the campanile** the panels that once decorated the coffers in the lower part of the campanile are exhibited; they were replaced by copies. The **hexagonal panels** cannot be attributed for certain, apart from five by Luca della Robbia, since the work was done in the common workshop. They depict the creation story and crafts, which were thought to have become necessary after mankind had been driven out of paradise.

The **diamond-shaped panels** with marble reliefs on a blue majolica background come from the school of Andrea Pisano. They depict the planets, virtues, arts and sacraments.

The next room is named after the two marble **choir lofts** by Luca della Robbia (1431–38) and Donatello (1433–39) that were intended for the choir. Luca della Robbia's theme is praising God in song according to Psalm 150, while Donatello depicted exuberantly dancing putti. The lofts were in the cathedral until 1688, when they were removed for the wedding of Grand Duke Cosimo III and Violante Beatrice of Bavaria.

The statues that stood in the niches of the campanile are also exhibited here. *Habakkuk* (1423–35) and *Jeremiah* (1436) are expressive masterpieces by **Donatello**; they combine classical forms with Gothic robed figures, which gives the figures passion and prophetic power.

The most precious work in the next room is the **silver altar** from the baptistery, one of the most beautiful examples of Florentine silver work. Its fabrication in the Gothic style was begun in 1366 and completed in the Renaissance period (1480). Prophets and sibyls, scenes from the life of John the Baptist and other scenes from the Bible decorate the altar. The emaciated wooden figure of *St Magdalene* as an old woman (1453–55) by Donatello is poignant. The collection in this room also includes precious liturgical objects like crosses, reliquaries and vestments. In the corridor **Brunelleschi's construction site** for the cathedral dome has been reconstructed with tools and hoists. The original wooden model of the dome lantern and the architect's death mask are also on display.

Panels of the Paradise Door The gilded bronze relief panels of the marvellous Paradise Door (1429 – 1447) of the baptistery by the artist **Ghiberti are on display in the attractive courtyard. They were replaced by copies in 1990 which are made of bronze and gold, just like the originals, and carefully restored recently. It is worth taking some time here to enjoy the picturesque effect of the many beautiful figures and landscapes up close, even if only through protective glass.

Museo Stibbert

✦ H/J 4

Location: Via Federico Stibbert 26
Bus: 4
❶ Museum: Mon – Wed 10am – 2pm, Fri – Sun 10am – 6pm,
Park: April – Oct Mon – Wed, Fri – Sun 8am – 7pm, Nov – March
8am – 3pm, www.museo stibbert.it, admission: €8

The Scottish army officer Frederick Stibbert collected works of art in the Villa Montughi outside Florence from 1860 and gave them to the city in 1906.

The collection of old European and Asian weapons is of interest. Complete suits of armour as well as helmets, swords, sabres, rapiers and powder horns are on display. The highlight is in the Sala della Cavalcata: a **life-sized cavalcade** (▶ill. p. 95) of the 16th century with 14 riders and 14 foot soldiers, armed and in full armour. The other exhibits – furniture, paintings, textiles and various pieces of artistic value – show the collector's appreciation of art and taste.
The villa is set in a beautiful **park** with a small temple and fountains, also accessible to the public.

Extensive collection of weapons

Ognissanti

✦ H 6

Location: Piazza Ognissanti
Bus: C2, C3, D
❶ Mon – Sat 7.15am – 12.30pm, 4pm – 8pm, Sun 9am – 1pm,
4pm – 8pm, admission: free, www.chiesaognissanti.it

Ognissanti was built from 1252 to 1256 as the monastery church for Humiliati; later it became one of the first churches in Florence to be converted into Baroque.

The church was completely renovated in the 16th and 17th centuries; in 1872 and after the severe flood in 1966 it had to be restored. A Romanesque campanile towers over the church. On the façade there is a majolica relief *Coronation of the Virgin* in the tympanum. Inside the ceiling is decorated with *Apotheosis of St Francis* (1770) by Giuseppe Romei. The second altar on the right-hand side, which was donated by the Vespucci family, bears the *Madonna della Misericordia* by Domenico **Ghirlandaio** (around 1473); the man under the Madonna's right arm is supposed to be the seafarer Amerigo Vespucci, after whom America was named. Don't miss the fresco with a Pietà (1472)

MARCO POLO Insider Tip

...ps of Florence

...he city's most traditional ...otels, the Westin Excelsi- or, is on Piazza Ognissanti. The restaurant Se.sto on Arno on the rooftop terrace on the 6th floor serves the finest food, but an espresso or a cocktail are enough to enjoy the spectacular view of the city on the river. The roof bar is open from 12noon to 2am.

by Domenico and Davide Ghirlandaio. Domenico Ghirlandaio also created the fresco *St Jerome Studying* (1480), while the fresco *St Augustine Studying* (also 1480) is considered to be an especially important picture by **Sandro Botticelli**, who is buried here in the crypt. Another high point can be seen in the sacristy: an impressively painted cross panel (1315), which has definitely been attributed to **Giotto** since its restoration in 2010.

Cenacolo di Ghirlandaio e Museo Ognissanti The cloister leads to the former refectory, with the *Last Supper* (1480) by **Domenico Ghirlandaio**, which takes up the entire back wall. It is painted so that the room appears to merge with the painting. It is impressive for its realistic portrayal of the figures; additions were made to the head of Jesus in the 17th century.

✴ Orsanmichele

✦ H 6/b III

Location: Via dei Calzaiuoli
Bus: C2, C3, D
❶ Church: daily 10am – 5pm, Aug. closed Mon, free admission
Museum: Mon 10am – 5pm, admission: free, www.uffizi.firenze.it

The delicate Gothic architecture of the church of Orsanmichele is complemented by major Renaissance sculptures.

Former trading hall The present church is a well-preserved 14th-century building; it was converted from an oratory – San Michele in Orto, a name that was shortened to Or San Michele – and an earlier trading hall and warehouse, where a miraculous picture in time attracted more pilgrims than shoppers. By the late 14th century the spiritual purposes of the building prevailed. The detailed decoration of the outside walls, ornaments, arches, niches, figures, cornices, the marble used to close up the windows and the ornate tracery make the church a fine work of architecture.

*Figures in niches Figures of the patron saints of the guilds occupy the 14 skilfully constructed niches in the façade; they were commissioned by the guilds in the late 14th century. Thus most of the figures, which have been replaced by copies, date from the early 15th century. They include

key works of Renaissance sculpture, not to say of Western sculpture. In Via dei Calzaiuoli, beginning with the left outer niche, the first figure is the early Renaissance bronze statue of *John the Baptist* (1414) that Lorenzo Ghiberti made for the cloth traders' and wholesalers' guild. The cascading folds of the robe give the figure the grace of a dancer and are carried over from the Gothic period, but the contrapposto stance and the expressive, energetic face are characteristic of the Renaissance. The bronze group of *Christ and Doubting Thomas* (1465–83) by Andrea del Verrocchio is a work of the High Renaissance for the niche of the court of commercial law. The next two niches contain the *St Luke* (1597–1603), by Giambologna for the guild of the judges and notaries, and *St Peter* (around 1420) by associates of Donatello for the butchers. For the next two niches Nanni di Banco created St Philip (1410–12), a robed figure for the tanners' guild that still appears flat despite its contrapposto, and four crowned saints (1414–17) for the guild of stonemasons and carpenters, representing a group of four early Christian sculptors who were martyred under Diocletian (with a relief around the pedestal). His figures, which were influenced by ancient art, show a definite contrapposto, toga-like robes and Roman beards.

Donatello depicted *St George* (around 1416) as a holy knight for the niche of the armour makers (copy; the original is in the Bargello). Even though the figure stands in a niche, the path of development to free-standing sculpture is already apparent. The bronze statue of the *St Matthew* (1424) by Lorenzo Ghiberti for the money-changers' guild shows more confidence in the physical form than that of St John. Instead of facing forward as in the traditional representation, it now faces slightly to one side and the right hand is no longer occupied with holding a robe or an attribute; instead the evangelist is holding it in front of his chest in the gesture of an ancient orator.

John the Baptist

Two more niches show *St Stephen* (1427–28) by Ghiberti for the traders in woollen cloth, and the tall, slender *St Eligius* (around 1420) by Nanni di Banco for the blacksmiths' guild. The *St Mark* (1411–15) was made by Donatello for the guild of linen drapers and scrap traders. His deeply furrowed beard, spare, unruly curls, deep-set eyes and prominent forehead give an impression of spiritual tension and inner agitation. In the next niches are *St James* (after 1422) by Niccolò di Pietro Lamberti for the furriers and fur traders, the *Madonna della Rosa* (1399) by Giovanni di Piero Tedesco, for the doctors and pharmacists, and the *St John* (1515) by Baccio da Montelupo for the guild of silk weavers and goldsmiths.

Interior   The interior of the two-aisled hall is striking for its frescoes, paintings and glass windows. In the left aisle at the back is the altar of St Anne with the marble group St Anne, Madonna and Child by Francesco da Sangallo (1526). The right aisle ends with the **famous Gothic marble tabernacle by Orcagna** (1349–59); its rich decoration honours the miraculous votive image of the Madonna by Bernardo Daddi (1347). Reliefs on the base show scenes from the life of the Virgin (front) and the Death and Ascension of the Virgin with a self-portrait of Orcagna. The tabernacle is decorated by angels and prophets, sibyls, apostles and allegorical figures of the virtues. The marble gate with a bronze grille (1366) by Pietro Migliore is also worth looking at.
The church is connected to the Palazzo dell' Arte della Lana by means of a bridge (1569) by Buontalenti, which leads to the **Museo di Orsanmichele**, where the original niche sculptures are exhibited.

Palazzo   Florence became wealthy in the Middle Ages by processing and sell-
dell' Arte   ing wool. This can be seen in the palace of the wool weavers' and wool
della Lana   traders' guild (Via dell' Arte della Lana), which once housed 200 shops. The irregular complex was begun in 1308; in 1905 the Dante Society moved in. Today the building houses a shop. On the corner of Via dell' Arte della Lana/Via Orsanmichele is the Gothic **tabernacle of Santa Maria della Tromba** (14th century).

＊ Ospedale degli Innocenti

✳ **J 6/c II**

Location: Piazza della Santissima Annunziata 12
Bus: C1, 6, 31, 32
❶ Mon – Sat 10am – 4pm, Sun 10am – 2pm (currently only the inner courtyards, loggia and Sala Grazzini are accessible), admission: €3

The 15th-century Ospedale degli Innocenti was a refuge for all mothers who could not keep their newborn children.

Renaissance   The guild of silk dealers and silk tailors commissioned Filippo
foundling   Brunelleschi in 1419 to build a foundling hospital: abandoned chil-
hospital   dren were called »innocenti« as a reminder of the children murdered

in Bethlehem. Mothers who wanted to give their children away without being seen could place them in a revolving wooden cylinder at the end of the colonnade until 1875. The Ospedale degli Innocenti marks the **beginning of Renaissance architecture in Florence**. Children are still the focal point here, with three daycare centres, societies for mothers and children in difficult situations and a research institute on the conditions of children. A museum is being established so that along with the artistic framework the historical development of children's rights can be depicted.

Loggia

The loggia with its arches supported by classical-style columns and the domes, which were constructed here for the first time, made the Ospedale famous. The superb architecture is complemented by frescoes under the arcades and in the lunettes above the doors, as well as by ten coloured **medallions portraying infants** in glazed terracotta, the work of Andrea della Robbia around 1463.

Galleria dello Ospedale degli Innocenti

In the Galleria dello Ospedale degli Innocenti on the first floor paintings and frescoes from the 14th to 18th centuries are on display. They include works by Giovanni del Biondo, Rossellino, Benedetto da Maiano and above all Domenico Ghirlandaio and Andrea del Sarto as well as the terracotta *Madonna* by Luca della Robbia. The altar panel depicting the *Adoration of the Magi* by **Ghirlandaio** is a major work. The collection of frescoes, which were removed from their original locations, includes the works of Florentine artists like Poccetti, Bicci di Lorenzo, Lorenzo Monaco, Allori, Rosselli, Ghirlandaio, Fra Bartolommeo, Perugino and della Robbia.

Palazzo Antinori

✳ H 6/a III

Location: Piazza Antinori 3
Bus: C1, C2, 6, 22, 36, 37
❶ Cantinetta: Mon – Fri 12noon – 2.30pm, 7pm – 10.30pm
www.cantinetta-antinori.com

The city palace of the Antinori family stands on the piazza of the same name; the family has been committed to the growing and selling of good wine for generations.

Winegrowers' palace

The austere, formal building was built between 1461 and 1466 in the style of Giuliano da Maiano. In a family-run **cantinetta** inside the palace wines can be sampled along with Tuscan specialties from the family estates. Don't forget to take a look at the pretty courtyard with fountain.

AROUND PALAZZO ANTINORI

San Gaetano **The most beautiful 17th-century façade** in Florence is that of the church of San Gaetano opposite; it was built in the 11th century but completely renovated in the early 17th century. Inside light figures are placed in front of dark stone, which gives the interior its special atmosphere. In the second chapel on the left is the Martyrdom of St Lawrence by Pietro da Cortona. The Cappella Antinori in the adjacent monastery has a Crucifixion by Filippo Lippi.

✳ Palazzo Medici-Riccardi

✦ H/J 6/b II

Location: Via Cavour 1
Bus: C1, 14, 23
❶ Mon, Tue, Thu – Sun 9am – 6pm, www.palazzo-medici.it, admission: €7, reservation for the Cappella dei Magi: tel. 055 2 76 03 40

The majestic stone building of the Palazzo Medici-Riccardi, diagonally opposite the church of San Lorenzo, shows the power of a wealthy patrician dynasty. At the same time in its lack of ostentation it reveals the clever modesty of the Medici before their elevation to the nobility; they were the heads of a democratic republican community in the 15th century and could not act like urban kings.

Residence of the Medici and of artists
The palace was built by Michelozzo between 1444 and about 1460 for Cosimo the Elder. Lorenzo the Magnificent, a great lover of art, hosted many young artists in the palazzo; thus Michelangelo spent his younger years here. The Medici family lived here until Cosimo I moved into the Palazzo Vecchio in 1540. In 1659 the Riccardi acquired and enlarged it, extending the front; in 1818 it passed to the Grand Duke of Tuscany. The building includes the well-known Cappella dei Magi and the Biblioteca Riccardiana. Plundering, destruction and sale decimated the collection of valuable works of art and furnishings.

Outside
The three storeys of this prototypical first Renaissance palace are strictly separated, which only emphasizes their uniqueness. In the ground floor there are »kneeling windows« – so called because of the consoles on which the windowsills rest – with over-arched triangular pediments. The round-arched windows of the first floor are divided in two. Little columns divide the windows in the second floor, too; it is topped by a roof cornice. The **Medici coat of arms** with its six spheres, the topmost one decorated with a lily, is on the south side of the building.

Walk through the arched entry into the beautiful, columned first courtyard, which is decorated along with the Medici coat of arms with twelve marble medallions, imitations of Roman cameos, above the arcades. The statue of *Orpheus* was created by Baccio Bandinelli.

Courtyard

Steps lead from the courtyard to the palace chapel, the Cappella dei Magi, in the first floor, which was built to plans by Michelozzo. **Benozzo Gozzoli** decorated the walls of the chapel with a cycle of frescoes that is one of his main works: **T**he Procession of the Magi to Bethlehem (1459/1460). Gozzoli included two historic events in Florence in the fresco: the magnificent council of 1439 on the unification of the eastern and western church and the visit of Pope Pius II, the great humanist Aeneas Silvius Piccolomini, in 1459 accompanied by the Duke of Milan. The artists depicted some of the people who took part in these events: Patriarch Joseph of Constantinople (the oldest), the Byzantine emperor John VII and Lorenzo de' Medici as a boy are the kings. The well-preserved frescoes with fine colours give an impression of how the Florentine ruling class thought of Renaissance art. The altar painting is a copy of a famous painting of the Birth of Jesus by Filippo Lippi; the original is in the Gemäldegalerie in Berlin.

Capella dei Magi

AROUND THE PALAZZO MEDICI-RICCARDI

Florence's patron saint, John the Baptist, stands next to St John the Evangelist. The architect **Ammanati** began the building of the church

San Giovanni degli Scolopi

Orpheus watches over the inner courtyard of Palazzo Medici-Riccardi and the adjacent college opposite the Palazzo Medici for the Jesuit order in 1579 in his honour. The church was completed by **Alfonso Parigi the Younger** (1661). When the Jesuits were driven out of Florence in 1773, the church was turned over to the Piarists (Padri Scolopi). The interior is decorated with frescoes.

** **Palazzo Pitti**

✳ H 7

Location: Piazza Pitti
Bus: C3, D, 11, 36, 37
❶ Tue – Sun 8.15am – 6.50pm, www.polomuseale.firenze.it, admission: €8,50, with exhibits €13

Palazzo Pitti was once the setting of the court of the grand dukes; today its valuable furnishings, especially the large collection of famous paintings, is open to the public. The palace also holds the Appartamenti Reali of the first kings of Italy.

The palace is striking for its size (32,000 sq m/345,000 sq ft in area; 205m/660ft long), its imposing exterior and its location on the expansive square of the same name. The Pitti were a respected and wealthy Florentine merchant family. For this reason Luca Pitti (after 1447) planned a magnificent city palace on the southern bank of the Arno, a short distance upstream of the city.

The architect **Luca Fancelli** carried out the first phase of the construction (1457–66), possibly to plans by Brunelleschi. Between 1558 and 1570 Eleonora of Toledo, the wife of Cosimo I, had the palazzo completely renovated by Bartolomeo Ammanati after acquiring it in 1549: It was enlarged considerably. To decorate the rooms the new Medici owners, especially Cosimo II, bought valuable paintings that later formed the basis of the Galleria Palatina. Ancient and contemporary statuary was added in time.

Palazzo Pitti was the residence of the Italian kings from 1864 to 1871 when Italy was not yet completely unified and Florence was the capital. In 1919 King Vittorio Emanuele III gave it to the state, which then expanded the museums.

The front of the palace with its massive stone blocks, high-arched windows and stepped storeys as well as the courtyard, which was built in Mannerist style between 1558 and 1558 by **Bartolomeo Ammanati** and looks like a grotto conceived by a »rustic« imagination, are great architectural achievements. Beyond a terrace with fountains and statues lies the ▶Giardino di Boboli. While Ammanati kept the three storeys on the courtyard side with their classical arrangement of columns (Doric, Ionian, Corinthian), he broke up the vertical structure of columns again by means of horizontal layers of stones that varied over three levels; in this way he re-incorporated the protruding columns into the walls.

** GALLERIA PALATINA

From the inner courtyard of the palace there is an entrance on the right to the stairs leading to the Galleria Palatina in the first floor. The pictures in the gallery are arranged not chronologically but on decorative criteria in order to adorn the rooms with their valuable furnishings. The rooms are named after themes or the artists displayed. The paintings of Raphael, Andrea del Sarto, Titian, Tintoretto and Rubens are especially worth seeing.

Collection

From the steps walk through the vestibule to the Sala delle Statue, a room with ancient sculptures where this tour begins. The order of the rooms described corresponds to the numbering on the plan. The first room is named after the **artist Giuseppe Castagnoli**, who did the ceiling painting after 1815. Two colossal marble statues from the Villa Medici in Rome adorn the walls. The valuable **Table of the Muses** with lapis lazuli in the middle of the room was made between 1800 and 1855 in the Opificio delle Pietre Dure and is decorated with plant and figure motifs using semiprecious stones.

Sala Castagnoli

The series of rooms beginning with the Sala delle Allegorie, the Quartiere del Volterrano, was the winter apartment of the grand duchess in the Medici period. Only the decorations from the first room come from the time of Medici rule; the other rooms were renovated after 1815. Grand Duchess Vittoria della Rovere commissioned the artist Volterrano (1611 – 1689) to fresco the Room of the Allegories. The sculpture *Michelangelo as a Child* (1861) by Emilio Zocchi shows the myth of the brilliant artist who chiselled a faun out of marble at an early age.

Sala delle Allegorie

The Music Room takes its named from the concerts that take place here and the furnishings, which were inspired by musical instruments. The painted frieze, made to look like a relief, is worthy of note.

Sala della Musica

Almost all of the tondi (round pictures) of the Galleria Palatina can be admired in the Sala di Prometeo (Prometheus Room). Like the other paintings in this room they are works of the 15th and 16th century. Filippo Lippi, Sandro Botticelli, Ridolfo del Ghirlandaio and Guido Reni are represented here. The *Madonna painting* (around 1450), the largest and the only tondo by **Lippi**, unites various themes in a medieval manner: *Madonna with Child*, scenes from the *Life of*

Sala di Prometeo

St Anne and the *Birth of the Virgin*. The room is named after the ceiling painting, which depicts Prometheus, who brought fire to mankind. The vase decorated with colourful bouquets of flowers and gilded bronze comes from the Sèvres porcelain manufacture.

Sala della Giustizia The hall of justice displays Venetian painting of the 16th century including **Titian's** **Portrait of Tommaso Mosti*, a member of the court of Urbino (1520–around 1530). The exact depiction of the face and the fur-lined jacket are typical of the artist's skill.

Sala di Ulisse The ceiling of the Sala di Ulisse (Ulysses Room) is decorated with the return of Ulysses, a reference to the return of Ferdinand III of Lorraine to Florence (1815). The showpiece, however, is Raphael's **Madonna dell' Impannata* (around 1514), named after the drapery material at the window. The painting has a complicated arrangement of figures.

Palazzo Pitti

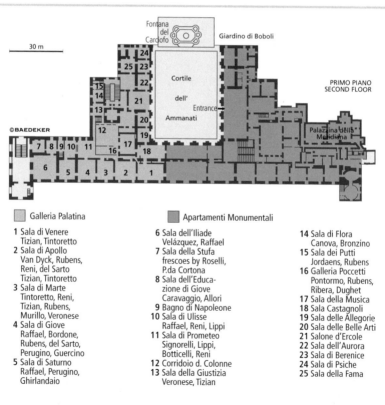

Galleria Palatina

1 Sala di Venere
Tizian, Tintoretto
2 Sala di Apollo
Van Dyck, Rubens,
Reni, del Sarto
Tizian, Tintoretto
3 Sala di Marte
Tintoretto, Reni,
Tizian, Rubens,
Murillo, Veronese
4 Sala di Giove
Raffael, Bordone,
Rubens, del Sarto,
Perugino, Guercino
5 Sala di Saturno
Raffael, Perugino,
Ghirlandaio

Apartamenti Monumentali

6 Sala dell'Iliade
Velázquez, Raffael
7 Sala della Stufa
frescoes by Roselli,
P.da Cortona
8 Sala dell'Educa-
zione di Giove
Caravaggio, Allori
9 Bagno di Napoleone
10 Sala di Ulisse
Raffael, Reni, Lippi
11 Sala di Prometeo
Signorelli, Lippi,
Botticelli, Reni
12 Corridoio d. Colonne
13 Sala della Giustizia
Veronese, Tizian

14 Sala di Flora
Canova, Bronzino
15 Sala dei Putti
Jordaens, Rubens
16 Galleria Poccetti
Pontormo, Rubens,
Ribera, Dughet
17 Sala della Musica
18 Sala Castagnoli
19 Sala delle Allegorie
20 Sala delle Belle Arti
21 Salone d'Ercole
22 Sala dell'Aurora
23 Sala di Berenice
24 Sala di Psiche
25 Sala della Fama

The »Room of the Education of Jupiter« was Napoleon's bedroom. **Caravaggio's** *Sleeping Amor* shows his extreme realism: he used a dead child as a model so that the mythological figure would not be idealized but rather depict a child's body realistically.

Sala dell' Educazione di Giove

The small Sala della Stufa (stove room) was first decorated in 1627 by the Florentine artist Matteo Rosselli. The paintings for this room are by **Pietro Cortona** (1637 and 1640–41). The subjects are the *Four Ages of Mankind*: gold, silver, copper and iron. The other rooms were heated from this room.

Sala della Stufa

The Iliad Room was only redecorated between 1819 and 1825, and its present furnishings are not 17th century. Luigi Sabatelli did the ceiling painting on the subject of Olympus and the lunettes with scenes from Homer's Iliad. Two large-scale pictures by Andrea del Sarto from 1526 and 1530, both of which glorify the *Assumption of the Virgin* into heaven, hang opposite each other and can be compared directly. The portrait *La Gravida (Pregnant Woman;* around 1507) by Raphael and the Baroque *Portrait of Count Waldemar Christian* (around 1660) by **Justus Sustermans**, the Medici court painter, are also worth seeing.

Sala dell' Iliade

The ceiling fresco (1662 – 1665) in the Saturn Room by Ciro Ferri depicts the duke as Hercules going up to Olympus. The *Madonna del Granduca* (around 1506) by **Raphael** is impressive in its simplicity and intimacy. The *Madonna della Seggiola* (c 1516), showing the Virgin and child with the young John the Baptist, is the only Madonna by Raphael in tondo form. The form gives the portrait a sense of density and monumentality. The portraits of *Agnolo and Maddalena Doni* (both 1505/1506) are also by Raphael. The influence of Leonardo da Vinci's *Mona Lisa* is recognizable, especially in the pose. The artist's preference for detail is clear in both portraits. The Doni were art collectors and patrons and also valued Michelangelo.

Sala di Saturno

The Jupiter Room (1642–44) is also decorated with ceiling paintings by Pietro da Cortona. The ceiling painting refers to the fact that the room served as throne room. The most important works in this room include the famous *The Young John the Baptist* (c 1525) by **Andrea del Sarto**. The three-dimensional figure is remarkable and is only intensified by the red coat. The *Pietà* (c 1511–12) by **Fra Bartolomeo** is one of the most significant paintings of the early 16th century; it impresses with its detailed depiction, depth and intense colours. The *Three Ages of Mankind*, which is attributed to Giorgione, has a singing lesson as its subject. The *Lady with a Veil (La Velata)*, one of **Raphael**'s most beautiful portraits of a woman, was made around 1516.

Sala di Giove

The ceiling painting (1644–46) in the Mars Room is by Pietro da Cor-   **Sala di Marte**
tona and shows the Medici coat of arms surrounded by allegorical
scenes of war and peace. **Rubens**' large-scale masterpiece *The Consequences of War* (1637–38) corresponds to the subject of the ceiling
painting. It depicts how Venus tries in vain to keep Mars from going to
war. Rubens created the work under the impression of the Thirty Years'
War. ****The Four Philosophers** (1611–12) by Rubens is a masterpiece of
portraiture; the artist painted himself on the left. He painted it in memory of his dead brother Philip and his brother's philosophy teacher,
Justus Lipsius; the man on the right is another student. The tulips near
the bust of Seneca symbolize the blossoming of life.

The *Portrait of Ippolito de' Medici* (1533) was painted by **Titian** in
memory of the cardinal's heroic deeds of war when Vienna was under
siege by the Turks. The colours and the facial expressions show the
cleric's warlike aspects. In the *Portrait of Cardinal Bentivoglio* (c 1625)
van Dyck glorifies the papal legate to the Netherlands with the red colour of the cardinal, noble facial features and fine hands. In the *Portrait
of Alvise Cornaro* (c 1560–1665) **Tintoretto** makes not only the rank
of his subject clear but also his human side.

Pietro da Cortona was also responsible for the frescoes of the Apollo   **Sala di Apollo**
Room, which he began in 1646 and which his pupil Ciro Ferri com-
pleted. Of the 16th and 17th-century works, the following deserve
mention: *St Maria Magdalena* and *Portrait of a Man* (c 1535), both by
Titian. The former painting, which was made around 1535 for the
Duke of Urbino, shows the typical Titian red in the saint's hair. In
Portrait of a Man the painter emphasizes the high status of the subject
in the proud look, the black clothing and the heavy gold chain. The
Pietà (*Pietà di Luco*) was painted by **Andrea del Sarto** in 1523/1524
for the high altar of the church of Mugello. The iridescent colours of
the painting already point to Mannerism. *Cleopatra* (1638–39) in a
passionate pose and lighting is thought to be a late work of **Guido
Reni**.

The ceiling frescoes, painted by Pietro da Cortona around 1641/1642,   **Sala di
Venere**
show the duke in the centre with Minerva taking him away from Ve-
nus in order to lead him to the arts. The oval stucco medallions depict
the Medici popes and dukes. In the centre of the room is the **Italic
Venus* by **Antonio Canova**, which Napoleon commissioned in 1810.
The sculptor revealed his mastery of the art of working marble in the
treatment of the surface of the body and the robe. In the paintings
Return of the Farmers from the Fields (c 1640) and *Odysseus on the
Island of Feaci* **Rubens** emphasizes the more cheerful side of nature.
Salvatore Rosa achieved a grand depiction of landscape in the **Sea**

Paintings cover the walls of ornate rooms

at Sunset (c 1645), where the setting sun gives the scenery a wonderful atmosphere. Three **portraits show the development of the Venetian **Titian**: *The Concert* (1510–12) as an unusual genre picture, *Portrait of a Noblewoman* (c 1536) and *Portrait of Pietro Aretino* (1545) with insightful portrayals of people.

OTHER MUSEUMS

*Apparta- menti Reali

In addition to the art collections in the Galleria Palatina, the Palazzo Pitti houses the Appartamenti Reali (royal apartments), where Vittorio Emanuele II, Umberto I, Queen Margherita and Vittorio Emanuele III lived. The stately rooms – notice the frescoes and stucco work here as well – are furnished with precious furniture, paintings, statues, tapestries and utensils, mostly from the 19th century; some rooms also have Florentine Baroque furniture.

The Galleria d' Arte Moderna

The **Galleria d' Arte Moderna** (▶ill. p. 64) is on the second floor of the Palazzo Pitti. It was established around 1860 and works from public galleries and donations have been added regularly. It gives an impressive overview of **19th and 20th-century Tuscan art** as well as other Italian schools; there are also examples of sculpture from this period. Part of the collection is dedicated to the Macchiaioli (»dabbers«). The members of this Tuscan school – including Giovanni Faltori, Silvestro Lega, Telemaco Signorini – got their names from their anti-academic use of the brush. Other Italian painters are also represented, among them Severini, Soffici, De Chirico and Morandi.

Museo degli Argenti

On the ground floor of the Palazzo Pitti (enter from the inner courtyard, on the left) is the **Silver Room**. Along with silver and gold objects, gems, jewellery, ivory and amber objects as well as painted glass and porcelain are on display. The museum was founded after the First World War and is based on the silver collection of the house of Medici; other exhibits are from the Uffizi Gallery, the Bargello Museum as well as the collections of the prince bishops of Salzburg and the Italian kings. The collection includes 17th and 18th-century jewellery boxes and reliquaries, vases, crystal objects, tapestries, 16th and 17th-century amber and ivory work, the Medici jewellery collection, cups, gold tableware as well as silver cups and bowls.

❶ Jan, Feb, Nov, Dec daily 8.15am – 4.30pm; March daily 8.15am – 5.30pm; Apr, May, Sep., Oct daily 8.15am – 6.30pm; June, July, Aug daily 8.15am – 6.50, admission: €7, www.polomuseale.firenze.it

Inside the Appartamenti Reali

Museo delle Carrozze The carriage museum is in the right wing of the ground floor of Palazzo Pitti. State carriages, chaises and wagons of all kinds that were used in the 18th and 19th century by the grand dukes and kings are on display.

❶ Currently closed for renovation

AROUND PALAZZO PITTI

Giardino di Boboli ▶p.206

Museo Zoologico La Specola Palazzo Torrigiani (Via Romana 17) now holds a zoological museum; it is also called »La Specola«, the observatory, because Grand Duke Pietro Leopoldo built an astronomical and meteorological observatory here in 1775. It was already opened for visitors in 1775, which makes it the oldest the oldest science museum in Europe. The museum has an enormous amount of animal exhibits. Of special interest here is the collection of wax anatomical models.

Insider Tip

❶ June – Sep. Tue – Sun 10.30am – 5.30pm, Oct – May Tue – Sun 9.30am – 4.30pm, some of the rooms are currently closed for renovation, www.msn. unifi.it, admission: €6

San Felice The history of the church of San Felice, opposite Palazzo Pitti, goes back far into the Middle Ages (1066). The façade, a classic example of simple but effective Renaissance architecture, was made around 1450. Works by the Giotto school (*Crucifixion*), the Filippino Lippi school (triptych), Ridolfo Ghirlandaio (*Madonna with Child*), Neri di Bicci (triptych) and a terracotta group from the school of Giovanni della Robbia adorn the church.

✱ Palazzo Rucellai

✦ **H 6/a III**

Location: Via della Vigna Nuova 18
Bus: C3, D

❶ Tours on appt., tel. 055 2 64 59 10, www.palazzorucellai.org.

Bernardo Rossellino built the palace from 1446 to 1451 to plans by Leon Battista Alberti; it is one of the most beautiful Renaissance houses in Florence. Giovanni di Paolo Rucellai, a wealthy merchant who achieved wealth and fame in the 15th century, commissioned it.

Palace of a wealthy merchant Architect and artist, Alberti and Bernardo Rossellino, were given a free hand in the work; the wealthy merchant was happy to foot the bill. The result was a palazzo that has a clear conception and generous execution in the exact design of the façade with pilasters and storeys that diminish in size higher up, windows with varying shapes and exactly cut stones – a milestone in the architectural history of the Renaissance. Above the windows of the first floor there is a frieze with wind-filled sails in stone, the trademark of the Rucellai. The Rucellai family still lives in the palace; it also houses an American college.

AROUND PALAZZO RUCELLAI

Palazzo Corsini (Lungarno Corsini 10) is a little south of Palazzo Rucellai on the Arno. It is incomplete; the left part, which would be in symmetry with the right, was not built. The palace is still owned by the Corsini family and was built by Pier Francesco Silvani and Antonio Ferri from 1648 to 1656 with Baroque elements.
Palazzo Corsini

Palazzo Corsini also holds the **Galleria Corsini** with the finest private collection in Florence; it was established in 1765 by Lorenzo Corsini, a nephew of Pope Clement XII. Beautiful examples of Italian and other 17th-century schools and Florentine 15th and 16th-century painting can be seen, including works by Raphael.
Currently closed, www.palazzocorsini.it

Ponte alla Carraia (not far to the west of Palazzo Corsini), the oldest Arno crossing after Ponte Vecchio, collapsed several times and had to be rebuilt: for example in 1304, after too many spectators went onto the bridge to watch a water show on the Arno, and after floods. The architect **Bartolomeo Ammanati** gave it its present form with five arches in 1559. Ponte alla Carraia was blown up during the Second World War by German troops, but it was rebuilt in a style that resembles the original.
Ponte alla Carraia

⋆ Palazzo Strozzi

✳ H 6/a/III

Location: Piazza Strozzi
Bus: C1, 6, 22, 36, 37
❶ Mon – Wed, Fri – Sun 9am – 6pm, Thu until 11am, admission: €10, www.palazzostrozzi.org

The residence of the powerful Strozzi family is one of the most beautiful Florentine Renaissance palaces and bears witness to their self-confidence.

The Strozzi considered themselves to be the equals of the Medici in the 15th century. However, in order not to challenge the influential
»Mighty« palace

Lorenzo de' Medici, the Magnificent with a building that would overshadow the Palazzo Medici-Riccardi in magnificence, the wealthy merchant Filippo Strozzi planned a residence for his family that would stand out for its careful execution rather than for its size and splendour. Palazzo Strozzi was built between 1489 and 1536. In the year of completion Cosimo I confiscated it; it was given back to the Strozzi family only in 1568. Today Palazzo Strozzi houses cultural institutes. The architects Benedetto **da Maiano** and – after his death – **Cronaca** united the achievements of Renaissance architecture through a classical, beautiful design both overall and in the details, with perfect execution of all architectural elements. The effect of the façade derives from the balanced division of the storeys, the entrance, the windows and the concluding cornice as well as the exact working of the stones, which have a flatter rustication higher up and remain in regular horizontal rows. The ironwork – rings for tying up horses in the walls, torch holders and corner lanterns – were made around 1500 by Niccolò Grosso, a famous smith known as »il Caparra« (»the advance«) because he refused to give credit to his customers. The elegant courtyard by Cronaca is worth noting.

In the **Galleria Strozzina** on the ground floor and first floor, worthwhile modern art exhibitions are held. There is also a chic café. Moreover, a small **museum** in the basement relates the history of the construction of the palazzo; a wooden model of the palace by da Maiano is on display here.

Palazzo dello Strozzino

The junior branch of the Strozzi family had a townhouse built by Michelozzo in 1458, before Palazzo Strozzi was built; it was completed by Giuliano da Maiano from 1462 to 1465.

✷✷ Palazzo Vecchio

✧ J 7/b IV

Location: Piazza della Signoria
Bus: C1, C2
❶ April – Sep Mon – Wed, Fri – Sun 9am – 12midnight, Thu 9am – 2pm,
Oct – March 9am – 7pm, tower: 10am – 5pm, Thu 9am – 2pm,
Admission museum: €6.50 with tower €10

The austerity and beauty of the city, the pride and the down-to-earth character of the Florentine people are uniquely embodied in Palazzo Vecchio, the seat of the city government. The massive fortified structure from the Gothic period was built at the beginning of Florence's rise to power and greatness and has remained a symbol of its time of prosperity.

Palazzo Vecchio

SECOND FLOOR
Quartiere degli Elementi
1 Sala degli Elementi
2 Camera di Cerere
3 Camera di Opi
4 Camera di Giove
5 Camera di Ercole
6 Loggiato di Saturno

Quartiere di Elenora
7 Sala Verde
8 Cappella di Eleonora
9 Sala delle Sabine
10 Sala di Ester
11 Sala di Penelope
12 Sala di Gualdrada
13 Cappella dei Priori
14 Sala dell' Udienza
15 Sala degli Gigli
16 Cancelleria
17 Sala delle
 Carta Geografiche
18 Salotta

FIRST FLOOR

FIRST FLOOR
1 Salone dei Cinquecento
2 Studiolo di Francesco I

Quartiere di Leone X
3 Sala di Leone X
4 Sala di Cosimo il Vecchio
5 Sala di Lorenzo il Magnificio
6 Sala di Cosimo I
7 Sala di Giovanni delle
 Bande Nere
8 Cappella di Leone X
9 Sala di Clemente VII
10 Sala dei Dugento

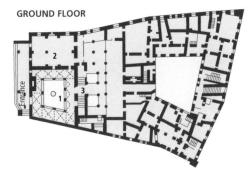

GROUND FLOOR
1 Primo Cortile
 (courtyard)
2 Camera dell' Arme
3 Stairs by Vasari

As an expression of the citizens' victory over the nobility, the seat of communal government and largest Medieval secular building represents Florence's self-confidence from the 14th to the 16th century; the daring, 94m/280ft-high tower with a clock (1353) and the rooms demonstrate farsightedness and show the citizens of Florence's love of art. The beginning of construction in 1299 is attributed to the famous **Arnolfo di Cambio**. The fortified Gothic central structure with the tower were finished in 1314. Awas afterwards several patrons and architects – including Michelozzo – continued the building, expansion and reconstruction: the palace was first the seat of the priori and the gonfaloniere, i.e. of the magistracy of the republic, the Signoria. It got its other names Palazzo del Popolo and del Comune from Florence's republican and democratic character when the citizens tried to resist various efforts by the Medici to establish ducal rule; they only succeeded in 1530. Cosimo I, Duke and later Grand Duke of Tuscany, occupied the city's main palace in 1540, which was then called the Palazzo Ducale. But the duke soon moved to the Palazzo Pitti, after which the name Palazzo Vecchio (old palace) came into use. Between 1865 and 1872, the period of Italian unification, it was the temporary seat of government, the chamber of the members of parliament and the foreign ministry. Then the city government moved in and the state rooms were opened to the public as museums.

Symbol of Florentine self-confidence

To the left of the main entrance is a copy of the Marzocco lion by Donatello with the coat of arms of Florence between its paws; next to it is a copy of the bronze statue Judith and Holofernes by Donatello (the original is in the Sala dei Gigli). To the right is a copy of the statue of David by Michelangelo (original in the Galleria dell' Accademia) as well as a marble group of Hercules and Cacus by Bandinelli (1533). On the upper part of the façade are frescoes with the coat of arms of Florence.

Outside

The first courtyard, the **Primo Cortile**, was redesigned in 1470 by Michelozzo, who added the magnificent columns. A graceful fountain stands in the centre with a putto and a water-spouting dolphin on top (around 1475; original by Verrocchio on the second floor). The 18 large **city panoramas** on the upper parts of the wall were painted for the wedding of Francesco de Medici and Johanna of Austria (1565). The marble group Samson and the Philistines by Perino da Vinci is in a niche in the corner. The **Camera dell' Arme** (Weapons Room) is interesting insofar as it is the only 14th-century room in the palace. It is used for exhibitions today.
In the second courtyard, the Cortile della Dogana, is the ticket office and the large staircase by Vasari (1560–1563) that leads to the first floor.

Ground floor

Palazzo Vecchio is the symbol of the city-republic's self-confidence

First floor

The giant **Salone dei Cinquecento** (Hall of the Five Hundred) – 54m/167ft long, 22m/72ft wide and 18m/59ft high – is the work of Simone del Pollaiolo, called Cronaca (1495). The walls were supposed to be decorated by two famous paintings, Michelangelo's *Battle of Cascina* and Leonardo's *Battle of Angari*. The current subjects of the wall paintings by Giorgio Vasari are the wars against Pisa (wall above the stairs) and Siena (wall opposite the stairs). The carved ceiling has 39 richly decorated fields with allegorical depictions and scenes of the history of Florence and the Medici.

In the part of the Salone called the **Udienza** (Audience Hall; left side), which was used for receptions and ceremonies, **statues of the Medici** stand in the niches: Cosimo I, Pope Leo X, Giovanni delle Bande Nere, Alessandro, Pope Clement VII crowning Emperor Charles V, and Francesco I, all by Bandinelli, De' Rossi and Caccini. Opposite is the famous marble statue *Genio della Vittoria (Genius of Victory*, after 1516) by Michelangelo; according to the most recent research, its purpose is not clear. It shows the artist's confident mastery in working the marble and his powers of expression in the beauty and complicated motion of the bodies. Side niches next to it contain Roman statuary: Ganymede, Mercury, Apollo and Bacchus. Paintings, frescoes, statues (figures of Hercules by Vincenzo de' Rossi) and wall paintings complete the room's decoration. The **Studiolo of Francesco I de' Medici** was designed by Vasari in 1570 – 1575 and is extravagantly decorated with paintings, frescoes and statues. Famous painters (Allori, Naldini) and sculptors (Giambologna) worked on this Florentine Mannerist »treasure chest«.

The Salone dei Cinquecento (on the side opposite the entrance, on the right) leads to the **Quartiere di Leone X** (Quarters of Leo X). The rooms in this complex, named after Giovanni de' Medici, the later Pope Leo X, are dedicated to other famous members of the Medici family: Cosimo the Elder, Lorenzo the Magnificent, Cosimo I, Giovanni delle Bande Nere and Pope Clement VII. Many of the paintings are by **Vasari** and his workshop, and often depict scenes from the life of the Medici.

Second floor

The **Quartiere degli Elementi** (Rooms of the Elements), which were painted by Vasari and his pupil Gherardi from 1556 to 1566, consist of the following chambers: the **Room of the Elements**, with allegorical depictions of fire, water, air and earth in Mannerist style; the Terrazzo di Saturno with a beautiful view of Florence; and the rooms of Ceres, the goddess of fertility, Ops, the goddess of opulence, Jupiter, Hercules with scenes from his life, and a small study. The **Quartiere di Eleonora di Toledo** are named after Duchess Eleonora of Toledo, Cosimo I's first wife, who died prematurely. Masterpieces of painting

Michelangelo's *Genius of Victory*

by Agnolo Bronzino (1503 – 1572) can be seen in the **Cappella di Eleonora**. The ceiling paintings of the **Sala delle Sabine** show the Sabine women mediating in a quarrel between their Roman husbands and their Sabine relatives. In the **Sala di Esther** the story of the virtuous Esther from the Bible is depicted, and in the **Sala di Penelope** the myth of Odysseus. The **Sala di Gualdrada** is dedicated to a beautiful woman from Florence who refused to give Emperor Otto IV a welcoming kiss because only her husband was allowed to do this, as the bedroom ceiling fresco shows. In the **Cappella dei Priori** (1511 – 1514) there is a large fresco by Ridolfo Ghirlandaio. The magnificent **Sala dell' Udienza** (Audience Hall) has a richly carved ceiling by Giuliano da Maiano and decorative frescoes by Francesco Salviati. The **Sala dei Gigli** (Room of the Lilies) is decorated with a fresco with the episcopal patron saint of the city, St Zenobius (1481- 1484) by Ghirlandaio. It also holds the famous bronze group *Judith and Holofernes* (1455–60) by Donatello; a copy was placed in its original location at the main entrance of the Palazzo Vecchio.

In the **Cancelleria** (Chambers) of the secretary of the republic there is a bust of Niccolò Machiavelli, who worked there, and the original of the *Genius with Dolphin* by Verrocchio (copy in the courtyard). The **Sala delle Carte Geografiche**, the cloakroom, is decorated with beautiful wooden cabinets that are adorned with paintings of historic maps (1563 – 1575). The globe on display here is the **largest of its time**.

Mezzanine The tour of the palace ends with the Quartiere del Mezzanino. Michelozzo created the mezzanine by lowering ceilings; works from the **Collezione Loeser**, pictures and sculptures by Tuscan artists from the 14th and 16th centuries, are on display. The American collector Alexander Loeser bequeathed the collection to the city on the event of his death.

Piazza del Duomo

————————————— ✳ **J 6/b III**

Location: Centre
Bus: C1, C2, 14, 23

The Piazza del Duomo, the cathedral square, with the cathedral and the campanile by Giotto (▶Duomo Santa Maria del Fiore) is the spiritual centre and focal point of tourism in the city (▶Duomo Santa Maria del Fiore).

Centre of art   The cathedral square, which merges with Piazza San Giovanni in the
history west, is bordered by several grand buildings: Palazzo della Misericor-

Piazza del Duomo is the spiritual centre of Florence

dia and Palazzo dei Canonici, Palazzo Guadagni and Palazzo Niccolini.

The »Arch-brotherhood of Mercy«, which has its seat next to the cathedral, is the **oldest brotherhood of Florentine citizens for social
and charitable purposes**. It is said to have been founded in 1326,
when the plague was ravaging Florence. Michelangelo once belonged
to the arciconfraternità, whose members used to wear red and now
wear black hoods. Among their duties was to accompany those condemned to death to their execution. Today the brotherhood has a
modern ambulance service as well as an emergency medical station.
The members of the brotherhood, which is supported by donations,
all work as volunteers.

**Arciconfrater-
nità
Misericordia**

Piazza San Giovanni

Piazza San Giovanni got its present size only when the archiepiscopal palace was set back 50m/165ft because of the traffic. The Baptistery (▶Battistero San Giovanni) stands in the middle of the square. The column of St Zenobius, which was erected here in 1384, commemorates the fact that a dead elm tree that was supposed to have stood on this spot began to sprout again in 429 when relics of the saint were transferred from San Lorenzo to Santa Reparata, the predecessor of the cathedral.

The south side of the square is occupied by the **Loggia del Bigallo**, a typical late Gothic construction, which was commissioned by the Society of the Merciful Brothers (Compagnia della Misericordia) in order to »display« abandoned children for adoption. The marble loggia and the palace that it belongs to were built from 1353 to 1358. In 1445 Ventura di Moro and Rossello di Jacopo Franchi painted frescoes on the sections below the double arch with scenes from the life of the martyr St Peter; today there are only copies here. Some of the originals are in the **museum** inside the palace, which also has 14th and 15th-century Florentine art on display. A remarkable picture of the Madonna della Misericordia (1342) shows one of the first views of Florence with the as yet incomplete cathedral.

The **Palazzo Arcivescovile**, archiepiscopal palace, on the west side of the square was built between 1573 and 1584 by Giovanni Antonio Dosio for Cardinal Alessandro Medici, the later Pope Leo XI; but completed only around 1735 by Ciurini. This long building period

Piazza del Duomo

1 Porta del Paradiso	A Portale Maggiore	F Santa Reparata
2 North portal	B Porta dei Cornacchini	(crypt)
(entrance)	C Porta della Mandorla	G Old Sacristy
3 South portal	D Porta del Campanile	H New Sacristy
4 Main altar	E Porta dei Canonici	

produced a mixture of medieval and »modern« building elements. In 1895 the whole palace was moved back 50m/165ft in order to make room for the increasing traffic in the city.

Loggia del Bigallo, Museum: Mon 9am – 12noon, 3pm – 5pm; closed July, Aug.

Piazza della Repubblica

✳ H 6/b III

Location: Centre
Bus: C1, C2

The many elegant cafés on the Piazza della Repubblica are in themselves a reason why almost every visitor to Florence comes to this large square in the centre of the city.

The ancient Roman forum was once located here; until 1888 it was used as the Mercato Vecchio (old market). Then the market stalls were torn down and the Loggia del Pesce was rebuilt elsewhere. A monumental triumphal arch, the so-called Arconte (1895), and a series of administrative palaces were built in their place. The statue *Abbondanza* (Abundance) towers over the piazza on a tall column. It is a copy. The original *Abbondanza* by Donatello was the first secular statue to be erected on a public square since ancient times.

Café district

! **Lots of tradition ...**

Insider Tip

MARCO ⊕ POLO TIP

... and the charm of the Belle Epoque are among the attractions of Café Gilli (▶ill. p.80) on Piazza della Repubblica, which is known for its excellent biscuits and candied chestnuts, which customers can enjoy on a terrace with a view of the square.

✳ Piazza della Santissima Annunziata

✳ J 6/c II

Location: Centre
Bus: C1

Piazza della Santissima Annunziata owes its charm to the arcades that border it and the harmony of the surrounding buildings.

The church of ▶Santissima Annunziata on the north side of the square has a columned portico, which is continued in the ▶Os-

Architectural complete work of art

pedale degli Innocenti, a work of Brunelleschi, and ends in the corresponding colonnades of the Confraternità dei Servi di Maria by Antonio da Sangallo and Baccio d' Agnolo. The **Palazzo Riccardi-Manelli** by Ammanati is part of this ensemble. Immediately to the left next to the columned arcade of the Ospedale is the entrance to the ►Museo Archeologico Nazionale im Palazzo della Crocetta (17th cent.). The **equestrian statue of Grand Duke Ferdinand I** by Giambologna, which was completed in 1608 by his pupil Pietro Tacca from Carrara, stands in the centre. The two bronze fountains with mythical creatures (1629) are also by the sculptor and architect Tacca.

Palazzo Budini Gattai The imposing three-storey Palazzo Budini Gattai (formerly Palazzo Grifoni) with its beautiful, dignified façade dominates the square from opposite the church Santissima Annunziata. Ugolino Grifoni, a wealthy official, commissioned **architect Bartolomeo Ammanati** to build a new palace on the site of some old houses, a task that the architect performed skilfully from 1557 to 1563. The combination of red brick and the dominant grey stone is especially effective. The palazzo is still owned by the family and housed the regional government of Tuscany until the late 20th century; it is now used for conventions and events.

★ Piazza della Signoria

✦ H/J 7/b III/IV

Location: Centre
Bus: C1, C2

Piazza della Signoria has been the political centre of the city since the 14th century. The impressive square has crowd-pulling attractions: the ►Palazzo Vecchio, which serves as the city hall; the Palazzo degli Uffizi (►Galleria degli Uffizi) with its world-famous art gallery; and the ►Loggia dei Lanzi with statues by Michelangelo and Donatello.

Heart of the city (►MARCO POLO Insight p. 258) Piazza della Signoria was less attractive in the 1980s. Archaeologists had found unimagined treasures when excavating below street-level: Etruscan, Roman and medieval remains, and even finds from the Bronze Age were discovered. However, the people of Florence did not want their most beautiful square to be marred by an everlasting construction site or by archaeological digs. So, bowing to public pressure, the excavations were filled in again in 1989. Then there were vigorous differences on how the square should be paved. Even though most of Florence wanted red terracotta to be used, as it was from the 14th to the 18th century, the city government decided to use the sandstone slabs that had been in place before the excavations. When this did not work out some of those responsible were prosecuted and sentenced to heavy fines.

Two special monuments are located here: a slab of granite in the pavement not far from the Fountain of Neptune commemorates the burning of Savonarola at the stake in 1418 at the orders of Pope Alexander VI, after the theocracy of this Dominican prior failed in Florence. Next to the fountain is an equestrian statue of Cosimo I de' Medici (1594) – for the first time on an open square in Europe – created by Giambologna, commemorating Cosimo's elevation to Grand Duke of Tuscany by Pope Pius V in 1569.

Monuments

The Fontana del Nettuno, the Fountain of Neptune, dominates the square. The intention was to decorate Piazza della Signoria with a magnificent work of art for the wedding of Francesco de' Medici with Princess Johanna of Austria (1565), as this wedding made the Medici into one of the great ruling houses of Europe. A fountain that was already under construction to the left of the entrance to the Palazzo Vecchio had to be completed in a hurry. For the occasion Bartolomeo Ammanati created the largest fountain in Florence from 1563 to 1575, with four seahorses, three tritons and a colossal Neptune brandishing a trident.

Fontana del Nettuno

The Loggia dei Lanzi next to Palazzo Vecchio, one of the most beautiful examples of Florentine Gothic architecture, got its name from the »Lanzichenecchi« – as the Swiss *landsknecht* soldiers were called in Italy – because they served as guards here. It was built from 1376 to 1382 under the direction of **Benci di Cione** and **Simone di Francesco Talenti**. Its dimensions were exactly coordinated with those of the Palazzo Vecchio. The arcaded hall was used in the republic for official ceremonies: ambassadors and rulers were received here; priori and gonfalonieri were inaugurated into office. When the republic was dissolved, the loggia lost its political function and only served decorative purposes. After being restored in the past century it resumed its official function for festivities.
Outside, above the arches, panels (1384 – 1389) show allegorical figures of the cardinal and theological virtues, which were made by various artists to designs by Agnolo Gaddi. In the hall there are important sculptures: to the right and left of the entrance **two lions**, one from the Greek classical period, the other a copy of the original by Flaminio of 16th-century originals by Vacca. Walking through the building clockwise, the first work is the bronze statue of *Perseus* (1545 – 1554). It is the masterpiece of the Mannerist Benvenuto Cellini, striking for the brutality of the theme, detailed execution and the

*Loggia dei Lanzi

** *Heart of the City*

The impressive square where public assemblies were held in the past is dominated by the massive tower of the Palazzo Vecchio. With other important sights like the Loggia dei Lanzi and especially the Uffizi Gallery it is the tourist heart of Florence.

❶ Palazzo Vecchio

Building of the massive and fortified Palazzo Vecchio, once the seat of the government of the city-republic of Florence, the Signoria, began around 1300. The palace is a symbol of the political and cultural glory of the city.

❷ Loggia dei Lanzi

The open triple yoked hall, the landsknecht hall, displays famous statues like *Perseus with the Head of Medusa* by Benvenuto Cellini. Under the right-hand arcade is the marble group *Rape of the Sabine Women* by Giambologna.

❸ David

In front of the Palazzo Vecchio stands a copy of the David by Michelangelo, one of the most famous sculptures in the world. Anyone who wants to see the original has to go to the ▶Galleria dell' Accademia.

❹ Fontana del Nettuno

The Fountain of Neptune was made for the wedding of Francesco de' Medici with Princess Johanna of Austria in 1565 by Ammanati. Maybe the building went too quickly because the results were not satisfactory. The Florentines mocked: »Ammanato, che bel marmo hai rovinato!« (»Ammanato, what a beautiful block of marble you have ruined!«).

❺ Palazzo degli Uffizi

The Galleria degli Uffizi is housed in the palazzo on the Piazza della Signoria, one of the most famous art galleries in the world with countless masterpieces, especially of Italian painting.

The Fontana del Nettuno was created as a wedding present

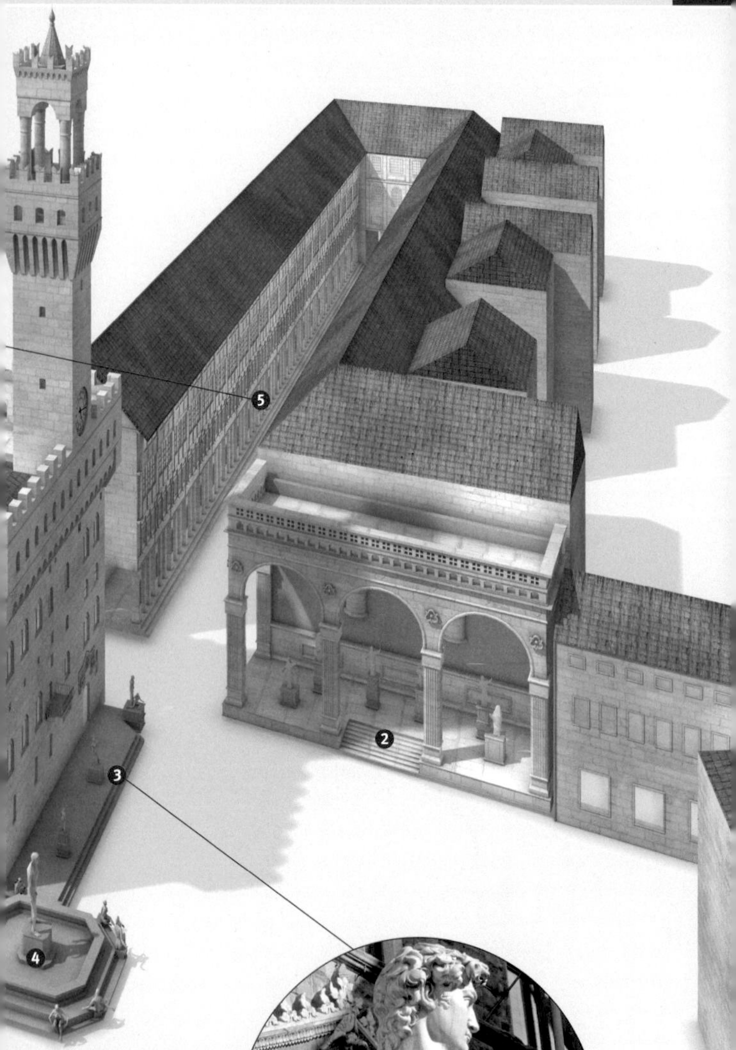

A copy of the world famous David by Michelangelo stands in front of the Palazzo Vecchio. It was interpreted in various ways: as a just fighter in a righteous cause, as the embodiment of ideal manliness and as a symbol of the Republic of Florence.

REX RE
DON
DOMINI

©BAEDEKER

As an elongated U the Palazzo degli Uffizi meets the Piazza della Signoria. The world famous picture gallery is located inside.

①

The equestrian statue of Cosimo I de' Medici made by Giambologna is the first publicly displayed monument since Antiquity.

A
Dav
in fro
It
ca

MARCO ⊕ POLO TIP

! Insider Tip

Quiet rest

Anyone who is looking for a quiet place to relax on the Piazza della Signoria full of people, where he can still watch the activity, should try the terrace of the Gucci café. The café serves tasty salads, pasta and fish, tarts and a rich selection of teas.

confidence of the composition. In the centre at the end is the *Rape of Polyxena*, a marble group by Pio Fedi (1866), followed by ancient statues of women on the long side (heavily restored). In the middle of the opposite end is another marble group depicting *Hercules Fighting the Centaur Nessos*, created by Giambologna in 1599. On the other long side is a sensational figure: **The** *Rape of the Sabine Woman* (1583), also by Giambologna, the first »figura sepentinata«, whose spiral form forces the viewer to walk around it.

Gucci Museum
The stately Gothic building to the left of Palazzo Vecchio was built in 1359 for the trade court of the traders' guild. The coat of arms of the trade and craft professions can still be seen on the façade. Today the world famous fashion label Gucci displays its legendary luggage, handbags, shoes and textile designs in an elegant museum with a shop and an attractive design café. In 1921 Florentine tailor Guccio Gucci began to specialize in processing fine leather, which he used to produce luggage and handbags; the rest is history.

❶ daily 10am – 8pm, www.gucci.com, admission: €6

✳ Piazzale Michelangelo

✧ J 7

Location: South-east of the centre
Bus: 12, 13

Piazzale Michelangelo is named after the artist Michelangelo, who was not always treated kindly by the Florentines; it commands the most beautiful view of Florence.

Lookout point
The piazzale at an elevation of 104m/340ft was designed by Giuseppe Poggi and built between 1865 and 1870. The statuary in the centre is a reminder of Michelangelo: a bronze copy of David (original in the Galleria dell' Accademia) surrounded by the reclining figures from the Medici tombs in the New Sacristy of San Lorenzo. The best-known city sights are easy to identify from Piazzale Michelangelo. The Palazzo Vecchio, the tallest building of the city, can be recognized by its crenellated tower. Nearby is the tower of the Bargello. The slender tower of the Badia Fiorentina rises in front of the cathedral. The Franciscans built the church of Santa Croce along the river. On the other side, far in the distance and near the main railway sta-

Enjoy the beautiful view from Piazzale Michelangelo

tion, the pointed bell tower of Santa Maria Novella can be seen. But the city's panorama is dominated by the massive cathedral with its magnificent dome and richly decorated campanile. The little white roof to the left of the **cathedral** belongs to the Baptistery, the red dome to the New Sacristy of San Lorenzo.

✱ Ponte Vecchio

H 7

Location: Centre
Bus: C3, D

The picturesque Ponte Vecchio over the Arno with its many jewellery shops attracts many visitors. It is a great place for window-shopping during the day and a popular meeting place for romantic people.

Ponte Vecchio with magnificent lighting

»Chic« bridge   The »Old Bridge«, which was built at the river's narrowest point, may even go back to Etruscan times. It is certain, however, that the Roman consular road Via Cassia crossed the Arno here over a wooden bridge. This bridge has been renovated many times more than any other bridge in Florence because of its age – whenever it collapsed or was washed away. Shops and homes were built on it from the 13th century. Butchers had a very practical way of disposing of their meat waste, by throwing it into the river to the joy of the fish and the Florentine street cleaners, but the stench grew until Grand Duke Ferdinando I »for the sake of the foreigners« ordered that only **goldsmiths** could have shops on the bridge, a law that is still in force.

In the middle of the bridge is a bust of Florence's most famous goldsmith, **Benvenuto Cellini** (1900). The **Corridoio Vasariano** (▶p. 202), the connecting corridor between the Palazzo Vecchio and Palazzo Pitti, runs through the first floor of the houses on the bridge.

AROUND PONTE VECCHIO

Not far north-east of the Ponte Vecchio, the church of San Stefano al   San Stefano
Ponte stands on the little Piazzetta San Stefano. It was documented   al Ponte
as early as 1116, and has traces of
building from various centuries: the
façade dates from the 13th, altars
from the 16th, the nave from the
17th century. **Ferdinando Tocca**, the
church architect, also created the
bronze relief *The Stoning of St Ste-*
phen (1656). The impressive marble
stairs to the presbytery is by Buontalenti (1574) and the high altar is by
Giambologna. The church is used for
concerts today.

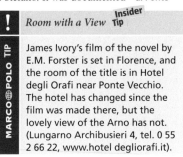

MARCO ⊕ POLO TIP

! *Room with a View* **Insider Tip**

James Ivory's film of the novel by
E.M. Forster is set in Florence, and
the room of the title is in Hotel
degli Orafi near Ponte Vecchio.
The hotel has changed since the
film was made there, but the
lovely view of the Arno has not.
(Lungarno Archibusieri 4, tel. 0 55
2 66 22, www.hotel degliorafi.it).

The church of Santa Felicità on the piazza of the same name not far   Santa Felicità
south of the Ponte Vecchio, is **probably the oldest church in Flor-**
ence. It was built over an early Christian cemetery, rebuilt in the 11th
and 14th centuries and completely remodelled in the 18th century.
The vestibule and the Vasari Corridor as a passage between the Palazzo degli Uffizi and the Palazzo Pitti were preserved. Inside the church
above the door is the balcony used by the grand dukes when they at-
tended mass. To the right of the entrance is the Cappella Barbadoni/
Capponi, which holds the church's major works of art, masterpieces
(1526–28) by **Pontormo**: the *Entombment of Christ* and the *An-*
nunciation, two of the best examples of Florentine Mannerism.

San Frediano

—————— ☀ H 6/7

Location: South-west
Bus: D, 6

San Frediano is the name of the south-western quarter on the
southern side of the Arno, the Oltrarno. While visitors do
come here for the famous Brancacci chapel in ▶Santa Maria del
Carmine, the otherwise rather rustic quarter is untouched by
tourism and lively

The quarter is characterized by workshops, small crafts studios and   Comfortable
eateries around the nicely greened Piazza Torquato Tasso. From here   quarter
walk (2 km/1.2mi) up **Bellosguardo Hill**, across Piazza San Francesco di Paola and on Via del Bellosguardo past beautiful villas on

Piazza del Bellosguardo with a wonderful view of the city. Villa Torre del Bellosguardo is now home of a luxury hotel.

San Frediano in Cestello The church and the Carmelite monastery were dedicated as the parish church of San Frediano and remodelled in the 17th century. This gave the complex a Baroque character, which can easily be seen in its elegant dome and dainty bell tower. Inside is the famous *Smiling Madonna*, a coloured Tuscan wooden statue from the 13th or 14th century.

★★ San Lorenzo

✦ H 6/a/b II/III

Location: Piazza San Lorenzo
Bus: 1, 6, 7, 10, 11, 17
❶ Mon – Sat 10am – 5.30pm, March – Oct Sun 1.30pm – 5.30pm,
www.operamedicealaurenziana.it
Church: admission: €4.50
Library: Mon – Sat 9.30am – 1.30pm, admission: €3

San Lorenzo is one of the most significant sites of Western art. The church of San Lorenzo, the Old Sacristy, the New Sacristy, the ducal chapel and the Laurenziana Library are an architectural ensemble of the highest quality that holds priceless art treasures.

Renaissance church As generous art patrons the **Medici** urged on artists of their city such as Filippo Brunelleschi, Donatello and Michelangelo to ever greater achievements in and around their parish church. The church of San Lorenzo is believed to have been founded by St Ambrose in 393, at that time outside the city walls. The church was rebuilt in the 11th century in the Romanesque style. It gained its present form in 1421 from the famous Florentine Renaissance architect **Brunelleschi**, who designed the definitive Renaissance church for the Medici. The work was completed in accordance with his plans after his death by Antonio Manetti between 1447 and 1460. Michelangelo designed a façade – the drawings and models are on display in the Casa Buonarroti, but these were never used, and the exterior still has no façade.

Piazza San Lorenzo In front of San Lorenzo among the market stands is a **monument to Giovanni delle Bande Nere** (1498–1526), the father of Duke Cosimo I and ancestor of the Medici dukes, by Baccio Bandinelli 1540.

Church interior The interior of the columned basilica shows the clarity of Brunelleschi's design: a beautiful marble floor, columns with Co-

San Lorenzo

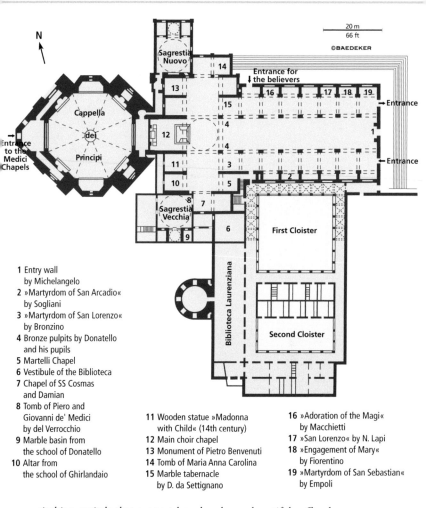

20 m
66 ft
©BAEDEKER

N

Sagrestia Nuovo

14

13

15

4

4

3

5

Entrance for the believers

16   17   18   19

Entrance

Entrance

Entrance

Cappella dei Principi

Entrance to the Medici Chapels

12

11

10

8

7

6

9

1

2

Sagrestia Vecchia

First Cloister

Biblioteca Laurenziana

Second Cloister

1 Entry wall
  by Michelangelo
2 »Martyrdom of San Arcadio«
  by Sogliani
3 »Martyrdom of San Lorenzo«
  by Bronzino
4 Bronze pulpits by Donatello
  and his pupils
5 Martelli Chapel
6 Vestibule of the Biblioteca
7 Chapel of SS Cosmas
  and Damian
8 Tomb of Piero and
  Giovanni de' Medici
  by del Verrocchio
9 Marble basin from
  the school of Donatello
10 Altar from
  the school of Ghirlandaio

11 Wooden statue »Madonna
  with Child« (14th century)
12 Main choir chapel
13 Monument of Pietro Benvenuti
14 Tomb of Maria Anna Carolina
15 Marble tabernacle
  by D. da Settignano

16 »Adoration of the Magi«
  by Macchietti
17 »San Lorenzo« by N. Lapi
18 »Engagement of Mary«
  by Fiorentino
19 »Martyrdom of San Sebastian«
  by Empoli

rinthian capitals that support broad arches, a beautiful coffered ceiling with fine rosettes. The harmonious proportions of the side chapels, aisles and nave create an **unusually harmonious space** and make the church an architectural achievement of the highest order.

At the back of the **nave** on the left and right, the two box-shaped ****Bronze pulpits** set on pillars are masterpieces by **Donatello**, the last works of the old and ill artist (around 1460). They were completed by his pupils Bartolomeo Bellano and Bertoldo di Giovanni. The left pulpit shows scenes of the passion of Christ in moving images; most of the reliefs derive from designs by Donatello but were executed by his pupils. The right pulpit, whose theme is also scenes from the life of Christ, and from the martyrdom of St Lawrence, shows clearer signs of the artist's hand. Both pulpits are decorated with friezes of vases, centaurs and horse-tamers. When Donatello died two years after Cosimo de' Medici, who had commissioned the pulpits, he was interred in the crypt next to his benefactor.

Opposite the left pulpit by Donatello is a fresco by **Agnolo Bronzino:** *Martirio di San Lorenzo* (*Martyrdom of St Lawrence*, 1565–69), one of the main works of this Mannerist artist. The Mannerist staging of the many figures in changing colours is impressive. In the Cappella Martelli behind it a diptych by Filippo Lippi, the *Annunciation* (around 1440), adorns the altar; it is one of his main works and the composition clearly shows the style of the Renaissance. In the left aisle there is a door to the **cloister**, which was built in 1475 in Brunelleschi's style. The entrance to the Biblioteca Medicea Laurenziana (see below) is here.

The left transept leads to the ***Sagrestia Vecchia** (Old Sacristy). Its donor Giovanni Bicci de' Medici intended it to be a funerary chapel that also had the public function of a sacristy. It is the first complete new work of architecture (1420–28) by **Brunelleschi**, and in its structure and proportions was considered to be the first space of the Renaissance with a central plan, a model for later European architecture. The innovation of the design lay in the use of geometric shapes like squares, circles and semicircles. **Donatello** was for the most part responsible for the decoration of the room.

Here again works of art were used to enhance the room: under the dome four round medallions show scenes from the life of St John the Evangelist and four stucco reliefs in the arches represent the four evangelists seated. Donatello used a breath-taking perspective for these works. The **bronze doors** of the apse (1440 – 1443), which depict martyrs and apostles, are by the same artist. Along the left wall is the **tomb of Piero and Giovanni de' Medici** (1472) by Andrea del' Verrocchio. The bronze grille shaped like ropes is still used today by Florentine shops. Under the marble table in the middle is the sarcophagus of Giovanni Bicci de' Medici and his wife Piccarda Bueri. In the side chapel opposite Donatello's right-hand bronze pulpit is a finely detailed and richly decorated tabernacle (1461) by Desiderio da Settignano. The second-last chapel (towards the entry) is decorated with a painting by **Rosso Fiorentino,** *The Betrothal of the Virgin* (1523).

Insider Tip

Inexpensive leather goods

On Piazza San Lorenzo and in Via dell' Ariento leading away from it a market is held on weekdays except Mondays, which mainly has a good and extensive selection of leather goods. The right place for anyone looking for inexpensive bags or belts. Summer Tue – Sat 9am – 7pm

The Biblioteca Medicea Laurenziana (Laurentian Library), attached to the church of San Lorenzo and accessible via the first floor of the cloister, owes its art historical significance to its architectural forms and the Medici collection of books and manuscripts that it holds. The building is considered to be the **most important example of Mannerist architecture in Florence**. The collection, which was begun by Cosimo the Elder as a collection of books and manuscripts and expanded by Lorenzo the Magnificent, was taken to Rome; part of it was returned to Florence under the Medici Pope Clement VII. Clement VII commissioned the building so that the collection would be available to the public.

Biblioteca Medicea Laurenziana

Michelangelo began it in 1524, but the library was not completed until 1571, after his death. Michelangelo, who continued to take part in the construction by means of letters and models after he left Florence in 1534, showed his Mannerist style in the sculpting of the façade, vestibule and reading room as well as in the stairs.

The ****Vestibule** is one of his most individual designs. As a triumphal ascent to the library, the high and narrow vestibule in a monumental style is unique in the history of architecture. The room is divided into individual sections by double columns and the wall sections have recesses that are part window and part niche. Everywhere the rules of architecture seem to have been reversed: The niches are too shallow to hold statues, the pilasters on the sides get narrower at the bottom instead of wider, the soft volutes of the lower storey are much too weak to carry the columns. The columns in turn serve purely decorative purposes. The staircase is also unique in that it rises a great height in a short distance. The visitor climbing the stairs feels insecure. This insecurity caused by reversing architectural forces is typical of Mannerism.

The **library manuscript collection** includes important documents ranging from the time ancient Egypt and valuable manuscripts of the Renaissance period to writings in Napoleon's own hand.

** CAPPELLE MEDICEE

🕐 daily 8.15am – 1.50pm; closed 2nd, 4th Sun of the month, admission: €6
www.polomuseale.firenze.it

Although the Medici Chapels belong to San Lorenzo, they are considered to be a separate museum and not part of the church. They include the ducal mausoleum and the New Sacristy. The oldest Medici Chapel is the Sagrestia Vecchia in San Lorenzo. The entrance leads first to a crypt with tombs of the Medici family including the tomb of the last, Anna Maria Luisa de' Medici, Electress of Pfalz-Neuburg (▶MARCO POLO Insight p. 77), and then into the monumental burial chapel of the famous Medici rulers, the Cappella dei Principi.

*Cappella dei Principi

In 1602 Grand Duke Ferdinando I planned to create an especially magnificent burial place for the Medici dynasty. The design was so costly that it started the rumour that they wanted to bring the grave of Jesus Christ from Jerusalem to Florence, for so valuable a building could not be not intended for mortals, not even for princes. The final plans were drawn up by Giovanni de' Medici, the illegitimate son of Cosimo I, and executed by **Buontalenti** from 1604. After he died **Mario Nigetti** continued the work until 1640. Despite great efforts the chapel was not completed before the death of the last Medici ruler of Florence (1737); the massive, 59m/195ft-high dome was only closed in the 19th century.

The grandiose decoration represents the power of the Medici dynasty: ceiling paintings with scenes from the Old and New Testaments, valuable mosaics on the walls, 16 coats of arms of Tuscan cities with semi-precious stones, the large Medici coats of arms high up, some made of wood and some even of cardboard. Six **Medici dukes** are interred in the chapel (from the left): Cosimo I (†1574), Francesco I (†1587), Cosimo III (†1723), Ferdinando I (†1609), Cosimo II (†1620), Ferdinando II (†1670). The wall tombs and sarcophaguses were beautifully made using valuable materials by craftsmen whose work was technically perfect. But the chapel still seems cold in its austere pomp – a sign that art in the city flowered in the Renaissance and declined after the 16th century. The entrance to the two rooms of the treasury is behind the altar.

**Sagrestia Nuova

Now walk from the ducal chapel to the Sagrestia Nuova. This »New Sacristy« was built between 1520 and 1534, with interruptions, by **Michelangelo** and decorated by Brunelleschi as the counterpart to the Sagrestia Vecchia. The name »Sacristy« is deceptive since it is actually a Medici funerary chapel.

While the chapel was Michelangelo's first work of architecture, he was also able to put his talents as a painter and sculptor to good use.

This can be seen in the articulation of the walls inside, the sculptural treatment of architectural elements, the niches and pediments as well as protruding and receded arches and triangles. The windows in the dome add light to the interior with its dominant colours of grey and white. The sculptor Michelangelo was commissioned along with the architect Michelangelo: he was entrusted with sculpting the tombs of the Medici family members, but only two of the **tombs** were completed, for **Giuliano, Duke of Nemour,** and **Lorenzo, Duke of Urbino**. Lorenzo the Magnificent, his murdered brother Giuliano and Duke Alessandro, who was also murdered, are all interred in the chapel, but without memorials. Neither Giuliano with the field commander's staff, nor Lorenzo wearing a helmet with a contorted face – maybe as a sign of his mental weakness – are depicted as unmistakable personalities. Michelangelo answered the criticism that the figures did not look like the deceased with the comment that after a thousand years no one would ask what they looked like. He deliberately went beyond simple portraits by creating timeless figures. Thus

Sagrestia Nuova: funerary chapel by Michelangelo for the Medici

the two figures are simply called »la vigilanza« (Vigilance) and »il pensiero« (Thought). Seated and dressed in the armour of a Roman commander, Giuliano turns his head sideways as he looks attentively at the Madonna and the two patron saints of the Medici, Cosmas and Damian, early Christian physicians who were martyred and were highly honoured by the Medici, above the grave of Lorenzo the Magnificent.

Under Giuliano on the slanted lid of the sarcophagus lie the **figure of *Night*, with half moon and stars in its hair and with poppies, an owl and a mask; and **Day*, who seems to be staring at nothing out of the uncarved stone with an undecipherable look. Both sarcophagus figures were modelled on ancient statues. Night resembles a figure of Leda from a Roman sarcophagus and Day is oriented on a torso of Belvedere. Michelangelo consciously analyzed ancient sculpture and at the same time gave it a new Christian and philosophical dimension.

Opposite them another niche figure depicts Lorenzo de Medici, whose head rests pensively in his hand with the index finger extended – a pose that expresses contemplation. On the sarcophagus lid below are the two allegorical **figures of *Evening and Morning*. The masculine figure of dusk stands for mental exhaustion, with the lethargic mass of the body going to sleep, while the feminine figure shows awakening and the slowly developing power of the body and spirit. This pair of opposites also depicts Lorenzo's inner battle, since he died demented. Like his counterpart, Lorenzo turns to the Madonna with Child in the hopes of salvation. The Madonna looks at the altar wall opposite her and thus points to the sacrificial death of Christ on the cross, the resurrection and eternal life. In this way all figures communicate with one another and penetrate the room with their looks – an idea typical of Michelangelo.

* San Marco

✦ J 5/6/b II

Location: Piazza San Marco
Bus: C1, 1, 6, 7, 10, 11, 17, 23, 25, 31, 32, 33
❶ Mon – Fri 8.15am – 1.50pm; Sat, Sun 8.15am – 5pm; closed 2nd, 4th Mon, 1st, 2nd, 3rd Sun in the month, www.polomuseale.firenze.it, admission: €4

San Marco was the first 15th-century Renaissance monastery and the home of the painter-monk Fra Angelico. It gained its significance from Prior Girolamo Savonarola (1452 – 1498), who established a republic in Florence based on ascetic Christian principles that lasted for some years until he was burned at the stake.

The church of San Marco, built in 1299, was given to the Dominicans of Fiesole together with the monastery in 1436 by Pope Eugene IV. Cosimo the Elder made a renovation of the church and construction of the monastery possible through generous donations. The architect **Michelozzo** was commissioned to complete the work between 1437 and 1452. Giambologna added the side altars and the Antoninus chapel as well as the Salviati chapel (1588). In 1678 **Pier Francesco Silvani** remodelled the church and gave it its present appearance; in 1777–80 the façade was altered. The Museo di San Marco is located in the oldest part of the monastery, which surrounds the church, while monks still live in the rest of the complex.

Monastery of Fra Angelico and Savonarola

The church houses valuable furnishings. The outstanding work is a crucifix from the school of Giotto on the middle of the entry wall. The **burial chapel of St Antonino** (1580 – 1589) on the left is considered to be the major architectural work by **Giambologna**, who also provided the decoration: six life-size **niche statues** and **six bronze reliefs** with scenes from the life of St Antoninus. Three treasures are to be seen on the right side: a **Baroque marble door** designed by Cigoli that leads to the sacristy, a Byzantine **mosaic of the** *Madonna at Prayer* (705–707) and Fra Bartolomeo della Porta's painting *Madonna and Child* (1509).

Interior

MUSEO DI SAN MARCO

The entrance to the monastery of San Marco is to the right of the church. It was built by Michelozzo in the Renaissance style; its wonderful collection of paintings and frescoes give a more fitting impression of the spiritual life and artistic interests of the Dominicans than the church does. In the late Middle Ages strong religious and spiritual impulses went out from this monastery and transformed Florence. They were given in part by the Dominican prior Antonino, the later archbishop of Florence, who was canonized, and especially by **Girolamo Savonarola**. After the Medici were driven out he established a republic based on ascetic Christian principles and was burned at the stake as a heretic in 1498. However, the monastery owes its fame to the Dominican monk **Fra Angelico** (▶Famous People), who painted the rooms of the monastery from 1436 to 1445, and thus left a museum that sprang up »naturally«. Fra Bartolomeo, a gifted painter of the early 16th century, also left paintings here.

Artist's Monastery

In the pilgrims' hospice are several **panel paintings by Fra Angelico**, which come from various Florentine insitutions. Fra Giovanni, as he was actually called, was named »angelico« (angelic) by his con-

Ground floor

temporaries. Among the greatest treasures are: *Madonna dei Linaioli* (1436), commissioned by the linen weavers' guild, miniatures of the life of Jesus (1450), a *Deposition from the Cross* (1435) and a *Last Judgement* (1430).

In the atmospheric **cloister of St Antonino** right opposite the entrance on the other side is the fresco *St Dominic at the Foot of the Cross*; diagonally opposite the entrance in the lunette is the fresco *Ecce Homo*, both by **Fra Angelico**.

In the **chapter house** the fresco *Crucifixion* by **Fra Angelico** covers an entire wall. It depicts well-known saints including church fathers, bishops and founders of holy orders. The Dominicans of San Marco were so impressed by the *Last Supper* fresco, which Domenico **Ghirlandaio** painted in 1480 for the monastery of Ognissanti, that they asked him to paint a copy in the **small refectory** (1486).

First floor On the first floor are more than 40 cells which **Fra Angelico** decorated with ****frescoes**, alone or with the help of his pupils. His style is unmistakable in the paintings and frescoes. He transformed the austere, stern and stiff medieval saints into soft, gentle and delicate ones. His saints are characterized by innocence and piety, yet they are not ethereal but human. Man seems to be transformed and the earthly has traces of the heavenly. There is hardly a more intimate depiction of the Annunciation than that of Fra Angelico on the wall opposite the stairway. The prior's apartment (at the end of the back transverse passage) is a reminder of **Savonarola**, and in one of the cells Archbishop Antonino of Florence is honoured. Two cells toward the church (front transverse corridor, the two last cells on the right) commemorate Cosimo the Elder, who often came here to meditate and pray.

The large hall of the **library** with valuable manuscripts, missals and Bibles was designed in an imposing and austere style. The room is divided up by arches with delicate columns. The library goes back to private collections, which **Cosimo de' Medici** bought. He commissioned Michelozzo in 1444 to build a house for the collection when San Marco was remodelled and thus founded the **first public library in Europe**. In the 19th century it was incorporated into the Biblioteca Medicea Laurenziana. Only recently some of the manuscripts were returned from the Biblioteca Medicea Laurenziana. Illuminated manuscripts from the 15th and 16th century are on display.

AROUND SAN MARCO

Casino Mediceo Casino Mediceo was built by Bernardo Buontalenti between 1568 and 1574 for Grand Duke Francesco I de' Medici as a laboratory for scientific experiments. The house is called »casino« (»little house«)

Quiet atmosphere in San Marco's cloister

because it used to be in a rural area on the former site of the Medici gardens. The grand duke also maintained **studios for young artists** here. Today Casino Mediceo is the seat of the court of appeals (Corte d' Appello). The pretty courtyard has a statue of the goddess Diana from the school of Giambologna.

The nearby Chiostro dello Scalzo (Cloister of the Barefooted), an elegant cloister with slender columns, was painted by **Andrea del Sarto** from 1514 to 1526 for the Confraternity of St John the Baptist; the members walked barefoot when carrying the cross in processions. The famous frescoes of scenes from the life of John the Baptist have been restored several times. The most important frescoes, all of which are monochrome, depict the birth of John the Baptist (1526), his preaching (1515) and Salome's dance (1522).

Chiostro dello Scalzo

❶ Via Cavour 69, Mon, Thu, 1st, 3rd, 5th Sat 8.15am – 1.50pm

San Giovanni-no dei Cavalieri	The adjacent church of San Giovannino dei Cavalieri (the Knights of St John) changed its name as often as it changed its architect: first it was the Oratory of Mary Magdalene as part of a home for »fallen« girls (1326), then San Pier Celestino, San Niccolò (1553), and finally San Giovanni dei Cavalieri, who was the patron saint of nuns from Jerusalem who had a convent here with a beautiful cloister. Inside the church, the *Birth of Christ* (1435) by Bicci di Lorenzo and a *Coronation of The Virgin* (around 1450) by Neri di Bicci are worth seeing.

Palazzo Pandolfini	The famous painter **Raphael** designed a palace for the Bishop of Troy, Giannozzo Pandolfini, which Giovanni Francesco and Aristotile da Sangallo built in 1520. The palace (Via San Gallo 74) not far to the north of the Casino Mediceo has an elegant and harmonious appearance; it expresses the elements of Renaissance architecture perfectly. The palace was probably planned to be extended to the right so that the entrance, which was beautifully integrated into the building, would have been in the centre. Under the Medici Pope Clement VII, whose name can be seen next to that of Leo X on the right-hand façade, it was decided that the building of the palazzo would be concluded as it now stands.

Sant' Apollonia	The former Benedictine convent Sant' Apollonia, which is a museum today, is worth a visit for its beautiful church (15th cent.) and cloister with elegant columns, but above all for the *Last Supper* by Andrea del Castagno. The convent was used as a military magazine after 1808 and today houses university institutes.

The **Museo Cenacolo di Sant' Apollonia** includes a refectory where Del Castagno painted the *Last Supper around 1447. This fresco has an important place in Renaissance painting: the exact portrayal of the figures in perspective and the realistic depiction of bodies – especially those of Jesus and of Judas sitting alone – make the painting intensely dramatic. The Crucifixion above it, the Burial and Resurrection as well as two lunettes *Pietà* and *The Crucified Christ with the Virgin, St John and a Saint*, all by Castagno, are also worth seeing.

❶ Via XXVII Aprile 1, daily 8am – 1.50pm; closed 2nd, 4th Mon, 1st, 2nd, 3rd Sun of the month

Giardino dei Semplici, Museo Botanico	The **Giardino dei Semplici** (garden of medicinal herbs) north of San Marco was started by Cosimo I to study exotic plants. Today it is part of the university's botanical institute. Most of the trees date from the late 18th century. The adjoining **Museo Botanico**, the largest botanical museum in Italy, displays mainly native herbs and a large collection of different types of wood.

❶ Entrance: Via La Pira 4, April – Sep Mon, Tue, Thu – Sun 10am – 7pm, winter Mon, Sat, Sun, www.msn.unifi.it

★ San Miniato al Monte

✦ J 8

Location: Monte alle Croci
Bus: 12
❶ Summer daily 8am – 7.30pm, winter Mon – Sat 8.15am – 1pm,
2.30pm – 6pm

The monastery of San Miniato al Monte is a jewel of Tuscan Romanesque architecture. The close relationship to Roman antiquity is noticeable outside and inside. The climb to the monastery is worth it for the view of the city alone.

A short path leads from Piazzale Michelangelo to the monastery San Miniato al Monte. It got its name from St Minias, who was martyred in Florence in the year 250. The monastery church, which was probably begun in 1018, stands on his grave. The church was largely complete by the early 13th century. The monastery first belonged to Benedictine nuns; from 1373 to 1552 and today is in the hands of Olivetan monks. — **Martyr's church**

The two-storey white and green incrusted façade (probably around 1100) with a triangular gable is covered with thin marble panels, which divide up the façade with geometric patterns with squares, rectangles, rhombuses, circles, together with large Romanesque/ Roman arches. The **mosaic** from the second half of the 13th century on the upper floor depicts Christ between the Virgin and San Miniato. The gable is crowned by a gilded eagle with a bunch of wool in its talons. It is the figure from the coat of arms of the textile merchants' guild, which financed the construction and maintenance of San Miniato for a long time. — **Exterior**

After the old campanile collapsed in 1499, a new one was begun in 1518 but never completed. In the turbulent early 16th century it defended the people of Florence – including Michelangelo – against the imperial troops. — **Campanile**

The impressive interior takes up the late antique, early Christian form of the **columned basilica**: a long church consisting of a nave and two aisles, with an exposed roof structure and without a transept. The lateral arches and the alternating supports give the nave an unusual rhythm. The raised choir, which was built in the traditional way over a martyr's grave, originally gave the pilgrim entering the church a view of the 11th-century hall crypt and the remains of St Miniato; today it is blocked off by the Renaissance tabernacle in the nave. San Miniato is mainly a medieval Romanesque structure but it holds two — **Interior**

San Miniato: a jewel of art history in a beautiful setting

outstanding examples of Renaissance art: a marble ciborium by Michelozzo and the Chapel of the Cardinal of Portugal, an attached central-plan construction by Antonio Manetti with sculpture by Antonio Rossellino.

Michelozzo's barrel-vaulted ***marble ciborium** in the nave was commissioned by Piero de Medici in 1448. The back is an altar painting by **Agnolo Gaddi** (around 1396) with scenes from the martyrdom of St Minias. It is interesting that the little structure is covered with signs of the proud donor: Piero's marks consist of a ring with an uncut diamond and peacock feathers. Not only the frieze zone but also the bronze grille of the little temple incorporates the emblems into its ornamentation. The back is decorated with an eagle: a guild mark and an indication that the cloth traders' guild built the structure and unwillingly gave Piero de Medici this sign of his pride as donor. The barrel ceiling of the tabernacle is made of glazed terracotta coffers, their white and light-blue colours a mark of the Renaissance artist Luca della Robbia.

The ***Cappella del Cardinale di Portogallo** (Chapel of the Cardinal of Portugal), commissioned by the Portuguese King Alfonso V and built by **Manetti** between 1461 and 1466 onto the left aisle, is reminiscent in its central plan of the Old Sacristy that Brunelleschi created for San Lorenzo. The interior decoration combines Christian and ancient ideas. Thus Antonio Rossellino's conception of the sarcophagus is reminiscent of Roman models; a Mithras sacrifice as well as putti and angels decorate the tomb niche. The reclining figure of the deceased faces an empty judge's seat as a reminder of the Last Judgement. In all, this tomb should be seen as a precursor to Michelangelo's sarcophaguses in the New Sacristy of San Lorenzo. The terracotta sculptures – the Holy Spirit and the four cardinal virtues – are by Luca della Robbia.

To the left and right of the marble ciborium, steps lead down to the **crypt** with 14th-century frescoes by Taddeo Gaddi.

The decoratively sculptured **marble screens** and the detailed **marble pulpit** from the second half of the 12th century are among the most valuable late Romanesque decorations of the church.

The **apse** is adorned with a mosaic *Christ with the Virgin and San Miniato*. Its Byzantine influence is recognizable. It was originally made in 1297 and in the second half of the 19th century almost completely renewed. From the elevated apse go right into the **sacristy**, where **Spinello Aretino** (after 1387) painted his masterpiece, *Legends of St Benedict*.

From the sacristy a door leads to the **cloister** with frescoes by Andrea del Castagno and Paolo Uccello.

Palazzo dei Vescovi

The Palazzo dei Vescovi (bishop's palace), which was begun by Bishop Andrea dei Mozzi in 1295 next to the church of San Miniato and completed in 1320, served for a long time as the summer residence of the bishops of Florence until it was incorporated into the monastery in 1534. Today it again belongs to Olivetan monks.

Cimitero delle Porte Sante

The cemetery Cimitero delle Porte Sante near the church was begun in 1857 to plans by Nicola Mata. Many famous people were buried here in the 19th century.

AROUND SAN MINIATO AL MONTE

San Salvatore al Monte

The church of San Salvatore al Monte is often overlooked because of the nearby church of San Miniato. Michelangelo called it »la bella villanella« (the beautiful country girl) and it is worth visiting for its strikingly clear outer and inner conception. **Cronaca** (from 1499) was mainly responsible for the construction and had to deal with many problems: the building could be constructed only with supporting walls because of the steep terrain.

** **Santa Croce**

✦ **J 7/c IV**

Location: Piazza Santa Croce
Bus: C1, C2, C3, 13

»Santa Croce is a pantheon of the most worthy kind. The church has a serious and dark solemnity, indeed a large funeral hall, which no rational person would enter without respect«, wrote Ferdinand Gregorovius, a German traveller in Italy in the 19th century.

Piazza Santa Croce

The church of Santa Croce is located on the square of the same name. By medieval standards it was a broad square, intended for festivals and assemblies of the people and for preaching by Franciscan monks. The 17th-century fountain, the large **monument to Dante** (1865) and two palazzi are highlights. Palazzo Serristori opposite the church façade was built between 1469 and 1474 to plans by Giuliano da Sangallo. Palazzo dell' Antella is on the south side of the square and was created by Gilio Parigi in 1619 by joining two 15th-century palaces. A kind of football was played here as early as the 16th century; a round plaque of 1565 at the Palazzo dell' Antella marks the centre line of the field. The tradition still continues: every year in June the piazza is the site of the »Calcio in Costume« (►MARCO POLO Insight p. 100), and the game is played in 16th-century costume.

CHURCH

Florentine hall of fame

With its many graves and monuments as well as numerous important paintings, Santa Croce **is one of the most impressive churches in Italy**. Its imposing dimensions (115m/125yd long and 38m/41yd wide) make it **the largest Franciscan church**. Building began in 1295, presumably under Arnolfo di Cambio. Pope Eugene IV was present when it was dedicated in 1443. The 19th-century façade of the church and campanile is decorated with marble in different colours.

Interior

The interior is a pillared basilica with an exposed wooden roof structure and a straight choir wall, as is common in the churches of mendicant orders. It is a hall church, suitable for the sermons of repentance of the Franciscan monks, who were very popular in this quarter of Florence where wool workers traditionally lived. The tomb of the famous natural scientist **Galileo Galilei** by Giulio Foggini is in the first part of the **left aisle**. The monument to the humanist and chancellor **Carlo Marsuppini** by Desiderio da Settignano, one of the most

Dante watches over Santa Croce

beautiful 15th-century tombs, is next to the side door. The grave-stones of **Lorenzo Ghiberti**, the creator of the bronze doors of the Baptistery, and his son Vittorio are set in the floor.

The tomb of the Florentine composer **Luigi Cherubini** (†1842) is also worth seeing (left transept corner). A series of chapels terminate the transept. In the **Cappella Bardi** is the Crucifixion by Donatello, which Brunelleschi criticized by saying that the artist had put a farmer on the cross. Brunelleschi himself created what he assumed was a more beautiful crucifix for Santa Maria Novella. In the **Cappella Bardi di Vernio** the wall frescoes on the life of St Sylvester were made in 1340 by Maso di Banco. The frescoes in the tomb niches are also by Maso di Banco and Taddeo Gaddi. In the **Cappella Tosinghi-Spinelli** the glass windows from the school of Giotto are remarkable. The main choir chapel is completely decorated with frescoes. The vault paintings (1380) are by **Agnolo Gaddi** and show the Risen

Santa Croce

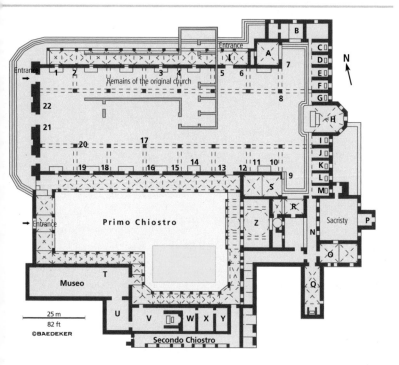

1 Saints' frescos
2 Tomb of Galileo Galilei
  by G. Foggini
3 Tomb of Lorenzo
  and Vittorio Ghiberti
4 »Pietà« by Bronzino
5 Tomb of Vittorio Fossombroni
  by Bartolini
6 Tomb of Carlo Marsuppini
  by D. da Settignano
7 Tomb of Luigi Cherubini
  by Fantacchiotti
8 Tomb of Leon Battista Alberti
  by Bartolini
9 Tomb of Prince Corsini
10 Tomb of Ugo Foscolo
11 Tomb of Gioacchino Rossini
  by Cassioli
12 Tomb of Leonardo Bruni
13 Niche of Donatello with
  tabernacle »Annunciation«
14 »Mount of Olives«
  by A. del Minga

15 Tomb of Niccoló Machiavelli
  by Spinazzi
16 Tomb of Vittorio Alfieri
  by Canova
17 Marble pulpit
  by B. da Maiano
18 Cenotaph of Dante Alighieri
  by Rici
19 Tomb of Michelangelo
  by Vasari
20 »Madonna with Child« relief
  by Rossellino
21 Tomb of G. B. Niccolini
  by Fedi
22 Tomb of Gino Capponi
  by A. Bortone

A Cappella Salviati
B Cappella Bardi with crucifix
  by Donatello
C Cappella Bardi di Vernio
D Cappella Pulci e Beraldi
E Cappella Ricasoli

F Cappella Capponi
G Capella Tosinghi/Spinelli
H Cappella Maggiore
I Cappella Bardi with
  frescos by Giotto
J Cappella Peruzzi with
  frescos by Giotto
K Cappella Giugni
L Cappella Calderini
M Cappella Velluti
N Corridoio della Sagrestia
O Passage to Scuola
  del Cuoio
P Cappella Rinuccini
Q Cappella del Noviziato
  by Michelozzo
R Cappella Baroncelli with
  frescos by T. Gaddi
S Cappella Castellani
T-Y Museo dell'Opera
  di Santa Croce
Z Cappella de' Pazzi
  by Brunelleschi

Christ, the Evangelists and St Francis. The wall frescoes, also by Gaddi and his assistants, depict the legend of the holy cross.

As with the left, the **right cross aisle** is also divided into five chapels. In the **Cappella Bardi** (around 1320) are frescoes by Giotto, Stories from the life of St Francis. They are among his most mature and significant works (around 1320). In the **Cappella Peruzzi** next to it there are also remarkable fresco cycles by Giotto that depict scenes from the lives of John the Evangelist and John the Baptist (around 1325). They were especially admired and thoroughly studied by Renaissance painters like Masaccio and Michelangelo. In the last chapel, the **Cappella Velluti**, there are damaged frescoes (Archangel Michael) by a pupil of Cimabue and the *Coronation of the Virgin* by Giotto. The wall paintings of the prophets (outside) and the life of the Virgin (inside) on the **Cappella Baroncelli** at the end of the transept are by Taddeo Gaddi, a pupil of Giotto, and are his masterpieces. In the next chapel, **Cappella Castellani**, are frescoes (*Lives of the Saints*) by Agnolo Gaddi and his pupils as well as a beautiful tabernacle by Mino da Fiesole.

A door to a corridor (Corridoio della Sagrestia), both designed by Michelozzo, leads to the sacristy. It contains valuable cabinets from the Renaissance and a Crucifixion by Taddeo Gaddi. Behind the sacristy is the 14th-century **Cappella Rinuccini** with frescoes by Giovanni da Milano showing scenes from the lives of the Virgin and Mary Magdalene. At the end of the sacristy corridor lies the novitiate chapel, **Cappella del Noviziato**, built by Michelozzo on the commission of Cosimo the Elder 1445 for the novitiates of the convent. The *Madonna* (1480) in glazed terracotta above the altar is by Andrea della Robbia (1480).

The **right-hand aisle** contains the funerary monument of the composer **Gioacchino Rossini** (†1868) as well as the tomb of the Florentine scholar and chancellor of the republic, **Leonardo Bruni** (†1444), in which Bernardo Rossellino created the prototype of the Florentine Renaissance tomb around 1450. The graceful relief of the Annunciation by Donatello (1435) is in a niche nearby. About in the middle of the aisle is the wall tomb with an allegory of diplomacy for the political philosopher **Niccolò Machiavelli** (†1527), the work of Spinazzi (1787).

At the fifth pillar the famous octagonal **marble pulpit by Benedetto da Maiano** (1472–76) depicts scenes from the life of St Francis and allegorical figures. The monumental cenotaph for **Dante** (1829) with its allegories of Italy and mourning Poetry is in the last third of the aisle. Florence wanted to honour the exiled poet in this way; he died in Ravenna in 1321. **Michelangelo's** tomb, designed by Vasari, is decorated by the personifications of Architecture, Sculpture and Painting. There is a relief by Antonio Rossellino at the first pillar: *Madonna col Bambino* (1478).

MUSEO DELL' OPERA DI SANTA CROCE

❶ Mon – Sat 9.30 – 5pm, Sun 1 – 5pm, admission: €6,
www.santacroceopera.it

Viewing To the right of the church is the entrance to the monastery of Santa
Croce. Two cloisters are open for visitors, as well as the Pazzi Chapel
and the Museo dell' Opera di Santa Croce, which is located in the
former refectory and other rooms of the monastery. The Cappella dei
Pazzi is at the end of the Primo Chiostro (First Cloister), which was
built in the late 14th and early 15th century.

**Cappella The Pazzi Chapel owes its fame to the architectural genius of
dei Pazzi **Brunelleschi**. He worked on this early, pure Renaissance structure
from 1430 to his death in 1446 for Andrea de' Pazzi. It was supposed
to be the tomb of the Pazzi and at the same time the chapter house of
the Franciscan monks. The vestibule is supported by columns with a
frieze of small medallions with heads of angels by **Desiderio da Settignano**, and the half dome of the portico is decorated with beautiful
rosettes by **Luca della Robbia**, as is the *St Andrew* relief (1445) over
the wooden doors; the doors are by **Giuliano da Sangallo** (1470–
78.

The interior of the Cappella dei Pazzi forms a harmonious whole,
clearly structured by pilasters, implied niches, rounded forms and
barrel vaulting, even though the rectangular plan of the chapel is broken up by the altar area. The four terracotta medallions with seated
evangelists are by Luca della Robbia, as are the twelve tondi of the
apostles.

Secondo A passageway leads from the first cloister to the large two-storey Sec-
Chiostro ondo Chiostro (Second Cloister), built around 1452 by **Bernardo
Rossellino**, who followed Brunelleschi's style closely.

Museo dell' The Santa Croce Museum is housed in the refectory and adjacent
Opera di rooms of the monastery of Santa Croce. Its main works include the
Santa Croce 120 sq m/1300 sq ft *Last Supper* (around 1360) by **Taddeo Gaddi**
and also his Entombment. A late masterpiece is the large painted
*Crucifix by Cimabue (around 1285 – 1290), which has been severely damaged since the flood in 1966. It is innovative in the human
features and the detailed physique of Christ.

Note also the expressive fresco fragments that are part of the *Triumph of Death* (around 1360) by **Andrea Orcagna**; the gilded
bronze statue of St Louis of Toulouse (1423) by **Donatello**; a fresco
by **Domenico Veneziano**, *Saints John the Baptist and Francis*
(around 1450 – 1460); *The Coronation of the Virgin* by **Maso di
Banco** as well as *Stigmata*, a terracotta group by **Andrea della Robbia**.

AROUND SANTA CROCE

The national library – built from 1911 to 1935 – next to Santa Croce **Biblioteca** holds 24,721 manuscripts, more than 70,000 letters and documents, **Nazionale** 3780 incunabula, more than four million books, about 4000 sheets of **Centrale** music, more than 600 atlases and about 1500 geographical and topographical maps. The oldest known copy of the *Divine Comedy* by Dante (early 14th century), manuscripts by Galileo, as well as missals and Bibles from before the invention of book printing are especially valuable. The library dates from the 13th century and has manuscripts from all famous citizens of Florence.

❶ Mon – Fri 9am – 7pm, Sat 9am – 1pm

The English art historian Herbert Percy Horne (1864–1916) gave a **Museo Horne** valuable collection of paintings, sculptures, drawings, furnishings, jewellery and utensils to the Italian government, which is now on display in Palazzo Horn (not far to the west of the church). The building was constructed in the 15th century for the Alberti family, and was probably designed by Cronaca; later it belonged to the Corsi. The collection was damaged severely in the floods in 1966, especially the exhibits on the ground floor.

There are paintings on the first floor from the 14th to the 16th century, including works by Simone Martini, Benozzo Gozzoli, Pietro Lorenzetti, Filippino Lippi and Bernardo Daddi. Giotto's panel of *St Stephen (around 1320) is the main attraction.

On the second floor there is furniture from Florentine workshops, drawings, tondos and terracottas from the 15th and 16th centuries.

❶ Mon – Sat 9am – 1pm, www.museohorne.it, admission: €6

The Palazzo Bardi (around 1420) opposite the museum is attributed **Palazzo Bardi** to Brunelleschi. It stands out for its good proportions. The inner courtyard is accentuated by slender columns

* Santa Maria del Carmine

━━━━━━━━ ✦ H 7

Location: Piazza del Carmine
Bus: D

The large church on Piazza del Carmine is known mainly for the Brancacci Chapel, a place of great significance for art history.

| Church remodeled as Baroque | The church, which was begun in 1268, was not completed until 1476; Romanesque and Gothic building elements on the sides bear witness to this. In the 16th and 17th centuries it was remodelled and so severely damaged in a fire in 1771 that it had to be completely reconstructed; this was done by Ruggieri and Mannaioni until 1782 in Baroque style. The church has a nave with chapels at the sides. |

Baroque Santa Maria del Carmine

Along with the Brancacci Chapel, the church is famous for its Baroque **Cappella Corsini** (1675 – 1683) by Pierfrancesco Silvani in the left transept; the dome fresco *Apotheosis of St Andrea Corsini* (1682) is by Luca Giordano. The chapel has the tombs of Neri and Piero Corsini with three marble high reliefs by Giovanni Battista Foggini.

The entrance to ***Cappella Brancacci** is on the right next to the church. Access the chapel is via a cloister added in the early 17th century, which Felice Brancacci, a rich Florentine merchant, had decorated with **frescoes** from 1424 to 1427 by **Masaccio** and **Masolino**. They represent an important stage in the development of European painting. Thanks to his rediscovery of perspective in his frescoes, Masaccio went beyond the rich forms and colours of medieval Gothic style and developed Giotto's initial efforts further. Following the tradition of Masaccio and Masolino, **Filippino Lippi** painted the five murals in the lower zone. Leading Renaissance artists studied the works of the Brancacci Chapel because of their use of perspective, the strict realism of the images, the detailed faces, the artistic freedom and concentrated expression. The frescoes had been disfigured by various attempts to restore them, but the original colours were recovered recently. They depict (left to right, top): Adam and Eve driven out of the Garden of Eden, the tribute (paid by Peter to the emperor; both masterpieces by Masaccio), St Peter's sermon, St Peter baptizes new believers, St Peter and St John heal the lame man and St Peter awakens Tabitha, the temptation of Adam and Eve. Bottom: St Paul visits St Peter in prison, St Peter awakens the son of Theophilus, St Peter preaches, St Peter (with St John) heals the sick, St Peter and St John distribute the believers' goods, crucifixion of St Peter, St Peter and St Paul dispute with Simon the magician in front of Nero, the angel releases St Peter from prison. It is said that **Michelangelo** became so enraged in a discussion over these pictures that it came to blows and his nose was disfigured.

❶ Mon – Sat 10am – 5pm, Sun 1pm – 5pm, reservations necessary, tel. 0 55 2 76 82 24, admission: €6

★★ Santa Maria Novella

———————————— ✦ H 6/a II/III

Location: Piazza di Santa Maria Novella, additional entrance: Piazza della Stazione 4
Bus: C 2, 12, 13, 14, 17, 22, 23, 36, 37
❶ Mon – Thu, 9am – 5.30pm, Fri, 10am – 5.30pm, Sat 9am – 5pm, Sun 12pm – 5pm, www.chiesasantamarianovella.it, admission: €5

The Dominican church of Santa Maria Novella with its epoch-making Renaissance façade and famous cycles of frescoes is one of Florence's most famous churches.

The church, which has architecture typical for the mendicant orders, lies on Piazza di Santa Maria Novella. The two marble obelisks with bronze lilies on top and supported by four turtles, are the work of Giambologna (1608).

Building history

Santa Maria Novella was begun in 1246 and more or less complete around 1300. Various architects made slight changes in the 14th and 15th centuries. As with the Franciscan church of Santa Croce, the building is entered by crossing a wide processional square. The façade was made from 1456 to 1470 by **Leon Battista Alberti** for Giovanni Rucellai, whose family mark, a sail, can be seen in the middle of the frieze-like cornice. Alberti gave it a unique design by harmonizing Romanesque and Gothic style with Renaissance forms (door, adjacent pillars, upper attic storey with volutes). The façade is adorned by marble of different colours. There is an old cemetery next to the church.

Church interior The interior of the church is balanced harmoniously between ascending Gothic forms and the wide, unified space, whose length of 99m/108yd is exaggerated by the narrowing curve of the pillars. In the lunette above the door is the fresco *Birth of Christ*, possibly an early work of Botticelli, while the rosette, the oldest in Florence, is the *Coronation of the Virgin*.

The marble pulpit at the second pillar in the left aisle was designed by **Filippo Brunelleschi** in 1443 and executed by Buggiano. *The Trinity* (1427), a fresco by **Masaccio**, is at the third altar; it has a place of honour among the works of this artist because of its intense expression and perfect perspective depiction.

There is a painted crucifix (around 1290) in the front of the nave, an early masterpiece by **Giotto**; its depiction of the human features of the suffering Christ made it a model for 14th-century painters.

In the elevated **Cappella Strozzi**, where the altar picture *Saviour and Saints* is by Andrea Orcagna, Nardo di Cione created the frescoes with themes from Dante's *Divine Comedy* in 1357. The **Cappella Gaddi** houses works by Bronzino including the painting above the altar, *Jesus Awakens the Daughter of Jairus*. In the adjacent **Cappella Gondi** is a famous wooden crucifix (1410 – 1425) by Brunelleschi, the first depiction of Christ without a loincloth.

Turning markers

Do you know what the obelisks on Piazza Santa di Maria Novella are for? They are a reminder that chariot races were held here during the times of the Medici dukes; the obelisks were the turning markers.

MARCO ⊕ POLO INSIGHT

The **main choir chapel** was completely decorated with frescoes of scenes from the life of John of Baptist and the Virgin by **Domenico Ghirlandaio** and his assistants between 1486 and 1490 for Giovanni Tornabuoni. Thanks to a complete restoration the last great cycle of frescoes of the 15th century radiates again in its soft, glowing colours. The bronze crucifix is by Giambologna.

In the right transept two chapels were added on the left. The **Cappella di Filippo Strozzi** is decorated with frescoes (1497–1502) by Filippino Lippi. The tomb of Filippo Strozzi is behind the altar; it was made by Benedetto da Maiano in 1491 – 1493. In the adjacent **Cappella Bardi** is the *Madonna of the Rosaries* (1570) by Vasari. At the end of the transept in the elevated **Cappella Rucellai** note a bronze tomb plate (1423) for the Dominican General Dati by Lorenzo Ghiberti and a marble statue *Madonna with Child* by Nino Pisano. Nearby is the tomb of Patriarch Joseph of Constantinople, who died here during the Council of Florence in 1440. A door leads to the **Cappella della Pura** with the picture *Madonna with Child and St Cath-*

Santa Maria Novella with its impressive Renaissance façade is one of Florence's most important churches

erine. Legend says that the Virgin called out of the picture in 1472 to two dirty children that they should wash themselves – a disciplinary measure that mothers in Florence still like to use.

Towards the door the next tomb, by Rossellino (1451), is that of Beata Villana. *The Martyrdom of Lawrence* by Macchietti (1573) adorns the side altar.

MUSEO DI SANTA MARIA NOVELLA

A visit to Santa Maria Novella should also include the refectory, **Monastery** cloisters and the chapels of the earlier monastery, today called the Museo di Santa Maria Novella. The huge Chiostro Grande with its 56 arches, which is decorated in part with 16th cent. fresco cycles, is part the school of the Carabinieri, but it can be viewed on special occasions.

Santa Maria Novella

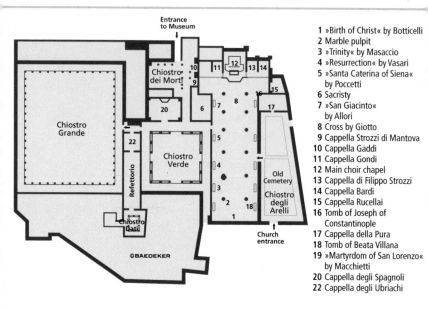

1 »Birth of Christ« by Botticelli
2 Marble pulpit
3 »Trinity« by Masaccio
4 »Resurrection« by Vasari
5 »Santa Caterina of Siena«
  by Poccetti
6 Sacristy
7 »San Giacinto«
  by Allori
8 Cross by Giotto
9 Cappella Strozzi di Mantova
10 Cappella Gaddi
11 Cappella Gondi
12 Main choir chapel
13 Cappella di Filippo Strozzi
14 Cappella Bardi
15 Cappella Rucellai
16 Tomb of Joseph of
  Constantinople
17 Cappella della Pura
18 Tomb of Beata Villana
19 »Martyrdom of San Lorenzo«
  by Macchietti
20 Cappella degli Spagnoli
22 Cappella degli Ubriachi

Chiostro Verde	The name of the Chiostro Verde (Green Cloister), a very beautiful cloister that is full of atmosphere, derives from the green colour of the **frescoes** by Paolo Uccello. The cycle begins with the Creation of the Animals and the Fall (around 1430); the depiction of the Flood was added 20 years later.
*Cappella degli Spagnoli	The frescoes in the Cappella degli Spagnoli (Spanish Chapel) are among the most magnificent of the 14th century in Italy; the chapel was built after 1340 by Jacopo Talenti as the chapter house of the Dominican monastery and used by **Eleonora of Toledo**, the wife of Cosimo I, from 1540 for her Spanish entourage – hence the name. Andrea da Firenze's ***wall paintings** depict the Dominican order. The artist combined scenes from the Bible, legends of the saints and the allegorical depictions of medieval sciences.

AROUND SANTA MARIA NOVELLA

*Museo Nazionale Alinari della Fotografia

The three Florentine Alinari brothers began to document the city and all of Italy with their cameras in the late 19th cent. With that they laid the foundation for one of the most important photography archives in the world.

The museum is housed in beautiful rooms in the beautiful portico building Loggiato delle Leopoldine – once a sanatorium, later a school – on the opposite side of the Piazza Santa Maria Novella. It shows photographs from the archives, old cameras and it organizes interesting pictures.

❶ Thu – Tue 10am – 6.30pm, www.mnaf.it,
admission: €9

Fortezza da Basso

Follow Via Valfonda northwards to get to the extensive, former Fortezza da Basso. Duke Alessandro de' Medici commissioned Antonio Sangallo the Younger to design the fortress in 1534, and Pier Francesco da Viterbo and Alessandro Vitelli to build it in 1534–35. Emperor Charles V made the construction of this bastion one of the conditions for the marriage of the illegitimate Alessandro and his daughter Margarete of Austria-Parma. With this fortress the duke wanted to demonstrate and secure his power. It is now used for exhibitions and conventions

Cascine

The Cascine park extends more than 3km/2mi along the Arno in the western part of the city. The farms of the Medici were once located here. In the late 18th century the property was opened to the public by the grand dukes of Habsburg-Lorraine. The extensive woods and lawns are a popular picnic area on weekends. Along with sports possibilities like the swimming pool, tennis and clay pidgeon shooting the park also has room for a horse race track (Ippodromo), for a small amusement park, an open air stage and for the new Parco della musica e della cultura (Viale Fratelli Rosselli 1) with a modern concert hall.

MARCO ⊕ POLO TIP

! *Not just medicines* Insider Tip

Just don't miss the old pharmacy Santa Maria Novella (Via della Scala 16 r), which has been in operation since 1612 and was appointed by the court of the Medici. The interior is very stylish (19th cent.). Perfumes, soaps and herbs are also sold. You are certain to find something you need.

✴ Santa Trinità

————————————————— ✦ H 6/a III

Location: Piazza Santa Trinità
Bus: C3, D, 6, 36, 37
❶ Mon – Sat 8am – 12pm, 4pm – 5.45pm, Sun 8am – 10.45am, 4pm – 5.45pm, free admission

The Florentines love the church of Santa Trinità on Piazza Santa Trinità above all for its dignified altar. The church is a Gothic basilica with sumptuous decorations.

First Gothic church of Florence
There was a church here in the 11th century. It was renovated in the 13th century, the first Gothic church in Florence, presumably by Niccolò Pisano, and in the late 14th century again by Neri di Fioravante. The façade was changed in the late 16th century to a design by **Buontalenti**.

Interior
The interior is 14th-century Florentine Gothic style. It is a basilica with a transept. Side chapels, all of which are elevated, have been added to the nave. Many works of art can be seen on a tour of the church.

Left aisle
In the third chapel there is an Annunciation on a gold background by **Neri di Bicci** and the tomb of Giuliano Davanzati (†1444), an early Christian sarcophagus with high relief work.
The fifth chapel is decorated with a wooden statue of Mary Magdalene (1464 – 1465) by Desiderio da Settignano and Benedetto da Maiano.

Left transept
In the left transept the marble tomb of Bishop Benozzi Federighi (1455–56) is impressive. **Luca della Robbia** created one of his best works here.

Right transept
In the right transept is the Cappella Sassetti with the famous ***frescoes by Ghirlandaio** (1483–86): *Legends of St Francis of Assisi*, including the well-known *Confirmation of the Rule of the Order*. Here the artist added contemporary persons and buildings, including Lorenzo de' Medici the Magnificent and himself with his hand on his hip as well as the Piazza della Signoria and Piazza della Trinita. The altarpiece *Adoration of the Shepherds* (1485) is also by Ghirlandaio.

Right aisle
In the Cappella Salimbeni there is a cycle of frescoes by **Lorenzo Monaco**, and in the first chapel at the entrance, the Cappella Gianfigliazzi, a miraculous wooden crucifix (14th century).

High Heels for VIPs

Hollywood's divas and numerous queens loved to have their feet flattered by the artistic shoes of Salvatore Ferragamo.

Until today the name Ferragamo stands for chic feet. A family business in Florence now in the third generation, it combines unique designs with detailed craftsmanship to achieve extravagant models for ►well-heeled" women with a craving for recognition. »La bella forma«, be it for flat or splayed feet, has always been the creed of Salvatore Ferragamo. He was born in 1898 as the eleventh of fourteen children of a poor farmer in a dismal village near Naples and emigrated to America at the age of sixteen, where his meteoric rise from shoemaker's boy to dream designer began. At first he made cowboy boots for western movies, which got him in touch with **Hollywood**; then historical movies required other shoes. In the end the divas only wanted hand-made shoes by Ferragamo. They even followed him to Florence, where the magician of shoes created ever more unusual shoes from 1927. In 1936 Ferragamo created the wedge sole made of cork, followed by sandals made of nylon thread and then the cage for the removable stiletto heel.

When **Greta Garbo** showed up in the Florentine shoe palace and Salvatore went on his knees for her feet, her visit brought him an order for seventy pairs of shoes. For **Audrey Hepburn** he cast 24 carat gold sandalettes with bells that rang with every step. In 1939 Ferragamo bought an old city palace for his family and for his headquarters on the Arno. Today business is as good as ever and the most brilliant creations of the artist of the high heel, who died in 1962, watch over it in the museum on the floor above.

Once many celebrities were wild about the Ferragamo's unusual shoe styles

AROUND SANTA TRINITÀ

Palazzo Spini-Ferroni The largest medieval palace in Florence was built to plans probably drawn up by Arnolfo di Cambio for the Spini family from 1289 on the Piazza Santa Trinità; it later passed into the ownership of the Ferroni family. The extensive complex on the banks of the Arno is an impressive sight with its massive walls, height and heavily emphasized crenellations.

In 1927 **Salvatore Ferragamo**, the famous »shoemaker to the stars«, opened a workshop and shop in the palazzo. The palace is still the headquarters of the Ferragamo company, which now also designs luxury fashion and accessories. Salvatore Ferragamo, who died in 1960, made shoes for Hollywood stars like Greta Garbo and Marilyn Monroe. In 1995 a museum was built in the Palazzo Spini-Ferroni, where 10,000 creations by the master are on display, including gold sandals and the famous »invisible shoe«, for which Ferragamo was given the fashion Oscar in 1947 (▶MARCO POLO Insight p.291).

❶ Daily 10am – 7.30pm, museoferragamo.it, admission: €6

Palazzo Bartolini-Salimbeni The Palazzo Bartolini-Salimbeni a short distance to the north was built by Baccio d' Agnolo from 1517 to 1520. The Florentines accused the architect of using too many elements of Roman building, i.e. the classical forms of Bramante and Raphael, which were thought better suited to a church than a residence. The architect defended himself in the inscription above the door »carpere promptius quam imitari« (»it is easier to criticize than to do it yourself«). Another inscription above the windows reveals the former owner's secret of success: »Per non dormire« (»Just don't sleep«).

Santi Apostoli A Latin inscription to the left of the façade states that the Church of the Holy Apostles (Piazza del Limbo, east of Palazzo Spini-Ferroni) was founded by Charlemagne and dedicated by Archbishop Turpinus. Historically it is only certain that the church was built in the late 11th century and renovated in the 15th and 16th centuries. Benedetto da Rovezzano added a beautiful entry to the Romanesque façade in the early 16th century.

The green marble columns from Prato with composite capitals stand out in the basilica; the first two are from the nearby Roman baths. The 1966 flood caused severe damage to the church and its art. Items worth seeing here are a large majolica tabernacle (around 1500) by **Giovanni della Robbia** and the tomb of Oddo Altaviti by **Benedetto da Rovezzano** (1507), both in the left aisle, as well as Vasari's panel *Immaculate Conception* (1541) in the third chapel of the right aisle.

Ponte Santa Trínità The most elegant bridge of Florence – near the church – is the Ponte Santa Trínità. It was built for the first time in 1252, but collapsed soon afterwards. Later it was rebuilt in stone but washed away in 1333 and 1557 by floods. **Ammanati** built it in its present form from 1567 to 1570, presumably getting artistic advice from Michelangelo. When German troops blew it up in 1944 the pieces were collected so that the bridge could be rebuilt in its original form from 1955 to 1957. There are allegorical figures of the Four Seasons (1608) on the four corners of the bridge.

The Frescobaldi palace stands on Piazza Frescobaldi, at the end of the Ponte Santa Trinità. It was built in the 13th century and served as the residence of **Charles of Valois**, the brother of the French king, when the peace commission set up by Pope Boniface VIII brought Charles to Florence in 1301 (as a result of his intervention Dante was banned from the city). In the 17th century the palace of the Frescobaldis was reconstructed; today they are among the largest and wealthiest land-owners in the country, and own excellent vineyards.

Palazzo Frescobaldi

From Ponte Trinità there is a beautiful view of the little Romanesque church of San Jacopo »above the Arno« next to the Palazzo Fresco-baldi. It was built in the 12th century but remodelled often. The beau-tiful campanile was built by Gherardo Silvani in 1660. The church has a vestibule from around 1000, the only one in Florence from this period. Inside there are frescoes and altar paintings by Florentine art-ists from the 18th century. The church is used for concerts and exhib-its today.

San Jacopo sopr' Arno

✴ Santissima Annunziata

✦ J 6/c II

Location: Piazza della SS. Annunziata
Bus: C, 6, 31, 32
❶ Daily 7am – 12.30pm, 4pm – 6.30pm

The church opens onto a stylish piazza and is an architectural masterpiece, although or perhaps because the ground plan of the church and monastery are so irregular.

The Church of the Annunciation, built in 1250 as an oratory of the Servite Order, was completely renovated between 1444 and 1477 by **Michelozzo**. It consists of a nave with side chapels to which a large round choir chapel was added, and a number of annexes to nave and choir. The church also houses many pioneering Mannerist works of art. Enter the **portico**, which was built from 1559 to 1561, through one of the seven arches which are carried by columns with elegant Corinthian capitals. There are three doors: the left one leads to the Chiostro dei

Church with major works of art

Morti, the right one to the Cappella Pucci and the middle one to the
Chiostrino dei Voti, built by Manetti in 1447 to designs by Michelozzo.

*Chiostrino
dei Voti

The **frescoes** of the Chiostrino dei Voti, which was named after the
votive offerings that were once kept here, are famous. There are (from
the left) masterpieces by Andrea del Sarto: cycle on St Filippo Benizzi,
who died in 1285 and was the main figure of the Servites, *Arrival of
the Magi* and *Birth of the Virgin* (1514), one of the artist's best works,
and by Franciabigio (*Betrothal of the Virgin*, 1513). In this work the
artist destroyed the head of Mary because the monks looked at the
picture before it was finished, but then no one wanted to repair the
damage. There are also masterpieces by Pontormo (*Visitation of the
Virgin*, 1516) and Rosso Fiorentino (*Assumption of the Virgin*, 1517).

Church
interior

Inside the nave is flanked by chapels on both sides; the choir is constructed like a rotunda. In the 17th and 18th centuries Santissima
Annunziata was panelled in marble inside and completely redeco-

Santissima Annunziata

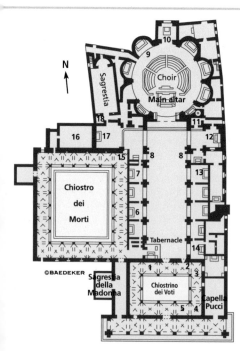

1 »Birth« by Baldovinetti
2 »Procession of the Magi«
   by A. del Sarto
3 »Birth of Mary«
   by A. del Sarto
4 »Visitation« by Pontormo
5 »Ascension« by Fiorentino
6 »Holy Trinity«, fresco
   by del Castagno
7 »Ascension of Mary«
   by Perugino
8 Organ
9 »Resurrection« by Bronzino,
   statue »San Rocco«
   by Veit Stoß
10 Cappella della Madonna
   del Soccorso
11 Pietà by Bandinelli
12 Cappella del Sacramento
13 Monument of Orlando
   de' Medici by Rosselino
14 »Madonna in Glorie«
   by Empoli
15 »Madonna with the Sack«
   by del Sarto
16 Cappella della Confraternità
   di San Luca
17 Cappella del Crocifisso
18 Cappellina delle Reliquie

rated. To the left of the entrance is a **marble tabernacle**, which was commissioned by Piero de' Medici to designs by Michelozzo for the miraculous picture of the Annunciation – of which there are many copies in Italy. It is said that when a monk painted this picture in the 13th century he was so despondent over his inabilitiy to paint a beautiful face for the Madonna that he fell asleep and an angel then finished the face of the Virgin. Bridal couples still come here and the bride leaves her bouquet with the Madonna. The nave has on both sides two beautiful organs from the 16th and 17th (left) centuries.

The Cappella Feroni on the left of the nave has a fresco by **Andrea del Castagno**, *Saviour and St Julian* (1455). The second chapel also has a work by Castagno: *Trinity*, noted for its realism. In the fourth chapel note the *Ascension of Christ* by **Perugino**. The **rotunda**, which is divided into nine chapels, was begun by **Michelozzo** (1444), then altered and completed by **Leon Battista Alberti**. The painting by Agnolo Bronzino in the fourth chapel from the left, *Resurrezione* (1550), and the Cappella della Madonna del Soccorso (Chapel of the Madonna of Refuge; 1594–98), which Giambologna designed to be his tomb, are impressive works. The chapel is richly decorated with frescoes, statues and reliefs. The dome of the rotunda has a fresco by **Volterrano** depicting the Coronation of the Virgin (1681–83).

In the first chapel in the right transept, which holds the tomb of Baccio Bandinelli and his wife, there is a fine **Pietà** by the artist himself.

From the vestibule the left door leads to the Chiostro dei Morti (Cloister of the Dead) past the Sagrestia della Madonna. In the cloister is the fresco **Madonna del Sacco* – named after the sack that St Joseph is leaning on. **Andrea del Sarto** painted it in 1525; it is one of his main works.

Chiostro dei Morti

In the Cappella del Crocifisso (Chapel of the Crucified Christ) note the ceramic figure of John the Baptist (1444–50) by **Michelozzo**.

Capella del Crocifisso

* Santo Spirito

✦ H 7/a IV

Location: Piazza Santo Spirito
Bus: C3, 6, 36, 37
❶ Mon, Tue, Thu – Sat 10am – 12.30pm, 4pm – 5.30pm, Sun 4pm – 5.30pm,
www.museicivicifiorentini.comune.fi.it

The bare exterior of Santo Spirito, which it was never completed to the original plans, belies the fact that it is one of the purest Renaissance churches.

Santo Spirito

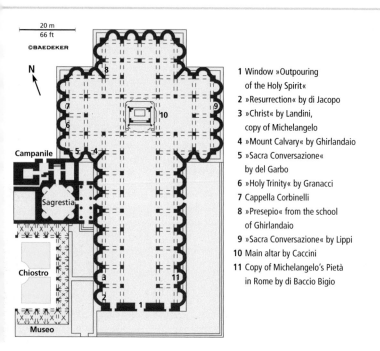

1 Window »Outpouring of the Holy Spirit«
2 »Resurrection« by di Jacopo
3 »Christ« by Landini, copy of Michelangelo
4 »Mount Calvary« by Ghirlandaio
5 »Sacra Conversazione« by del Garbo
6 »Holy Trinity« by Granacci
7 Cappella Corbinelli
8 »Presepio« from the school of Ghirlandaio
9 »Sacra Conversazione« by Lippi
10 Main altar by Caccini
11 Copy of Michelangelo's Pietà in Rome by di Baccio Bigio

In the early 15th century several Florentine families got together to build a new church on the site of one that had burned down. They were able to commission the city's most famous architect, **Brunelleschi**. When he died in 1446 the building itself was not much past the foundation. Brunelleschi's heir **Antonio Manetti** was able to complete the building according to Brunelleschi's plans; it was not finished until 1482 when the dome over the crossing was vaulted. **Giuliano da Sangallo** began with the sacristy in 1488, and **Cronaca** completed the narthex by 1494. The façade was added in the 18th century without any ornamentation.

Church interior
Santo Spirito has the shape of a Latin cross 97m/320ft long, 32m/105ft wide in the nave and 58m/191ft in the transept – with forty semicircular chapels, which are covered by a straight wall outside. Numerous works of art, tombs and monuments make Santo Spirito an impressive museum. Paintings and statues, reliefs and sacred objects deco-

The main altar of Santo Spirito stands in the crossing

rate the side altars. The rose window on the inner façade was designed by **Perugino** (*Descent of the Holy Spirit*).
The left aisle leads to a beautiful antechamber (1492–94), by Cronaca,
and from there into the ***sacristy**. This is built on an octagonal floor
plan, was designed by **Giuliano da Sangallo** from 1488 to 1492 and
is a masterpiece of European architecture. It is an High Renaissance
construction with a double-skinned dome. The triple wall zones divided by entablatures are an innovation. The capitals of the lower
pilasters are decorated with figures.
In the crossing is the early Baroque canopy altar with rich pietra dura
decoration (around 1600) by **Caccini**. In the first chapel note the
painting *Andate al Calvario* (Ascent to Mount Calvary) by **Michele
Ghirlandaio** and the glass windows. In the adjacent chapel the panel
Madonna col Bambino in Trono e Santi (Enthroned Madonna with
Child and Saints) by **Raffaele di Carli** (1505) is impressive. At the
head (left) is the panel *La Santissima Trinità adorata dalle Sante Ca-*

terina e Maddalena (Trinity Worshipped by Saints Catherine and Mary Magdalene), which is attributed to **Francesco Granacci**. Next to it is the Cappella Corbinelli (Chapel of the Sacrament; 1492), a work of exquisite taste by **Andrea Sansovino**, who also made the sculptures.

In the right transept note the altar painting *Madonna col Bambino e San Giovannino* (Madonna with Child and the Young John the Baptist, 1490), by **Filippino Lippi**, the most famous work in the church.

In the apse on the left is *Annunciation* from the Florentine school of the 15th century and a Nativity scene (*Presepio*) from the school of Ghirlandaio, on the right a polyptych by Maso di Banco (around 1340).

The first **cloister** (1580) is the work of **Alfonso Parigi**. The second cloister was built by **Ammanati** between 1564 and 1569.

Cenacolo   To the left of the church in the first cloister is the entrance to the **Cenacolo** (refectory), which houses a small museum today. The refectory is all that remains of the old Augustinian monastery; the large fresco *The Last Supper* (around 1360) is attributed to **Andrea Orcagna**. Ghiberti was already of this opinion, which was confirmed after thorough research and restorations. The heavily damaged fresco, of which only a crucifixion scene remains, is one of the greatest 14th-century works in Florence. The museum also has beautiful sculptures from the Fondazione Salvatore Romano (Salvatore Romano Foundation), works from pre-Romanesque to the 15th century including two sea monsters (13th century).

❶ Mon, Sat, Sun 10am–4pm, admission: €3

AROUND SANTO SPIRITO

Palazzo   Palazzo Guadagni on Piazza di Santo Spirito has a classical austerity
Guadagni   and beauty. **Cronaca** built it – presumably from 1503 to 1506 – for Riniero Dei. The three storeys all have different decorations and terminate in an open loggia. In 1684 the palace was acquired by Marchese Guadagni, then the Dufour-Berte family took it over. The building housed the German Art Historical Institute until 1964. There is a hotel on the top floor with a wonderful roof terrace.

Casa of   Not far east of the church, the Casa (house) of Bianca Cappello,
Bianca   daughter of a Venetian patrician and mistress, later wife of Grand
Cappello   Duke Francesco I, is a beautiful example of an aristocratic house of the time. In 1567 it was remodelled completely by Bernardo Buontalenti. The grotesque bats underneath the windows are unusual.

Settignano

Location: 8 km east of Florence
Bus: 10
www.settignagno.com

The town of Settignano is a charming venue for an excursion because of the magnificent villas nearby with large gardens.

These include the Villa I Tatti near Ponte a Ménsola, which is the seat of the Centro per la Storia del Rinascimento (Centre for the History of the Renaissance) of Harvard University. The **Collezione Berenson** has valuable works of art.

Villa »I Tatti«

❶ Via Vincigliata 22, tours only with reservations at tel. 0 55 60 3 51, www.itatti.harvard.edu

Also close to Settignano, the famous Villa Gamberaia (Via del Rossellino 72), **one of the most beautiful villa estates of the 16th century**, was heavily damaged in the Second World War but then completely reconstructed according to the old plans. The park today still looks like a Renaissance garden with geometrically cut boxwood hedges and a fountain in the middle as well as an axis from one end of the garden to the other.

*Villa
Gamberaia

❶ Mid April – Oct daily 9am – 6pm, Nov – mid April daily 9am – 5pm, admission: €10, www.villagamberaia.com

Synagoga e Museo Ebraico

—————————— ✴ **J 6/ c/d III**

Location: Via Luigi Carlo Farini 6
Bus: C1, 6, 31, 32
❶ Mon – Thu, Sun 10am – 5.30pm Fri 10am – 3pm, admission: €6.50

The monumental synagogue with its green dome is a distinguishing element of the skyline of Florence; it is one of the most magnificent European synagogues of the 19th century.

It was financed by a donation and built between 1874 and 1882 by three architects who modelled it on Hagia Sophia in Istanbul with a domed central plan. Some of the elements of decoration are Moorish. Inside note especially the ornamental painting and the glass windows.

Modeled on
Hagia Sophia

The Museo Ebraico (Jewish Museum) is adjacent, where visitors can gain insight into the history of the Jews in Florence with the aid of documents. Cult objects from various centuries are also displayed.

AROUND THE SYNAGOGA

Sant' Ambrogio
Saint Ambrose south of the synagogue is one of the **oldest churches in Florence**. The building was remodelled in the late 13th century and restored several times in the following centuries. The neo-Gothic façade was added in 1887.

Inside the church are the **tombs of famous Renaissance artists** such as Cronaca (†1580), Mino da Fiesole (†1484) and Verrocchio (†1488). The paintings and frescoes, e.g. the *Madonna del Latte* by Nardo di Cione, a triptych by Bicci di Lorenzo and the fresco *Procession* by Cosimo Rosselli, are noteworthy. A marble tabernacle (1481–83) by Mino da Fiesole in the Cappella del Miracolo (Chapel of Miracles) depicts the event after which the chapel was named: in 1230 a priest omitted to dry the chalice after mass and the next morning the remaining wine had turned to blood.

i Via Pietraplana 2 r

Uffizi Gallery

▶Galleria degli Uffizi

** Ville Medicee

Location: around Florence

Several members of the large Medici clan built attractive villas with expansive gardens as summer residences in the beautiful hilly Tuscan landscape near Florence. The architects were able to give free rein to their abilities and imagination in the buildings and gardens – albeit within the limits of Renaissance architecture: The painters and sculptors used the opportunity to show the more cheerful sides of their art in many varied forms.

*Villa la Petraia
Villa la Petraia is located 6km/3.5mi north of Florence in Castello. Francesco de' Medici bought it in 1575 and had **Buontalenti** remodel it; the old defensive tower was preserved. In the 19th century the

villa was the summer residence of the kings of Italy; it is still state property and is open to the public. The beautifully designed **park** is charming and offers a good view as far as Florence.

● Jan, Feb, Nov, Dec daily 8.15am–4.30pm; Mar daily 8.15am–5.30pm; Apr, May, Sep, Oct daily 8.15am–6.30pm, June–Aug daily 8.15am–7.30pm; closed every 2nd, 3rd Monday of the month, free admission; www.polomuseale.firenze.it

Only a few hundred metres to the west of Villa la Petraia lies Villa Medicea di Castello (Via Castello 47), which dates from the 16th century in its present form. The villa, seat of the Accademia della Crusca is not accessible, but the extensive park with its elaborate waterworks, grottoes and statues is open to the public. In the sculptural group on the central fountain Hercules battles against the giant Antaeus.

Villa di Castello

● Via Castello 47, opening times like Villa la Petraia, free admission, www.polomuseale.firenze.it

One of the most magnificent Medici villas, Villa di Poggio, stands on the edge of Poggio a Caiano, 18km/11mi north-west of Florence. The villa was built as a summer home for Lorenzo il Magnifico from 1485 by **Giuliano da Sangallo**. The owner did not live to see it completed; but Leo X, the first Medici pope, enjoyed the rural luxury to the utmost. It possessed residential quarters of considerable size. The ground floor is decorated by arcades; large terraces surround the first floor and a stately loggia with columns and architrave recalls the architecture of ancient temples and palaces.

**Villa di Poggio a Caiano

The painting of the interior was done by the **most famous fresco artists of the 16th century**, including Andrea del Sarto, Pontormo and Alessandro Allori. The noble Medici country residence shows a few architectural changes today (for example, the outside stairs), after being converted to the royal residence in the second half of the 19th century. It lies in the middle of a wonderful park with hothouses and exotic decorative gardens. The interior furnishings have unfortunately survived only in part, but the main hall (Salone di Leone X) with frescoes painted by Allori in 1580 is original.

● Opening times like Villa la Petraia, free admission, www.polomuseale. firenze.it

PRACTICAL
INFORMATION

Important and helpful information from arrival and planning through sources of information to a small Italian phrase book and local transportation.

Arrival · Before the Journey

By air The small Amerigo Vespucci Airport (www.aeroporto.firenze.it) lies 6km/3.5mi outside Florence in Peretola. The airline Meridiana (www.meridiana.it) flies there from London Gatwick. The most important airport in the region is Aeroporto Galileo Galilei (www.pisa-airport.com), just over one mile outside Pisa. There are currently connections to Pisa from the following destinations in the United Kingdom and Ireland: Belfast International (Jet2.com), Birmingham (Ryanair), Bournemouth (Ryanair), Bristol (easyjet), Coventry (Tomsonfly), Dublin (Ryanair), East Midlands (Ryanair), Edinburgh (Jet2.com, Ryanair), Glasgow Prestwick (Ryanair), Leeds-Bradford (Jet2.com), Liverpool (Ryanair), London Gatwick (British Airways, easyjet), Luton (easyjet) and Stansted (Ryanair), Manchester (Jet2.com) and Newcastle (Jet2.com). Intercontinental flights land at Leonardo da Vinci airport in Rome. Trains and buses run regularly between Pisa (railway station at airport) and Florence and take about one hour.

By car There are no car-carrying »motorail« trains from Calais or Paris to Italy, so motorists from the UK normally need to make the long journey on European highways. For those driving south-east through France the most obvious route is to go south to Lyon, then cross the Alps on the E70 to Turin; or, alternatively and further north, to pass Geneva and take the Mont Blanc tunnel to Turin (European route E25), then south to Genoa and along the coast into Tuscany. The coastal route is the E80 from the south of France parallel to the shore of the Mediterranean to Genoa, La Spezia and Livorno.

Drivers who have been in the Swiss or Austrian Alps before travelling to Tuscany or are coming from Germany or other points further north have a number of options. One is to take the St Bernard Pass, entering Italy at Chiasso, and on to Milan and then either via Bologna on the E35 to Florence, or on the E62 to Genoa and then via the E80 to La Spezia and south to the Tuscan coast. Alternatives from Switzerland are the Simplon Pass and St Gotthard Pass. Further east there is the route E45 from Munich to Innsbruck and the Brenner Pass, then on past Verona to Bologna and west into Tuscany.

Motorway Almost all motorways (autostrada) in Italy charge tolls (pedaggio). The tolls can be paid either in cash, with a credit card or with the so-called Viacard (►Transport). They are available in Italy from the automobile clubs, the ACI offices at the borders, motorway entrances, in tobacco shops as well as at petrol stations (information: www.autostrade.it).

By train For those who do not like flying, the train is an option for getting to Florence, which is a major rail hub, and can be reached from London via Paris in about 17 hours as an overnight trip. There are also good direct connections from Germany, Austria and Switzerland. For those arriving from the south, there are two main routes between Florence and Rome. The coastal line runs from Rome via Livorno and Grosseto to Pisa, the interior line from Rome via Florence to Pisa. Most of the Italian rail network is maintained by the Italian national railway, the Ferrovie dello Stato (FS); this is complemented by several private lines (schedules in the FS timetable). There are different kinds of trains: Regionale (slow local train), Interregionale (mainline train) and Espresso (express train). Intercity, Eurocity, Eurostar and the Pendolino, a high-speed luxury train, require seat reservations; there is also a surcharge on the regular fare (supplemento). There are one-way (andata) and return tickets (andata e ritorno) for first (prima) and second (seconda) class (classe). International tickets are valid for two months, and the journey may be interrupted as often as the traveller wishes. For tickets bought in Italy the following applies: for distances up to 200km/125mi the ticket is valid for 6 hours, for journeys over 200km/125mi for 24 to 48 hours. **Don't forget:** tickets must be validated at the departure station! There are special rates for groups, senior citizens over 60 years, young people under 26 years and families.

Bus tours directly to Florence or including Florence as part of a tour of Tuscany are offered by many operators. These are mostly group tours. The Euroline long-distance bus services which connect many European cities have no direct link from London; with changes in Paris and Milan the journey time to Florence is about 28 hours. Arrival by bus may be convenient for travellers who are moving on from other parts of continental Europe.

By bus

IMMIGRATION AND CUSTOMS REGULATIONS

The identity cards and passports of EU citizens are often no longer checked. However, since random inspections are carried out at the border and identification is required at airports, all visitors should be able to show their **passports** when they enter the country. Children under 16 years of age must carry a children's passport or be entered in the parent's passport.

Travel documents

Always carry your driving licence, the motor vehicle registration and the international green insurance card. Motor vehicles must have the oval sticker showing nationality unless they have a Euro licence plate.

Car documents

Since 2011 the EU has required that pets have an implanted microchip when they travel as well as an EU pet pass with proof of rabies vaccination. The shots must have been given at least 30 days, but no

Pets and travel

AIRPORTS
Florence
Amerigo Vespucci
tel. 055 3 06 13 00
www.aeroporto.firenze.it

Pisa
Galileo Galilei, tel. 050 84 93 00
www.pisa-airport.com

AIRLINES
Alitalia
tel. *89 20 10 (within Italy)
tel. 06 6 56 49 (from other countries)
www.alitalia.com

Meridiana
Aeroporto Amerigo Vespucci
tel. 05 53 02 49 10, 199 11 13 33 or
Aeroporto Galileo Galilei

tel. 05 04 30 48
www.meridiana.it

RAIL TRAVEL
In London
Rail Europe Travel Centre
178 Piccadilly, London W1V 0BA
tel. 0870 8 37 13 71
www.raileurope.co.uk

In Italy
Trenitalia tel. 892021
www.trenitalia.com

BUS
Eurolines
Bookings online and in UK through
National Express tel. 087 05 80 80 80
www.eurolines.com and
www.nationalexpress.com

mare than 12 months before arrival in the EU. A muzzle and leash are required, as is indemnity insurance.

Customs regulations for EU citizens
The European Union member states (including Italy) form a common economic area, within which the movement of goods for private purposes is largely duty-free. There are merely certain maximum quantities which apply (for example 800 cigarettes, 10 litres of spirits and 90 litres of wine per person). Gifts up to a value of €430 are also duty-free. During random inspections customs officers must be convinced that the goods are actually intended for private use.

Customs regulations for non-EU citizens
For travellers from outside the EU, the following duty-free quantities apply: 200 cigarettes or 100 cigarillos or 50 cigars or 250g of tobacco; also 2 litres of wine and 2 litres of sparkling wine or 1 litre of spirits with an alcohol content of more than 22% vol.; 500g of coffee or 200g of coffee extracts, 100g of tea or 40g of tea extract, 50ml of perfume or 0.25 litres of eau de toilette.

TRAVEL INSURANCE

Health insurance
Citizens of EU countries are entitled to treatment in Italy under the local regulations in case of illness on production of their **European**

health insurance card (EHIC). Even with this card, in most cases some of the costs for medical care and prescribed medication must be paid by the patient. Upon presentation of receipts the health insurance at home covers the costs – but not for all treatments. Citizens of non-EU countries must pay for medical treatment and medicine themselves and should take out private health insurance.

Since some of the costs for medical treatment and medication typically have to be met by the patient, and the costs for return transportation may not be covered by the normal health insurance, additional travel insurance is recommended.

Private travel insurance

Electricity

Italy uses 220 volt electricity; an adapter is generally necessary.

Emergency

General emergency numbers
tel. 118 (national)

Fire department
tel. 115 (national)

Police emergency number
tel. 112 (national)
Florence police: tel. 055 3285

Breakdown service of the ACI
tel. 80 31 16; 800 116 800 (mobile phone)

Etiquette and Customs

Bella figura, a beautiful appearance, is a deep-seated need for most Italians. Everyone who goes out in public likes to dress up, even for a trip to the post office or market, following Coco Chanel's motto: always be dressed to meet the love of your life. When there is a choice, money is always spent on fashion (and good food) rather than furniture or a coat of paint for the façade. »Label-free« tourists who stroll into cathedrals with flip-flops on their feet, wear shorts to visit the art gallery, sit in a restaurant in sandals or even dare to stroll bare-chested through the old city are looked down upon with amusement or a complete lack of comprehension.

What is acceptable in Italy and what isn't?

What to pay attention to in a restaurant: guests do not just walk to a table, but wait for the head waiter to seat them. He will, of course, respect the guests preferences. Restaurants also do not make separate bills at a table. Instead the waiter makes one bill and the guests divide it up amongst themselves.

Italians are spontaneous behind the wheel. Although the government of Silvio Berlusconi decided to introduce a points system for traffic offences in 2004, Italians constantly prove their mastery of the art of living, airily attempting to overtake on the wrong side or parking their Fiats three deep – it's a relief when the chaos then unsnarls and as many people as possible join in with all the gestures at their command. Then the street becomes a living piazza, the machine-like routine of day-to-day life is interrupted. The purpose of all this is to communicate, and only rarely to be proved right, a fact shown by the Italians' chivalrous regard for pedestrians, which is a pleasing contrast to other Mediterranean countries.

Arrangiarsi
To enjoy life in Italy, approach individual Italians and let them know through a smile or a gesture just how much you appreciate dealing with such a competent and winning counterpart. Do not hesitate to ask for the waiter's first name, and call out a »bravo«, »grande« or »bello« too many rather than one too few. And if things are not working out, bring the ancient Italian art of »arrangiarsi« into play. A sympathetic compliment is usually more effective than a threatening attitude, which – you guessed it – is detrimental to the bella figura. This is a nation that prefers to be adored than to be told what to do.

Health

Medical help
In case of an emergency it is best to contact the Guardia Medica, which is based in Careggi university hospital (Largo Bambilla 3). First aid (pronto soccorso) is also available at Archispedale Santa Maria Nuova (Piazza Santa Maria Nuova) hospital. First aid for children (pronto soccorso pediatro) is available at Ospedale A. Meyer (Via Giordano 13).

First aid is also provided by the White Cross (Croce Bianca), Green Cross (Croce Verde) and Red Cross (Croce Rossa Italiana). The addresses are all on the first page of the telephone book (Avantielenco). Dentists can be found in the telephone book under »Medici dentisti«.

> ! **MARCO POLO TIP**
>
> *Medieval pharmacy* **Insider Tip**
>
> Take the time to visit Farmacia Moltenni (Via Calzaiouli 7 r), which dates from the 13th century and is thus the oldest pharmacy in the world. The great poet Dante is supposed to have bought his medicines here regularly. There's sure to be something that needs replenishing.

PHARMACIES

24 hour pharmacies

Farmacia Communale No 13
Santa Maria Novella railway station
Farmacia Communale No 5
Piazza dell'Isolotto 15 r
Farmacia Moltenni►MARCO POLO tip
p.308

MEDICAL HELP

24 hour Medical Service

Via Roma 4
tel. 0 55 47 54 11
(all major languages)
www.medicalservice.firenze.it

Medical emergencies

tel. 118

Pharmacies (farmacie) are generally open from Mon to Fri from 9am to 1pm and from 4pm to 7.30pm. They close either on Wednesdays or Saturdays. Some pharmacies are open around the clock.

Pharmacies

►p. 308

Medical
insurance

Information

IN ITALY

Italian National Tourist Office ENIT (Ente Nazionale Italiano per il Turismo)

Helpline in many languages:
tel. 0 39 03 90 39
Service number
within Italy:
tel. 8 00 00 00 39
www.enit.de
www.italia.it

IN AUSTRALIA

Italian Government Tourist Office

Level 4, 46 Market Street
NSW 2000 SIDNEY
tel. 02 92 621 666

IN CANADA

Italian Government Tourist Office

175 Bloor Street E, Suite 907

Toronto M4W 3R8
tel. 416 925 48 82

IN UK

Italian State Tourist Board

1 Princes Street
London W1B 2AY
tel. 207 408 12 54

IN USA

Italian State Tourist Board

630 Fifth Avenue, Suite 1565
10111 New York
tel. 212 245 48 22

IN FLORENCE

Agenzia per il Turismo di Firenze

Via Cavour 1 r
tel. 055 29 08 32
www.firenzeturismo.it

Info offices
Piazza Stazione 4 a
tel. 055 21 22 45

Loggia del Bigallo
Piazza San Giovanni (near the cathedral)
tel. 055 28 84 96

EMBASSIES AND CONSULATES
IN ITALY
Australian Embassy in Rome
Via Antonio Bosio 5
tel. 06 85 27 21
www.italy.embassy.gov.au

British Embassy in Rome
Via XX Settembre 80A
tel. 06 422 00 001
www.britishembassy.gov.uk

British Consulate in Florence
Lungarno Corsini 2
tel. 055 28 41 33

Canadian Embassy in Rome
Via Zara 30
tel. 06 44 59 81
www.canada.it

Embassy of the Republic of Ireland in Rome
Piazza Campitelli 3
tel. 069 697 91 21
www.ambasciata-irlanda.it

New Zealand Embassy in Rome
Via Zara 28
tel. 06 441 71 71
www.nzembassy.com

United States Embassy in Rome
Via Vittorio Veneto 119
tel. 06 4 67 41
www.usis.it

United States Consulate in Florence
Lungarno Amerigo Vespucci 38
tel. 055 26 69 51

Language

Development of the Italian language

Italian is the direct descendant of Latin, the closest to it of all the Romance languages. The earlier political unrest is the main reason for the development of the many Italian dialects. The great poets of the 13th and 14th century, especially Dante, wrote in the Tuscan dialect, which is still used today. English is generally spoken in the larger hotels and restaurants in Florence. Beyond that it will help to know a few simple phrases.

Italian phrases

At a glance

Sì/No	Yes/No
Per favore/Grazie	Please/Thank you
Non c'è di che	You're welcome
Scusi!/Scusa!	Excuse me!

Come dice?	Excuse me?
Non La/ti capisco	I cannot understand you
Parlo solo un po' di ...	I only speak a little ...
Mi può aiutare, per favore?	Can you please help me?
Vorrei ...	I would like ...
(Non) mi piace	I (do not) like that
Ha ...?	Do you have ...?
Quanto costa?	How much does it cost?
Che ore sono?/Che ora è?	What time is it?
Come sta?/Come stai?	How are you?
Bene, grazie. E Lei/tu?	Fine, thank you. And you?

Getting around

a sinistra	left
a destra	right
diritto	straight ahead
vicino/lontano	close/far
Quanti chilometri sono?	How far is that?
Vorrei noleggiare ...	I would like to rent ...
... una macchina	... a car
... una bicicletta	... a bicycle
... una barca	... a boat
Scusi, dov'è ...?	Excuse me, where is ...?
la stazione centrale	the central railway station
la metro(politana)	the metro/subway
l'aeroporto	the airport
all'albergo	to the hotel
Ho un guasto.	I have broken down.
Mi potrebbe mandare un carro-attrezzi?	Can you please send a tow truck?
Scusi, c'è un'officina qui?	Is there a garage nearby?
Dov'è la prossima stazione di servizio?	Where is the next gas station?
benzina normale	regular gasoline
super/gasolio	super/diesel
Deviazione	detour
Senso unico	one-way street
sbarrato	closed
rallentare	drive slowly
tutte le direzioni	all directions
tenere la destra	drive on the right
Zone di silenzio	honking forbidden
Zona tutelata inizio	start of the no-parking zone
Aiuto!	Help!
Attenzione!	Attention!

Chiami subito ...	Quickly, call ...
... un'autoambulanza	... an ambulance
... la polizia	... the police

Going out

Scusi, mi potrebbe indicare ...?	Where can I find ...?
... un buon ristorante?	... a good restaurant?
... un locale tipico?	... an typical restaurant?
C'è una gelateria qui vicino?	Is there an ice cream parlour nearby?
Può riservarci per stasera un tavolo per quattro persone?	Can I reserve a table for four, for this evening?
Alla Sua salute!	Good health!
Il conto, per favore.	The bill, please.
Andava bene?	How was everything?
Il mangiare era eccellente.	The meal was excellent.
Ha un programma delle manifestazioni?	Do you have an events diary?

Shopping

Dov'è si può trovare ...?	Where can I find ...?
... una farmacia	... a pharmacy
... un panificio	... a bakery
... un negozio di articoli fotografici	... a photo shop
... un grande magazzino	... a department store
... un negozio di generi alimentari	... a grocery store
... il mercato	... the market
... il supermercato	... the supermarket
... il tabaccaio	... the tobacconist
... il giornalaio	... the newsagent

Accommodation

Scusi, potrebbe consigliarmi ...?	Can you please recommend ...?
... un albergo	... a hotel
... una pensione	... a bed and breakfast
Ho prenotato una camera.	I have a room reservation.
È libera ...?	Do you have ...?
... una singola	... a single room
... una doppia	... a double room
... con doccia/bagno	... with shower/bath
... per una notte	... for one night
... per una settimana	... for one week
... con vista sul mare	... with a view of the sea
Quanto costa la camera ...?	What is the cost of the room ...?

... con la prima colazione?	... with breakfast?
... a mezza pensione?	... with half-board?

Doctor and pharmacy

Mi può consigliare un buon medico?	Can you recommend a good doctor?
Mi puo dare una medicina per ...	Please give me medication for ...
Soffro di diarrea.	I have diarrhoea.
Ho mal di pancia.	I have a stomach ache.
... mal di testa	... headache
... mal di gola	... sore throat
... mal di denti	... toothache
... influenza	... influenza
... tosse	... a cough
... la febbre	... fever
... scottatura solare	... sunburn
... costipazione	... constipation

Numbers

zero	0	diciannove	19
uno	1	venti	20
due	2	ventuno	21
tre	3	trenta	30
quattro	4	quaranta	40
cinque	5	cinquanta	50
sei	6	sessanta	60
sette	7	settanta	70
otto	8	ottanta	80
nove	9	novanta	90
dieci	10	cento	100
undici	11	centouno	101
dodici	12	duecento	200
tredici	13	mille	1000
quattordici	14	duemila	2000
quindici	15	diecimila	10000
sedici	16		
diciassette	17	un quarto	1/4
diciotto	18	un mezzo	1/2

Menu

Prima colazione	breakfast
caffè, espresso	small coffee, no milk
caffè macchiato	small coffee with a little milk

caffè latte	coffee with milk
cappuccino	coffee with foamed milk
tè al latte/al limone	tea with milk/lemon
cioccolata	hot chocolate
frittata	omelette/pancake
pane/panino/pane tostato	bread/roll/toast
burro	butter
salame	sausage
prosciutto	ham
miele	honey
marmellata	marmelade/jam
iogurt	yogurt
Antipasti	Appetizers and soup
affettato misto	mixed cold cuts
anguilla affumicata	smoked eel
melone e prosciutto	melon with ham
minestrone	thick vegetable soup
pastina in brodo	broth with fine pasta
vitello tonnato	cold roast veal with tuna mayonnaise
zuppa di pesce	fish soup
Primi piatti	Pasta and rice
pasta	pasta
fettuccine/tagliatelle	ribbon noodles
gnocchi	small potato dumplings
polenta (alla valdostana)	corn porridge (with cheese)
agnolotti/ravioli/tortellini	filled pasta
vermicelli	vermicelli
Carni e Pesce	Meat and fish
agnello	lamb
ai ferri/alla griglia	grilled
aragosta	crayfish
brasato	roast
coniglio	rabbit
cozze/vongole	mussels/small mussels
fegato	liver
fritto di pesce	baked fish
gambero, granchio	lobster, crab
maiale	pork
manzo/bue	beef
pesce spada	swordfish
platessa	plaice
pollo	chicken
rognoni	kidneys

salmone	salmon
scampi fritti	small fried shrimp
sogliola	sole
tonno	tuna
trota	trout
vitello	veal
Verdura	Vegetables
asparagi	asparagus
carciofi	artichokes
carote	carrots
cavolfiore	cauliflower
cavolo	cabbage
cicoria belga	chicory
cipolle	onions
fagioli	white beans
fagiolini	green beans
finocchi	fennel
funghi	mushrooms
insalata mista/verde	mixed/green salad
lenticchie	lentils
melanzane	aubergine
patate	potatoes
patatine fritte	french fries
peperoni	paprika
pomodori	tomatoes
spinaci	spinach
zucca	pumpkin
Formaggi	Cheese
parmigiano	parmesan
pecorino	sheep's milk cheese
ricotta	ricotta cheese
Dolci e frutta	Dessert and fruit
cassata	ice cream with candied fruit
coppa assortita	assorted ice cream
coppa con panna	ice cream with cream
tirami su	dessert with mascarpone cream
zabaione	whipped egg cream
zuppa inglese	cake soaked in liqueur with custard
Bevande	Drinks

acqua minerale	mineral water
aranciata	orangeade
bibita	refreshing drink
bicchiere	glass
birra scura/chiara	dark/light beer
birra alla spina	beer on tap
birra senza alcool	alcohol-free beer
bottiglia	bottle
con ghiaccio	with ice
digestivo	digestive
gassata/con gas	sparkling, carbonated
liscia/senza gas	not carbonated
secco	dry
spumante	sparkling wine
succo	fruit juice
vino bianco/rosato/rosso	white/rose/red wine
vino della casa	house wine

Literature

Fiction   **Giovanni Boccaccio**: *The Decameron*. Penguin Classics, 2003. Collection of 100 stories, which were written after the great plague in Florence in 1348 and are considered to be the genesis of Italian prose.

Dan Brown: *Inferno*. Anchor, 2014. This time the American author of best sellers picked Florence with its palazzi, churches and art treasures as the setting of his exciting thriller. Harvard professor Robert Langdon tries to uncover another wordwide conspiracy and the code iss in Dante's medieval epic *The Divine Comedy*.

Dante Alighieri: *The Divine Comedy*. Everyman's Library. Dante's chief work, an allegorical epic poem in the Tuscan dialect composed from 1311, contains many references to current events and contemporaries of Dante.

E. M. Forster: *Room with a View*. Bantam Classics, 1988. Florence 1907: an Englishwoman on a educational journey falls in love with a young aesthete. At first she denies her feelings, but then she finds the courage to choose against all conventions.

Ross King: *Brunelleschi's Dome: The Story of the Great Cathedral in Florence*. Pimlico, 2005 Exciting fictional account of Brunelleschi's construction of the cathedral dome.

Magdalen Nabb: *Death of an Englishman.* Soho Crime, 2001. Gripping crime novel with the somewhat slow Inspector Maresciallo Guarnaccia as the focus.

Vasco Pratolini: *A Tale of Poor Lovers.* Monthly Review Press, 1988. Life and love in Florence in Fascist times.

Michelangelo Buonarotti: *Life, Letters and Poetry.* Oxford World's Classics. A first-hand impression of his life.   Non-fiction

Peter Burke: *The Italian Renaissance: Culture and Society in Italy.* Polity Books, 1999. A standard work on a great period in the history of Tuscany.

James Cleugh: *The Medici: A Tale of Fifteen Generations.* Hippocrene, 1994. Portrait of the most important family in the history of Florence.

Christopher Hibbert. *The Rise and Fall of the House of Medici.* Penguin Books. Readable account by a leading cultural historian.

Christopher Hibbert: *Florence: The Biography of a City.* Penguin Books, 1994. An excellent account of the history of the city.

Giorgio Vasari: *The Lives of the Artists.* Oxford World's Classics, 1998. Biographies of the most famous painters, sculptors, and architects of the Renaissance from Cimabue to Michelangelo – a major work on Renaissance art. Written around 1550.

Lost and Found

Municipal Lost Property Office
(Ufficio Oggetti Trovati)
Via Francesco Veracini 5/5

tel. 055 33 48 02
Hours: Mon, Wed, Fri 9am–12.30pm
Tue, Thu also 2.30–4.30pm.

Media

La Repubblica, Italy's biggest-selling daily newspaper, is published in Florence with a local section.   Daily newspapers

Corriere della Sera is the number two national newspaper.
La Nazione is the largest Tuscan daily newspaper and published in Florence.
Leading international newspapers are available in Florence.

Calendar of events
The bi-monthly *Firenze Spettacolo* in Florence has information on all important events.
The tourist information centres and the hotels *Firenze Concierge Information*. It is published in English and Italian.

Money

Euro
The euro is the official currency of Italy.

Banks
With few exceptions the banks are open Mon–Fri 8.30am–1pm; afternoons vary (about 2.30–3.30pm).

ATM machines
Cash is available at ATM machines without problems round the clock by using credit and debit cards with a PIN.

Lost cards
If debit and/or credit cards as well as medical insurance cards and mobile telephones are lost it should be reported immediately.

Credit cards
Most international credit cards are accepted by banks, hotels, restaurants, car rentals and many shops.

Receipts
In Italy customers are required to request and keep a receipt (ricevuta fiscale or scontrino). It can happen that a customer is asked to show a receipt after leaving a shop. This is intended to make tax evasion more difficult.

Post · Communications

Post offices
Italian post offices offer regular mail and package delivery services as well as postal banking services. They are usually open Mon–Fri 8.15am–1.30pm and Sat 8.15am–12.30pm. The main post office (Via Pellecceria 1) in the arcades of the centrally located Piazza della Repubblica is open Mon–Sat from 8.15am to 7pm.

Postage stamps
Postage stamps (francobolli) can be bought in post offices or – quicker – in tobacco shops, which have the »T« sign (tabacchi). Letters up to 20g/0.7oz and postcards within Italy and to EU countries cost 0.85 euros.

There are only a few public telephones left, which can be used with a   Telephoning
telephone card (carta telefonica) that can be bought in tobacco shops,
Internet shops and post offices. Before using it the perforated corner
has to be broken off.

The area code is part of the Italian telephone number; it should be
dialed when making local calls and when calling abroad (including
the initial zero). This does not include emergency, service or mobile
phone numbers (these do not begin with a zero). Service numbers
with an 800 area code are free.

Cell phones (Italian *cellulare*) with the usual networks work well in
Italy by means of roaming, but the charges are higher. Anyone who
visits Italy often should get a prepaid chip from the Italian TIM; that
will be cheaper. Tarif comparisons can be found online.

Prices and Discounts

Florence offers significant tourist
discounts with its special Florence
Card. Pulic transportation is free for
card holders. Children, youth and
senior citizens get discounts on entrance fees at museums (▶p. 119).

?	*What does it cost?*
INSIGHT	Main dish ▶p. 97 Double room: ▶p. 134 1 espresso: from € 1.20 1 l petrol: ca € 1.75

Time

Italy is in the Central European Time zone (CET), one hour ahead of
Greenwich Mean Time. For the summer months from the end of
March to the end of October European summer time is used
(CEST = CET+1 hour).

Toilets

The information portal of Florence's tourism office (www.firenzetur-
ismo.com) has a downloadable list and map of public toilets:. The
charge is usually between €0.70 and €1:There are public rest rooms at
the cathedral square, in the San Lorenzo and Mercato Centrale markets as well as at the main railway station, among other places. Of
course, all museums have free public toilets and patrons may use the
rest rooms in the many bars (a glass of water or an espresso at the bar
is sufficient).

Transport

Public transport

The public transport in Florence are buses of the ATAF and one tram line (Line 1 from Scandicci to Santa Maria Novella, two other lines are being built). There are **tickets** for 90 minutes, 24 hours or several days. There is also a Carta Agile, a magnetic card with 10 rides at a reduced price. The tickets are available at all official sales locations, at automats, tobacco shops marked with a »T« as well as newspaper stands and bars with signs »*biglietti et abonamenti ATAF*«. The tickets must be validated on the bus.

Transport maps are available at the ATAF info kiosk at the main railway station Santa Maria Novella. The pedestrian zone around the cathedral and the Ponte Vecchio is circumvented by small electric buses (C 1, C 2, D), which run every 10 minutes through the city centre. The SITA bus company offers tours into the region. There is a computerized information service with arrival and departure times in four languages at the bus terminal (Via Santa Caterina da Siena 15, near main railway station).

Petrol stations

The import and transport of petrol in jerry cans is not allowed. Unleaded petrol (95 octane, benzina senza piombo or benzina verde), super petrol (97 octane) and diesel (gasolio) are available. Petrol stations are generally open from 7am until noon and from 2pm until 8pm. Along the motorway they are usually open 24 hours. Automatic petrol pumps are available on weekends, increasingly also during the midday hours and at night.

City centre closed!

The centre of Florence is for the most part closed to vehicles as it is a »zona di traffico limitato« (ZTL) with very limited access times, which are shown on lighted displays. Hotels will help with directions to public parking places and temporary special permits. There is a large parking lot below the main railway station Stazione Santa Maria Novella and a large, inexpensive parking lot at the Porta di Prato.

Traffic regulations

The blood-alcohol limit is 0.5 per mille. In summer 2002 some new traffic regulations were introduced in Italy. The permitted alcohol level was reduced from 80mg to 50mg of alcohol per 100ml of blood. On motorways dipped headlights are required during the daytime and the speed limit in rain has been reduced to maximum 68mph (110 km/h) from 80mph (130 km/h)! Beyond that the following limits apply. Cars, motorcycles and campers up to 3,5 t: within city limits 30mph (50km/h), outside city limits 55mph (90 km/h), on four-lane roads (2 lanes in each direction) 68mph (110 km/h), on motorways (autostrada) 80mph (130 km/h); cars and campers over 3.5 t: outside city limits 50mph (80 km/h), on four-lane roads 50mph (80 km/h)

AUTOMOBILE CLUBS
Automobile Club d'Italia (ACI)
tel. 80 31 16, www.aci.it

PUBLIC TRANSPORTATION
ATAF
Piazza Stazione
tel. 800 42 45 00
www.ataf.net

CAR RENTALS IN ITALY
Avis
tel. *01805 55 77 55
www.avis.com

Budget
tel. *01805 24 43 88
www.budget.de

Europcar
tel. *0180 5 80 00,
www.europcar.com

Hertz
tel. 01805 33 35 35,
www.hertz.com

Sixt
tel. *0180 5 25 25 25
www.sixt.com

PARKING
www.firenzeparcheggi.it

TAXI
Radio taxis
tel. 0 55 42 42

and on motorways 62mph (100 km/h). Anyone caught breaking the speed limit can expect heavy fines. Remember that speeding fine notices will be sent to your home address. Important: **safety vests** are required in Italy for motorists who have a breakdown.

Further regulations

Private towing is not allowed on motorways. If a car breaks down, foreign travellers in cars or on motorcycles will be towed to the nearest garage by the Italian automobile club ACI. Helmets are required on motorcycles of over 50cc. If a vehicle is wrecked completely, customs must be notified since there might be an import duty on it. **Telephoning** by drivers of cars is only allowed with a hands-free system in Italy.

Taxi

Taxis charge a minimum rate that does not depend on the number of passengers. There is a surcharge at night between 10pm and 6am as well as on Sundays and holidays. Taxis can be flagged down in the street, but not near taxi stands. A receipt (»ricevuta«) will be issued on request.

Travellers with Disabilities

Detailed information and individual help before your journey and when you arrive, links for barrier-free offers as well as hotels, restaurants and museums, first aid, dialysis emergencies, taxi service, pub-

Turismo senza barriere
Viale XX Settembre 157 a
Sesto Fiorentino

I-50019 Florenz
tel. 05 54 48 13 82
www.turismosenzabarriere.it

lic rest rooms and parking for the disabled are offered by Turismo senza barriere (»barrier-free tourism«) in Florence. This project was established by the Region of Tuscany and includes the regional capital.

When to Go

The best time to travel to Florence is in the months April to June and September to October, when the average temperatures are between 15 and 20°C (60° to 70°F), but the weather can also get very hot already in June. But try not to go around Easter or Pentecost. On these holidays the city is so full of tourists that sightseeing is no fun anymore. There are fewer tourists between November and March – a good enough reason for many visitors to put up with the less cheerful weather.

Index

List of Maps and Illustrations

Photo Credits

AKG   p. 68, 70, 75, 78, 156, 173
aboveright
AKG-Images/Poklekowski p. 259 below
left
AKG-Images/Rabatti Domingie p. 33
Baedeker Archiv p. 120
Bilderberg/Madej p. 2 right below, 19,
221, 42, 186
Bilderberg/Horacek p. 8, 9, 261, 276
Bilderberg/Rescio p. 21 below
Borowski p. 38, 41, 45, 58, 64
Dumont Bildarchiv p. 3 right below,
125, 235, 287
Dumont Bildarchiv/Widmann p. 2 left
above, 100, 153, 222, 259 above
Galenschovski p. 1
Getty Images/Cosulich p. 297
Getty Images/Dea/Dagliorti p. 95
Getty Images/Dea Picture Library p. 127
Getty Images/Leemage p. 201
Getty Images/Lonely Planet p. 92, 102,
138
Getty Images/Maremagnum p. 96
Getty Images/Mayfield p. 304
Getty Images/Mountford p. 99
Getty Images/Rutz p. 9, 118
Getty Images/Scicluna p. 211
Getty Images/Simonis p. 110
Getty Images/Thaxton p. 20 below
Getty Images/Tondini p. 107 above
Getty Images/Watson p. 82
Getty Images/Why p. 12, 262
Huber c 2, p. 4 above, 251, 260, 284
Huber/Bernhart Udo p. 106
Huber/Borchi p. 3 left above, 225
Huber/Cellai p. 174
Huber/Gräfenhain p. 10, 179
Huber/Pignatelli p. 150

Istockphoto p. 258
Laif p. 66
Laif/Celentano c 4 above, p. 5 below,
13, 80, 85, 117, 267, 289,
Laif/Gaasterland p. 140
Laif/Galli p. 198
Laif/Hoa-Qui U 4 below, p.3 left below,
248, 291
Laif/Steinhilber p. 21 above, 107 below
Laif/Zanettini p. 7, 105
Look/Cosulich p. 135
Look/Maeritz p. 5 above and center, 20
above, 122, 128, 136, 273
Look/Richter p. 2 left below, 2 center,
22, 188, 163, 203
Hotel Mangiane p. 87
Picture Alliance/AKG-Images p. 213
Picture Alliance/AKG-Images/Rabatti-
Domingie p. 77
Picture Alliance/Bildagentur online/
Lescouret p. 3 leftcenter, 208, 240
Picture Alliance/Cromorange/Tipsimages
p. 4 below, 63, 217
Picture Alliance/dpa p. 14, 37
Picture Alliance/Huber c3 below, p. 185,
253, 259 below right
Picture Alliance/Rabatti-Domingie
c3 above, p. 133
Reincke p. 173 below
Renckhoff p. 142
Strüber p. 28, 31, 47, 48, 49, 59, 76, 161,
194, 195, 231
Wrba p. 2 right above, 166, 3 right
above, 269, 3 right center, 243, 279
Wurth p. 162, 173 above left 269, 279

Cover photo: mauritius images/
Radius Images

Publisher's Information

1st Edition 2015
Worldwide Distribution: Marco Polo
Travel Publishing Ltd
Pinewood, Chineham Business Park
Crockford Lane, Chineham
Basingstoke, Hampshire RG24 8AL,
United Kingdom.

Photos, illlustrations, maps:
107 photos, 30 maps and and
illustrations, one large city plan
Text:
Carmen Galenschovski with contribu-
tions by Reinhard Strüber
Editing:
John Sykes, Rainer Eisenschmid
Translation: Barbara Schmidt-Runkel
Cartography:
Franz Huber, Munich; MAIRDUMONT
Ostfildern (city map)
3D illustrations:
jangled nerves, Stuttgart
Infographics:
Golden Section Graphics GmbH, Berlin
Design:
independent Medien-Design, Munich
Editor-in-chief:
Rainer Eisenschmid, Mairdumont
Ostfildern

Printed in China

Despite all of our authors' thorough
research, errors can creep in. The pub-
lishers do not accept any liability for thi
Whether you want to praise, alert us to
errors or give us a personal tip Please
contact us by email or post:

MARCO POLO Travel Publishing Ltd
Pinewood, Chineham Business Park
Crockford Lane, Chineham
Basingstoke, Hampshire RG24 8AL
United Kingdom
Email: sales@marcopolouk.com

FSC
www.fsc.org
MIX
Paper from
responsible sources
FSC® C011918